THE HENRY L. STIMSON
LECTURES SERIES

A BLUEPRINT FOR WAR

FDR and the Hundred Days That
Mobilized America

SUSAN DUNN

Yale

UNIVERSITY PRESS

New Haven and London

The Henry L. Stimson Lectures at the Whitney and Betty MacMillan Center for International and Area Studies at Yale.

Published with assistance from the Louis Stern Memorial Fund.

Yale University Press books may be purchased in quantity for educational, business, or promotional use. For information, please e-mail sales.press@yale.edu (U.S. office) or sales@yaleup.co.uk (U.K. office).

Set in type by
Printed in the United States of America.

Library of Congress Control Number: 2017954129
ISBN 978-0-300-20353-0 (hardcover: alk. paper)

A catalogue record for this book is available from the British Library.

This paper meets the requirements of ANSI/NISO Z39.48-1992 (Permanence of Paper).

10 9 8 7 6 5 4 3 2 1

For Joseph J. Ellis

Contents

CHAPTER ONE

The God of No Foreign War

"**M**R. PRESIDENT,**"** A REPORTER asked Franklin Roosevelt
at a press conference on March 4, 1941, "would you
care to give us a reminiscent thought on eight years
ago today?" It was the first day of his ninth year
in the White House—a milestone no other U.S. president had
reached. "We have a different kind of crisis," Roosevelt replied, "a
world crisis instead of a domestic crisis. It is probably more serious
than the one eight years ago. I think we might let it go at that."[1]

Everyone knew what the president meant. Another journalist
noted that FDR, suffering from a bad cold, spoke in such a low
voice that those in the back could hardly hear him. The fifty-
nine-year-old president joked with reporters and, as usual, puffed
on a cigarette in an amber holder set in his mouth at a jaunty
angle. But, the reporter wrote, he did not radiate any of the "cheer-
fulness and hope" that marked his accession to the White House in
1933, when people could optimistically sing "Happy Days Are
Here Again."[2]

At that first inauguration in 1933, on a grim, overcast March day
in the depths of the Great Depression, FDR had taken the oath of
office and then addressed the vast crowd outside the Capitol: "I
assume *unhesitatingly*," he said, "the leadership of this great army of
our people dedicated to a disciplined attack upon our common

problems." The new president's self-confidence—and his unforget-table declaration that "the only thing we have to fear is fear itself"—signaled the brave, buoyant beginning of the period historians have named the first Hundred Days.

Those months saw significant changes in economic policy. FDR's administration restored solvency to the battered banking system, provided jobs to millions of the unemployed, extended relief to farmers plagued by drought and foreclosures, constructed power plants in the Tennessee Valley, and imposed sweeping regulations on a financial system on the brink of ruin.

Two years later, in the summer of 1935, Roosevelt swung further to the left and took more bold steps to ease the domestic crisis. Congress passed some of the New Deal's most significant and enduring social programs: Social Security; the National Labor Relations Act; the Works Progress Administration, which gave millions of jobs to blue-collar workers as well as to artists, writers, actors, and teachers; the Rural Electrification Act; and the Revenue Act, which lowered taxes on small businesses and increased them on large inheritances. Historians have called this innovative period Roosevelt's second Hundred Days.

On November 5, 1940, when the president was elected to that unprecedented third term, he faced still another crisis—a worldwide military, political, and moral catastrophe. On the other side of the planet, Japan had extended its tentacles deeper into China and was rapidly rearming its navy to challenge American power in the Pacific Ocean. In the Atlantic world, almost all of the European democracies had fallen under the extraordinary onslaught of the unstoppable Nazi army and air force. Adolf Hitler's relentless aggression had transformed the continent into one huge prison house. As Hitler described the stakes of the war he had provoked, "Two worlds are in conflict, two philosophies of life." Only one could survive.[3]

Unlike in Roosevelt's first Hundred Days in 1933 or his second in 1935, far more than the nation's economic and social well-being was now at stake. The lives of tens of millions of people around the world and the fate of free and democratic governments everywhere hung in the balance. Judeo-Christian morality along with the Enlightenment principles of freedom under law, individual rights, and due process trembled on the verge of extinction.

Those cold and wet winter months between November 1940, when Roosevelt and his team began delineating a strategic plan for possible war, and March 1941, when he signed the Lend-Lease Act, constituted his third Hundred Days. It was ultimately the most vital and consequential period of his presidency: during those hundred days, the president would initiate the pivotal programs and approve the strategic plans for America's successful leadership in World War II—leadership on which hinged the survival of the civilized world.

This period marked a critical change for FDR. A master of communication and persuasion, he had fluctuated, temporized, calculated, and shifted for years in response to a public that was more receptive to isolationist leaders who rejected the foreign entanglements that had pulled the country into the First World War. It had been simpler in 1914 when, as Woodrow Wilson's young, bellicose assistant secretary of the Navy, he had freely criticized the president for not taking stronger action at the outbreak of the war. He complained then to his wife, Eleanor, that gullible Americans were being fed "a lot of soft mush about everlasting peace."[4]

Hitler and his Nazis, who swept into power in Germany in 1933, changed the dynamic of global politics; they were a malignant menace that grew year by year. But for most of the 1930s, FDR took no stronger action than words. In January 1936, as Hitler was threatening to march into the Rhineland in flagrant violation of the Treaty of Versailles, FDR proposed in his State of the Union message that the United States adopt a "well-ordered neutrality" and use its "moral influence" to combat intolerance and autocracy in the world.[5]

The following August, speaking in Chautauqua, New York, he emotionally expressed his horror of war. "I have seen war," he said, recalling his visit as assistant secretary of the Navy to the frontlines in war-ravaged France in 1918. "I have seen war on land and sea. I have seen blood running from the wounded. I have seen men coughing out their gassed lungs. I have seen the dead in the mud. I have seen cities destroyed. . . . I have seen the agony of mothers and wives. I hate war." His fervent hope was that "envy, hatred and malice among Nations" had reached their peak and would be succeeded by a "new tide of peace and good-will." The "noblest monument to peace" was the American-Canadian border—"3,000 miles of friendship." Did his horror of war and passion for peace mean that the president had embraced isolationism? Well, no—and definitely yes. "We are not isolationists," he stated, "except in so far as we seek to isolate ourselves completely from war."[6]

In public, especially before the 1936 presidential election, the president allied himself with the anti-interventionism that grew ever more intense as the European scene darkened. But privately, he knew that promises of "no political commitments which might entangle us in foreign wars" could not stop Hitler and his Italian ally, Mussolini, from starting a war that would indeed entangle the United States.[7] By the fall of 1937, after the Japanese launched a new and brutal incursion into China and after Secretary of State Cordell Hull warned FDR that the Germans were "hell-bent on war," the president began to distance himself from isolationism. Peace-loving nations, he insisted in a speech that October in Chicago, could no longer "escape through isolation or neutrality" from the "epidemic of world lawlessness." The United States could not expect "complete protection in a world of disorder in which confidence and security have broken down." He proposed that democratic nations "quarantine" the aggressors. But exactly how would that be done? How would other countries be persuaded to join in? He put forward no concrete plan and called for neither economic sanctions, an embargo, nor military action.[8]

Even so, internationally minded newspapers reacted positively. The quarantine talk was "statesmanlike in theme and compelling in argument," editorialized the *Atlanta Constitution*, noting approvingly that "the call today is no longer merely to make the world safe for democracy, but to make the world itself safe from the conflagration of hate and destruction." The *New York Times* praised Roosevelt for expressing "the increasing indignation in this country" over predatory governments that flouted international law. But the *Hartford Courant* panned the idea of the United States "perpetually fighting other people's battles all over the world."[9]

In Congress, Roosevelt came under instant siege from isolationists. Massachusetts representative George Tinkham and New York's Hamilton Fish threatened to impeach the president for having "torn to shreds" America's neutrality laws. The public largely agreed. A Gallup poll taken after Roosevelt's speech showed that 69 percent of Americans wanted Congress to pass stricter neutrality laws. Asked if America should take part in another war like World War I, 95 percent of respondents answered "No" and demanded that the government do "everything possible to keep us out of foreign wars."[10]

In his Chicago speech, Roosevelt had coined what became a well-known term though "quarantine" was little more than a dramatic flourish that he quickly turned his back on. As conflict shattered Europe in the late 1930s, the United States clung to the sidelines, offering only moral indignation.[11]

In March 1938, when German tanks invaded Austria, Roosevelt did not even speak out, leaving it to Secretary of State Hull to publicly warn against "international lawlessness." A year later, in March 1939, when Germany took over Czechoslovakia, Roosevelt sent an urgent plea to Hitler and Mussolini, asking them to vow not to attack thirty-one nations that he listed. His message elicited a two-hour harangue to the Reichstag. "Herr Roosevelt!" Hitler exclaimed, "I fully understand that the vastness of your nation and the immense wealth of your country allow you to feel responsible for the history of the whole world and for the history of all nations. I, sir, am placed in a much more modest and small sphere." All he had ever done, Hitler insisted, was assert his "abhorrence of war." The master of demagoguery assured the American president that, contrary to rumors, he had no intention of attacking any country on Roosevelt's list. As the Führer mockingly pronounced the names of all thirty-one nations, his audience in the Reichstag rocked with laughter.[12]

And on September 3, 1939, when German troops plunged into Poland and Nazi bombers flew over Warsaw, Roosevelt promised Americans in a fireside chat that "this nation will remain a neutral nation." All the same, he added, "I cannot ask that every American remain neutral in thought as well. Even a neutral has a right to take account of facts. Even a neutral cannot be asked to close his mind or his conscience." Yet facts and conscience would not alter the president's course. He affirmed that he had "seen war and ... I hate war.... As long as it remains within my power to prevent, there will be no black-out of peace in the United States."[13]

On September 21, his request that Congress repeal the arms embargo was couched in noninterventionist language. He again assured Congress that his administration would "exert every possible effort to avoid being drawn into the war" and that the nation would remain "a citadel wherein [Western] civilization may be kept alive. The peace, the integrity, and the safety of the Americas— these must be kept firm and serene."[14]

Roosevelt's own words nurtured the rapidly swelling isolationist movement. A Gallup poll taken in October 1939, after France and England declared war on Germany, found that 84 percent of Americans wanted to see the Allies win, but 95 percent believed the United States should not enter the war. In 1938, Indiana congressman Louis Ludlow's proposal for a constitutional amendment requiring a national referendum to approve any congressional declaration of war failed to muster enough votes to bring it out of committee—but the margin was small: 209 opposed, 188 in favor. In the House and Senate, powerful isolationists blocked any measure that might promote intervention, above all an attempted repeal of the Neutrality Act. That failed effort ended in mid-1939 with the verdict that Vice President John Nance Garner delivered to the president: "Well, Captain, we may as well face the facts. You haven't got the votes; and that's all there is to it."[15]

But Roosevelt's anxiety heightened after Russia's invasion of Finland on November 30. "No human being can tell what the Russians are going to do next," he told a friend two weeks after the Soviet attack on its neighbor. He acknowledged that the world situation was "getting rather progressively worse" and that the recent Nazi-Soviet pact and their combined military forces placed the United States "in peril." In his State of the Union address in early January 1940, he said that he understood Americans who passionately opposed sending American youth to fight once again "on the soil of Europe" but, he cautioned, "there is a vast difference between keeping out of war and pretending that this war is none of our business. . . . It is not good for the ultimate health of ostriches to bury their heads in the sand."[16]

In early February 1940, the president announced that he would soon send Undersecretary of State Sumner Welles to Berlin, Rome, London, and Paris to see if it was still possible to hold peace talks. An exchange of views, FDR stressed to the British prime minister and the French minister of defense, "may be of real value towards a peace which is neither 'inconclusive nor precarious.' " But on the eve of Welles's arrival in Berlin, the Führer served notice that he had no interest in peace. In a directive sent to the German officials who were to meet with Welles, he wrote: "It is requested that Mr. Sumner Welles be not left in the slightest doubt that Germany is determined to conclude this war victoriously." Back in Washington, the undersecretary informed the president and secretary of state that there was not "the slightest chance of any successful negotiation at this time for a durable peace."[17]

And then the storm struck. On April 9, 1940, German forces invaded Norway and Denmark. After their swift march of victory through the rest of western Europe, climaxing with the fall of France in June, Roosevelt finally grasped that Great Britain was the last fragile bastion between Nazi Germany and American immersion in cataclysmic war. "The scene has darkened swiftly," Prime Minister Winston Churchill urgently wrote the president on May 15. "We expect to be attacked here ourselves." Ten days later, masses of British, Indian, and French troops, pinned against the sea and stranded in the northern French port of Dunkirk, began their evacuation across the English Channel. On June 4, the day their exodus was completed, Churchill warned the country against attempting to give "this deliverance" the attributes of a victory. As he suspected, Hitler had the British Isles in his sights with a plan for a cross-Channel invasion called Operation Sea Lion. In July, the Luftwaffe assured the Führer that it would soon achieve air superiority over the British and then be able to attack and sink the Royal Navy. With the British fleet neutralized, the Nazi invasion of England could move forward.[18]

The question for the president was what the United States could—or would—do to ensure the survival of its own democracy as well as Great Britain's. The first logical step was to strengthen America's own defenses. In a fireside chat on May 26, Roosevelt outlined the progress that had been made in rearming the army and navy and explained the goal of vastly speeding up defense production. But he nevertheless reassured his listeners that, despite the great emergency, there would be "no breakdown or cancellation of any of the great social gains we have made in these past years" and no lowering of the standards of employment. A few days later, he asked for more than $1 billion in defense expenditures from Congress, an amount equal to the entire army budget for the previous five years.[19]

In his formal request to Congress on July 10, he made no mention of his promise to Americans that no social gains would be cancelled, but instead gravely underscored that "the threats to our liberties, the threats to our security, the threats against our way of life, the threats to our institutions of religion, of democracy, and of international good faith, have increased in number and gravity from month to month, from week to week, and almost from day to day." It had become all too clear that "if the United States is to have any defense, it must have *total defense*." He called for "sacrifice and work and unity" and for "the participation of the whole country in the total defense of the country." And indeed, in September, after stormy sessions, Congress passed and the president signed the Selective Service Act, authorizing the first peacetime draft in American history.[20]

The year 1940 was an election year—and the president had to both win the support of anxious voters and defeat his intelligent and well-informed Republican opponent, Wendell Willkie. He wanted to convince Americans of the dire threat the free world faced; and yet he decided to hold out the chimerical promise of peace, the promise that the terrors and staggering losses of the First World War would not be repeated. Peace came into play especially when FDR, focused on the short-term goal of winning the election, wore his candidate hat. On October 28, the day Italy attacked Greece, in a campaign speech in Madison Square Garden he praised the Neutrality Act and pledged that "there will be no entanglement." In Boston Garden on October 30, after boasting about the boom in defense industries all over the country, he offered a sweeping and emotional vow to the mothers of America's draft-eligible young men. "I shall say it *again and again*: your boys are not going to be sent into any foreign wars." Roosevelt knew well that his apparently unequivocal pledge contained a weasel-worded caveat. "If somebody attacks us," he said to his counselor and speechwriter Sam Rosenman, "then it isn't a foreign war, is it?" When the overflow crowd in Boston Garden heard the unambiguous promise that American boys would not be sent into foreign wars, they burst into the only deep-throated cheers of the evening. "This is going to beat me," Willkie said when he heard about FDR's speech. It did.[21]

Years later, FDR's speechwriter, the Pulitzer Prize–winning playwright Robert Sherwood, would deeply regret yielding to the anti-interventionists' "hysterical demands for sweeping reassurance." But in October 1940, both he and Roosevelt felt that the risk of future embarrassment over violating these guarantees was negligible compared to the risk of losing the election.[22]

In speech after speech, as historian James MacGregor Burns memorably remarked, FDR "made his obeisances to the God of No Foreign War."[23]

In the fall of 1940, it seemed reasonable for Americans to wonder about the future not only of liberal democracy but of the planet. That fall, at the height of the fraught election season, Anne Morrow Lindbergh, the wife of the aviator Charles Lindbergh, who was the premier spokesman at the isolationist rallies of the America First Committee, weighed in with a short, elegant book called *The Wave of the Future*. Fifty pages long and costing $1, it sold tens of thousands of copies and jumped to the top of the bestseller list. Readers eagerly drank her lyrical prose laced with poison.

The conflict taking place in Europe between democratic and fascist nations, Mrs. Lindbergh argued, was not between good and evil but between the forces of the past and those of the future. Fascism was energetic and dynamic, democracy inefficient and exhausted. Disdainfully she pointed to the "decay, weakness, and blindness into which all the 'Democracies' have fallen since the last war." The quotation marks with which she repeatedly surrounded the word *democracy* relegated self-government, perhaps the greatest achievement of the Enlightenment, to a quaint, worn-out past. In Germany, meanwhile, a "new conception of humanity" was struggling to be born. "But because we are blind we cannot see it, and because we are slow to change, it must *force* its way through the heavy crust violently." There might be some maleficent elements in the birth of the new order, she conceded, but they were merely "*scum on the wave of the future.*" The "greatness" of fascism remained, and "*no price* could be too high" to reach it.[24]

Or, on the contrary, was fascism "the wave of the past"? asked Columbia University history professor Allan Nevins in the *New York Times*. Nevins was repelled by the thought that the crimes of Hitler and Mussolini represented nothing but "froth and spray on a great wave of the future." Hardly an "anticipation of man's most modern needs," Lindbergh's futuristic vision was in reality "a step toward the old Stone Age" and a "resuscitation of medievalism." Nevins denounced the isolationists' "frigid indifference to moral considerations" at a time when the Western world was being shaken "by the mightiest conflict of moral forces in centuries."[25]

Just when Anne Morrow Lindbergh was mindlessly welcoming the fascist wave of the future, Eleanor Roosevelt published a short book of her own, *The Moral Basis of Democracy*. Hers was a different vision. Framed around Christ's message of kindness, the golden rule she believed was essential to the flourishing of a healthy and open democracy, her book asked all Americans to rise to their better selves and "practice a Christ-like way of living." This was not a question of belief in his divinity, she underscored; but his example of a life of gentleness, mercy, and love would bring "the spirit of social cooperation . . . more closely to the hearts and to the daily lives of everyone . . . [and] change our whole attitude toward life and civilization." Democracy, more than any other form of government, "should make us conscious of the need we all have for this spiritual, moral awakening."[26]

Americans cherished their individual rights, but did they also understand their responsibility for the common good? As if reviving Alexis de Tocqueville's idea of "self-interest properly understood," Eleanor argued that the true essence of democracy is fraternity, sharing, sacrifice, and an ethic of responsibility for the neighbors we know as well as for people we don't know. "That means an obligation to the coal miners and share-croppers, the migratory workers, to the tenement-house dwellers and the farmers who cannot make a living." Americans had a strong work ethic, she wrote, but it was not enough to work only for themselves; rather, they must "serve the purposes of the greatest number of people." Then American democracy would be truly inclusive; all citizens would enjoy prosperity and equal rights and would find meaning, satisfaction, and even pleasure in being active participants in a morally sound, robust, and vital democracy.[27]

And together those citizens would bravely fight and risk their lives to defeat the Nazi gangsters and refute the vile notion that fascism represented any sort of future.

Roosevelt handily won the 1940 presidential election. His rival, Wendell Willkie, also a strong internationalist, competed in trying to placate the majority of Americans opposed to their country's intervention in foreign wars. Political opportunism triumphed over their internationalist principles, democratic ideals, and staunch anti-fascism. Neither candidate gave voters an honest, realistic picture of the challenges both knew lay ahead. After the election, FDR wrote to a friend, "There is no question that the election did not change certain fundamentals in any particular." In his mind, Americans were still not ready to hear the stark truth about the growing clouds of war.[28]

From besieged London, Prime Minister Churchill cabled his congratulations. Roosevelt's victory, he wrote, filled him with "indescribable relief" and with "the sure faith that the lights by which we steer will bring us all safely to anchor." He confessed that he had prayed for the president's success and was "truly thankful for it." Still, he added darkly, Britain was entering a "a protracted and broadening war" and things were "afoot which will be remembered as long as the English language is spoken in any quarter of the globe."[29]

But did Roosevelt steer by the same lights? If the election changed no fundamentals, what should the president do now? When should he be honest with Americans? A *Time* magazine reporter wrote that FDR was coming "into office this time committed to no man, indebted to no group, bound by no strings." *Time*'s publisher, the staunchly internationalist Henry Luce, exhorted the president to remember the words he had spoken in his first Inaugural Address: "This nation asks for action, and action now."[30]

In November 1940, Britain reeled every night under the Luftwaffe's rain of bombs. The kingdom was running out of armaments, running out of money, and anticipating a cross-Channel invasion at any time. Meanwhile, imperial Japan continued to surge through Asia.

Franklin Roosevelt was not yet fully engaged in the urgency of this global crisis. He would spend the weeks after the election hesitating, discussing, reading, cruising, fishing, reflecting, vacillating, starting, stopping, postponing. Only when some people thought it was nearly too late would he finally act. Under his leadership, the nation would begin its transition into the preeminent military, industrial, and moral power on the planet, foreshadowing what Henry Luce famously called the "American Century," dominated by the United States as "the most powerful and vital nation in the world."[31]

CHAPTER TWO

Lousy November

NOVEMBER 1940 WAS A lousy month.

"We are facing difficult days in this country,"
Franklin Roosevelt told a crowd of neighbors and
friends in Hyde Park on November 5, election night.
He had just won a splendid victory, but it was not a time to celebrate. He knew that days of anxiety, decision, sacrifice, and violence
lay ahead for the nation and its allies; and as for himself, his an-
guish was softened perhaps by this brief respite at his childhood
home on the Hudson River. Even while he spoke to his neighbors,
German planes were dumping fifteen hundred bombs on London,
destroying factories and railroad tracks, reducing docks to smoking
rubble and buildings to skeletons. At sea, a German warship turned
its guns on a British convoy of thirty-eight ships, setting them
aflame. Thirty-two of the ships reached port safely.[1]

A crowd of thousands turned out to greet Franklin and Eleanor at
Union Station when they returned to Washington two days after the
election. Army, Navy, and Marine bands played festive music, and two
hundred thousand people lined the route to the White House, waving
and cheering as the president passed by in an open car. Now that the
campaign was past, many hoped, even expected, that Roosevelt would
lead Americans through a perilous and uncertain hour. But the president, *Time* magazine remarked, "looked tired and grey."[2]

13

That day brought the accustomed bad news. A hundred high-speed German bombers buzzed over London and Portsmouth, delivering savage destruction to houses, shops, factories, airfields, warehouses, docks, and power stations. Irish premier Eamon de Valera declared that Ireland would not permit Britain to use its naval bases. Between Germany and the democracies of Europe, Ireland would remain neutral. Any pressure from Britain, de Valera warned, would lead to bloodshed. "A most heavy and grievous burden," a disappointed Churchill sighed.[3]

At noon the following day, November 8, Roosevelt held his first post-election press conference. Two hundred newsmen jammed into his office. As usual at his twice-weekly press conferences, the president was good-natured, answering reporters' questions with banter and flashes of wit while offering as few specifics as he could. Journalist John Gunther later remarked that he had "never met anyone who showed greater capacity for avoiding a direct answer while giving the questioner a feeling he had been answered." During any given press conference, Gunther noted, the president's mobile features would express "amazement, curiosity, mock alarm, genuine interest, worry, rhetorical playing for suspense, sympathy, decision, playfulness, dignity and surpassing charm."[4]

Had the president, one reporter dryly asked, received any congratulatory messages from Herr Hitler or Mussolini? "No," FDR replied. Another reporter wanted to know if Mr. Roosevelt could say anything about a British request for twelve thousand new planes. The request was being studied, he answered vaguely, explaining that he had a new "rule of thumb" when it came to providing bombers and other weapons to Britain and Canada. "The rule is a 50–50 rule. In other words, we take half; they take half." But, he stressed, it was just a "general rule" and was "absolutely subject to exceptions."[5]

Secretary of War Henry Stimson, though eager to provide maximum aid to Britain, noted that the United States was "nearly down to the bottom of the can." Army Chief of Staff General George C. Marshall also harbored strong reservations about the president's "even-Stephen" proposal. That month, he remarked in frustration to his colleagues, the Royal Air Force had received four hundred new planes and the Army Air Corps about six. Although Churchill had recently remarked to his War Cabinet, "The Navy can lose us the war, but only the Air Force can win it," Marshall worried what would happen to American planes given to Britain if the Royal Air Force were defeated by Germany. If Britain collapsed, "we will be the sole defenders of the Atlantic and Pacific."[6]

The military was still struggling to overcome its virtual disarmament in the aftermath of World War I. By 1934 the entire regular army, according to General Douglas MacArthur, could have fit into Yankee Stadium. It stood seventeenth in size among the world's armies and was at its lowest effectiveness since the Great War. In January 1938, President Roosevelt had told Congress candidly that "our national defense is, in the light of the increasing armaments in other nations, inadequate for purposes of national security." Even with the huge new military appropriations enacted by Congress in the summer of 1940, Stimson remarked in the fall that "planes were still being counted one by one."[7]

The November 8 press conference was far from FDR's best performance. Perhaps he was just fatigued. The dual roles of president and candidate in such anxious times would have drained any man. He let on to the newsmen how badly he needed a rest, saying that on Tuesday or Wednesday of the following week, he planned to board the USS *Potomac* and "go down the river for three or four days of sleep and read a lot of documents that have not been read for the last two weeks."[8]

An hour after Roosevelt's press conference, Adolf Hitler was onstage in a very different mood, delivering a fiery, combative speech in the swastika-splashed Löwenbräu beer cellar in Munich, overflowing with Germany's high military officials. Seventeen years to the day after his failed attempt at revolution was launched in that very hall, he returned to celebrate his successes as Führer and warlord, and to assert his "absolute conviction" that German military might would triumph. The man with an iron grip on most of Europe announced, "Today I reject any compromise." After denouncing Jews and democratic regimes—especially Great Britain—as the satanic sources of war, the Führer injected a spiritual note: "I am convinced that Providence has brought me this far and has spared me from all the dangers in order to let me lead the German people in this battle." Now the British and the Jews had much in common, remarked Sir Norman Angell, a well-known British author and winner of the Nobel Peace Prize. They "share the honor," he said, "of being the two peoples of all the earth upon whom Hitler visits his deadliest enmity."[9]

Soon after Hitler left the hall, British war planes pounded it with explosives. It was bad timing. The British maintained that they had bombed the cellar by mistake, overshooting their real targets—railroad lines and freight yards. But upon returning to base, one candid Royal Air Force pilot remarked that "our target was almost in the center of the city and before we started, an intelligence officer mentioned that it was the anniversary of the beer hall putsch of 1923 and that Hitler probably would be in Munich during the raid." The near miss added to the dictator's mystique. Providence had again spared its servant so that he could bring his life's work to completion.[10]

A day later, Neville Chamberlain died. As prime minister on a rainy autumn evening two years earlier, he had waved a piece of paper with the Führer's signature before a wildly cheering crowd in front of 10 Downing Street and exuberantly announced that his meeting in Munich with Herr Hitler had secured "peace with honor." Germany's dictator had baited the hook well. He had assured Chamberlain, "with great earnestness," the prime minister innocently told the House of Commons, that the Sudetenland of Czechoslovakia was his last territorial ambition in Europe. Peace would reign. "I have no hesitation in saying—from the personal contacts I had with him," the British leader said, "I believe he means what he says."[11]

Even after Hitler's tanks and troops annexed the rump of Czechoslovakia six months later, Chamberlain continued to urge his people to have faith in the word of Adolf Hitler. "The aim of this government," he said, "is now, as it has always been, to promote the method of discussion over the method of force in the settlement of differences."[12]

Hitler preferred the method of force. When Germany invaded Poland in September 1939, a stunned Chamberlain moaned that everything he had "hoped for and believed in during my public life has crashed in ruins." But it was more than the prime minister's hopes that were dashed. His arrogance and gullibility and his faith in handshake agreements had opened the way for Germany's efficient crushing of Czechoslovakia, Poland, Denmark, Norway, Holland, Belgium, Luxembourg and, most ominously for Britain, France. By the end of his life, Chamberlain's country stood alone in Europe, braced for more attacks, more devastation, more suffering, more death.[13]

On the day of his funeral, heavy rain together with Nazi bombs fell on London, and the air was pierced by thunder and the high pitch of air-raid sirens. The time and place of the service had been kept secret, a safeguard against any attempt by the Luftwaffe to kill off Britain's war leaders with one blow. Most of them had opposed Chamberlain's appeasement policies—none more outspokenly or harshly or presciently than the man who had replaced him in May, as France was falling. But in a measured eulogy, Winston Churchill was as generous as the truth allowed. He granted that his predecessor had acted "with perfect sincerity according to his lights, and strove to the utmost of his capacity and authority . . . to save the world from the awful, devastating struggle in which we are now engaged."[14]

Earlier that week, on November 11, Americans and Europeans had observed Armistice Day, the commemoration of the 1918 agreement between the Allies and Germany that brought hostilities to an end, when Germany had at last surrendered. Adolf Hitler on that day had been in a hospital recuperating from a mustard gas attack. He marked the anniversary, bitter to so many Germans, with vicious air attacks on British ships and on Britain itself. In past years, at 11:00 in the morning on the eleventh day of the eleventh month, the British people had observed two minutes of silence for their war dead. This year there was no silence. German war planes screamed overhead. The war to end all war had failed.[15]

The mood was no less gray in the United States. "It is raining and the landscape is dreary and gloomy, as it may well be," Eleanor Roosevelt wrote in her "My Day" newspaper column, "for it matches the mood of most of us who remember what Armistice Day meant to us in the year 1918. Nature should weep with us, for the high hopes which humanity had of ending war on this earth lie in ruins all about us." An early winter storm ranged from the Rockies to the Appalachians and from Canada to the Gulf of Mexico. Blizzards, heavy snow, icy gales, huge waves, and tornadoes pummeled the country, killing and injuring hundreds of people, leveling homes, trees, and power lines, sinking boats and wrecking freighters on the Great Lakes, and imperiling fruit crops, causing millions of dollars in property damage.[16]

The storm had not yet struck Washington when President Roosevelt, accompanied by War Secretary Stimson, observed Armistice Day with a speech at Arlington National Cemetery. At the Tomb of the Unknown Soldier, with the Washington Monument and the Capitol in the distance, the president praised the courageous young men of 1917 and 1918 who, he said, "helped to preserve the truths of democracy for our generation." But even here the country's divisions intruded. To many Americans, those heroes, over one hundred thousand of them, had fought and perished in a war an ocean away from their home and even more distant from American principles and interests. The nation's impulse to isolation rose from the fear of repeating that mass slaughter, of renewing a foolish crusade that had falsely promised, as Woodrow Wilson put it, to make the world "safe for democracy."[17]

Some isolationists, scarred by memories of trench warfare and poison gas, embraced the mission of a 1934 Senate committee, headed by North Dakota's arch-isolationist Republican Gerald Nye, to investigate whether it had been profit-seeking financiers and munitions companies that had propelled the nation into war. Other isolationists simply believed that the United States, protected by two vast oceans, was invulnerable to attack. Others were convinced that the fate of the United States did not hinge on that of Great Britain and that American participation in another war would destroy the already fragile democracy at home. According to hardcore anti-interventionists, the die had already been cast and Hitler was the victor. Since American intervention, they argued, could make no difference, the task of the United States was to adapt, however painfully, to a new world order dominated by fascist ideology and the ethic of conquest and subjugation that lay at its heart. Some anti-interventionists manufactured optimism from this new reality. Echoing Anne Morrow Lindbergh's mantra that the future lay in the dynamism of a forceful and dazzling fascist order, they argued that democracy's time had passed.[18]

And, of course, there were politicians for whom the international crisis was merely a useful forum for domestic politics; their aim was to defeat not Hitler but Franklin Roosevelt, with isolationism as their cudgel. They challenged the president's every move, parsing his words, eager to discredit him in the eyes of Americans. In 1942, after American and Russian entry in the war, FDR wryly commented that those isolationist politicians wanted to win the war only "(a) if at the same time, Russia is defeated, (b) at the same time, England is defeated, (c) at the same time, Roosevelt is defeated."[19]

At Arlington, a lone bugler from the Army Band played "Taps." The president had given a moving, intelligent, and high-minded address on the paramount values of self-government and democracy, contrasting them to Hitler's "modern form of ancient slavery." Yet without specifics or muscle—without determined action—how could democratic ideals be secured? How could Great Britain, their last bulwark in Europe, survive? How could the United States itself prepare to defeat the Nazis and their Wehrmacht and terroristic Luftwaffe when its own defense production had barely begun and its military was still in its training stages?[20]

There could be no more urgent questions facing Americans in November 1940, yet President Roosevelt, to all appearances, scarcely addressed them in the weeks following his reelection.

The campaign had left Roosevelt "distinctly marked with fatigue," Steve Early, his press secretary, explained when he canceled the usual Tuesday press conference on November 12. The president's family and aides felt he should rest. Early confirmed that on the following day, the 13th, the president would leave on a cruise of several days on the Potomac River and Chesapeake Bay.[21]

Another cold, hard rain fell on Washington on November 13, and the forecast was for more of the same, along with thickly overcast skies and temperatures close to freezing. But the president, desperate to throw off the fatigue of recent months, drove through the wet city streets, pocked with puddles, to the yacht *Potomac*'s mooring. For Roosevelt, who as assistant secretary of the navy from 1913 to 1920 had decorated his office and bedroom with naval prints and models of ships, water meant rest, health, and pleasure. He enjoyed sailing off Campobello Island, fishing in the Caribbean, swimming in the therapeutic pool in Warm Springs, and playing cards with cronies aboard a yacht.[22]

Accompanying Roosevelt on the cruise were his attorney general and friend Robert Jackson, Postmaster General Frank Walker and his wife, as well as two of the most indispensable people in the president's circle: his close aide and confidant Harry Hopkins and the charming Missy LeHand, his longtime secretary and assistant. Through the years of FDR's presidency, his circle had shrunk with deaths and departures, but Harry and Missy were stalwarts.[23]

"Harry could disarm you," FDR's son Franklin Jr. remembered later. "He could make you his friend in the first five minutes of a conversation." The Iowa-born Hopkins, a social worker with a genius for politics and administration, had served FDR and the New Deal as head of the massive Works Progress Administration and then as secretary of commerce. He once had high political ambitions, even for the presidency, but a nearly fatal stomach cancer dashed all that. Though Hopkins never fully recovered, Roosevelt was determined to keep him close, and in 1940, the widowed Hopkins and his young daughter moved into private quarters in the White House.[24]

As for the forty-two-year-old Missy, she intuitively knew what the president needed in order to relax—when to bring out his stamp collection and when to invite people to the White House for dinner and poker. Secretary of the Interior Harold Ickes commented that Missy "sees the issues that are involved and she is so close to the President that she is in a position to keep him steady at times when he needs advice. The President is the kind of person who needs help of this sort from someone very close to him." Sam Rosenman, who had worked closely with FDR since his campaign for governor of New York in 1928, called Missy "one of the five most important people in the U.S."[25]

No one expected major decisions to emerge from this river jaunt. On such occasions, the president, as his son Jimmy once remarked, "wanted lighthearted, attractive persons around him. He

did not want to be burdened with heavy intellectual talk and discussions of serious problems. He needed—as a tonic—a little touch
of frivolity and sparkling, aimless gossip and conversation." On the
Potomac that week, the president served martinis to his guests before dinner, and afterward he and his friends played poker, with
FDR insisting that the stakes be kept small. The game over around
10:00 p.m., the whole company retired to bed.[26]

But despite everyone's best efforts, the cruise turned into a dismal affair, with blustery winds and persistent freezing rain.

A far more ferocious rain of fire was descending on the ancient
city of Coventry in the English Midlands. On the evening of
Thursday, November 14, the Luftwaffe dropped explosives indis-
criminately on that small and ancient industrial city and its quar-
ter-million people, dingy factories, and drab two-story brick
dwellings. The attack started with "pathfinder" planes releasing
flares to illuminate targets; then the real assault began. Over the
next ten hours, Coventry lay almost defenseless as more than five
hundred Nazi bombers released hundreds of tons of high explosives, dozens of parachute mines that exploded above roof level,
and, most destructive of all, more than thirty-five thousand incendiary bombs that spread fire throughout the city, engulfing
Coventry's majestic fourteenth-century cathedral in a swirling
mass of flames. Hitler had warned in September that if the British
attacked German cities, he would "obliterate" their own cities with
a hundred pounds of explosives for each pound the British
dropped. The attack on Coventry was savage retaliation for the
RAF's raid on Munich and the beer cellar; a German propaganda
official called it a "decent and soldierly punishment for an unsol-
dierly deed."[27]

Although the city's automobile and airplane factories played
a key role in Britain's war machine, its residential areas, business
district, hospitals, and cathedral bore the brunt of the punishment.
The Nazi aim was simply the greatest possible destruction, including destruction of human lives. A thousand people or more were
killed or injured that night; gas lines lay smashed and blazing;
electrical power was gone; unexploded bombs littered the streets.
"Coventry is now like a city that has been wrecked by an
earthquake and swept by fire," reported the *New York Times*. It had

become "the voiceless symbol," wrote the *New York Herald Tribune*, "of the insane, the unfathomable barbarity, which had been released on Western civilization."[28]

People crawled out of the shelters that Friday morning into a different world. Stunned by the devastation, they wandered through the streets, poking through the smoldering ruins of their homes. "You can stand on what used to be a main corner in downtown Coventry and in three directions see nothing but waste," wrote reporter Ernie Pyle when he visited the city four months later. Overcome by the catastrophe, he added, "Nobody has ever been able to put that night of Coventry's into words."[29]

Now the Nazis threatened to "Coventryize" the whole British island. But the Royal Air Force was beginning to take the fight to Hitler. On successive nights in mid-November, the RAF hit Hamburg's power stations, docks, gas works, and railway yards, targeting German military and industrial sites in order to tear at the sinews of Hitler's war machine and deposit hell upon German citizens, as the Luftwaffe had done in England.[30]

A few days after the attack on Coventry, Raymond Daniell, the London correspondent for the *New York Times*, attended a funeral there for two hundred of the victims. Their common grave, he wrote, "spoke so poignantly of the human suffering in this new kind of war."[31]

On November 21, 1940, thirty-two states, including New York, celebrated Thanksgiving Day. In 1939, Roosevelt had proposed a two-year experiment: moving the date of Thanksgiving up one week from the customary last Thursday in November would extend the lucrative shopping season between Thanksgiving and Christmas. In her "My Day" column, Eleanor Roosevelt concurred: "Christmas shopping provides jobs for many people and turns the wheels in many a factory."[32]

On a cloudy and occasionally rainy morning, an eighty-foot-tall Superman, a seventy-five-foot clown named Laffo, and a giant Santa Claus floated high above the streets of New York as the Macy's Thanksgiving Day parade made its way from Central Park West to 34th Street, delighting a million happy children and grinning adults. The Salvation Army and the Red Cross served turkey dinners around the city. Down at Fort McClellan, Alabama, twelve thousand National Guardsmen from New York attended church services, played football and baseball in seventy-degree weather, and welcomed a visit from Dixie Walker, the star outfielder for the Brooklyn Dodgers. And for the first time, English refugee children, safe in the United States from the nightly havoc and terror of aerial warfare, enjoyed familial Thanksgiving feasts with their American hosts.[33]

The mood was more solemn in churches and synagogues, as ministers, priests, and rabbis evoked the terrible suffering inflicted on peaceful nations by the Nazi rampage. At New York City's Cathedral of St. John the Divine, the Reverend Charles Gilbert praised the "unbelievable courage with which all Britain carries on its unequal struggle," while at the B'nai Jeshurun synagogue, Manhattan borough president Stanley Isaacs, a descendant of that congregation's first rabbi, said that no one had greater reason to cherish democracy than the American Jew. "Democracy is the great safeguard of minorities," he said, "whether they be minorities of race, or religion or political beliefs." At the First Methodist Church in Los Angeles, the pastor expressed gratitude for the freedom that still reigned in America, but he also invited parishioners to repent, adding bluntly that "we supplied our full share of the stupidity that paved the way for Hitler."[34]

Franklin and Eleanor Roosevelt celebrated Thanksgiving in Hyde Park, not at the "Little White House" in Warm Springs where they usually spent the holiday. That weekend, the rector at Hyde Park's St. James Episcopal Church reminded his congregation, including the president and First Lady, that "this great country enjoys so much"—above all, peace and security. "But we cannot just sit back and gloat on that. We have work to do. We must pass these blessings on to others."[35]

There was indeed work to do. The front-page headline of that day's *New York Times* read "Nazis Continue Battering Midlands; Industry Is Target." Wave upon wave of German bombers were pulverizing Birmingham and Liverpool.

In London that day, November 21, Parliament commenced its second wartime session. Much of the traditional pageantry of

Parliament's opening had been abandoned: no crowds waited in St. James's Park to cheer the royal carriage, and King George VI, dressed in the blue service uniform of an admiral of the fleet, wore no crown. But seated on the throne in the House of Lords as air-raid sirens screeched outside, the king declared Britain's determination to fight "until freedom is made secure" and expressed confidence in ultimate victory. In the House of Commons, Prime Minister Churchill elaborated on the royal optimism. "Even in the midst of our struggle for life, even under the fire of the enemy," he declared, Britain's tradition of parliamentary government would continue to "throw open the portals of the future." He predicted that the "arsenals, training grounds and science of the New World and the British Empire" would bring "victory and deliverance to mankind." Months earlier, in his first cable to FDR as prime minister, Churchill had underlined the starkness of the situation: "If necessary we shall continue the war alone, and we are not afraid of that." But "the voice and force of the United States may count for nothing if they are withheld too long."[36]

Now, in November 1940, would the New World's arsenals be thrown open to Britain? This was the only question that mattered. The British chiefs of staff reported that without the full economic support of the United States *"we do not think we could continue the war with any chance of success."* Nothing but American ships, planes, and arms could rescue Europe's last democracy from the barbarity of the Third Reich.[37]

In Hyde Park the day after the new shopping-friendly Thanksgiving, President Roosevelt assured reporters that everything possible was being done to aid England. The British were already scheduled to receive half the output of American planes, weapons, and other war materiel. FDR was asked whether that 50–50 rule of thumb might be altered, given the heavy Nazi bombings of England. Well, that question was altogether too general, the president responded. He challenged reporters to explain how plane production could possibly be sped up.[38]

The following day, November 23, the British ambassador, Lord Lothian, returned to Washington after a brief stay in London. "Nineteen forty-one will be a hard and difficult year," he soberly told the newspapermen who greeted him at the airport. Admitting that Britain was running out of funds to purchase war supplies, he stressed that England urgently needed planes, munitions, ships, and, he added with notable understatement, "perhaps a little financial help." His remarks were intended to provoke a constructive, collaborative discussion that would get Americans used to the idea that Britain alone could not defeat the Nazi monster, in part because it could not afford it. Lord Lothian's ultimate audience, however, was Roosevelt and his advisors—and Congress. If Lothian stirred enough anxiety about Britain's future, perhaps he could spur the government to action.[39]

Once a committed appeaser, Philip Kerr, the eleventh Marquess of Lothian, had become an ardent advocate of Anglo-American cooperation. Early on he had approved, as he wrote, the Führer's "desire to purify and discipline the national life" of the German people, and after meeting Hitler in 1935, had praised him as "the prophet of the new Germany." America's ambassador to Germany, William Dodd, who met Lothian in Berlin in 1937, commented that he "seemed to be more of a Fascist than any other Englishman I have met."[40]

By 1939, though, the motives and intentions of the Nazi gangsters had dawned on Lord Lothian. "What we are confronted with is the most ruthless use of the most ruthless power to remake the world according to the plans which are set forth in *Mein Kampf*," he told the House of Lords that April, the month of his appointment as ambassador to the United States. Churchill later wrote that Lothian was "a changed man." From an "aristocratic detachment from vulgar affairs," the prime minister noted, "now, under the same hammer that beat upon us all, I found an earnest, deeply stirred man."[41]

But Lothian's remarks at the Washington airport misfired. Reporters reduced his words to a sentence he never uttered: "Well, boys, Britain's broke. It's your money we want." His plea for economic assistance "did not help one damn bit!" exploded Treasury Secretary Henry Morgenthau, who correctly anticipated that isolationists in Congress would now object to letting Britain place additional orders for weapons. The extent of British assets in the Western Hemisphere became a matter of wild speculation. Was it

$2 billion, or $9 billion? For weeks, the issue roiled the capital, even spurring Senator Nye to call for a congressional investigation. Nazi propagandists pitched in, spreading the line that England was deceiving the United States about its wealth. All the speculation about hidden British assets, said Morgenthau, "just drives me nuts."[42]

"I don't think I have anything," the enigmatic president said at the beginning of his November 26 press conference, adding that his press secretary Steve Early, didn't have anything to say either. Newsmen tried anyway. "Mr. President, did the British Ambassador present any specific requests for additional help?" one inquired. Lothian had met Roosevelt a few hours earlier to advise him that Britain would soon ask for assistance from the United States on a larger scale than ever before. Also that day, the *New York Times* reported on its front page the chancellor of the exchequer's announcement that Britain was spending £9 million a day on the war, a sum that would soon empty his nation's treasury. "Nothing was mentioned in that regard at all, not one single thing—ships or sealing wax or anything else," the president replied, drawing a laugh.[43]

In fact the president was painfully aware of Britain's financial realities. Long before most of his advisors, he had anticipated that Britain might eventually need American loans or credits to finance its defense against the Nazis. Yet he was genuinely uncertain about how best to aid Britain within the constraints of U.S. politics and public opinion. On the day of FDR's press conference, Lothian informed the Foreign Office in London that Washington seemed to be suffering a "post-election lassitude." "Both in Congress and in the administration," he remarked in his cable, "there has been disinclination to do anything at all difficult in order to help us. The tendency is to postpone such things until the new session in January." Another alarmed British official complained that FDR was "blithely wasting the time that was running so short."[44]

Roosevelt's friend Supreme Court justice Felix Frankfurter was also concerned. "Dear Frank," he wrote on November 29 to FDR, "As you know, since the election a vacuum was created. . . . And now *your* decisive actions and controlling and encompassing voice will be filling the minds and purposes of our people to the realization of the objectives which *you* represent, and for which they summoned you for four more, albeit very hard, years."[45]

What kind of leadership, in this chaotic world, was Roosevelt willing and able to provide? In September 1940 he had demonstrated his improvisational brilliance in deflecting American opposition while helping Britain obtain vital military supplies. With Lothian's crucial assistance, he had concluded a bargain to send Britain World War I–vintage American destroyers in exchange for bases in the Caribbean. Churchill had been pleading for fifty or sixty American warships since June, calling it "a matter of life or death." "In the long history of the world," he wrote FDR, "this is the thing to do now." The president wanted to comply, but he knew that in order to avoid fireworks in Congress, there had to be some element of reciprocity.[46]

"What I am trying to do is to acquire American bases in the Caribbean," FDR told reporters at an August 16 press conference. He explained that he was asking London for ninety-nine-year leases or an outright gift of sites for naval and air bases in Newfoundland, Bermuda, and the Caribbean. But wouldn't he have to give Churchill something in exchange? "The quid pro quo is under discussion," he replied, insisting disingenuously that the attempt to get more American bases had nothing to do with destroyers. When some reporters continued to press him about the deal, the president bristled, repeating, "I am not discussing destroyers."[47]

The strategy worked: the United States acquired from Britain leases for eight valuable sites for bases in the Western Hemisphere in exchange for fifty virtually obsolete World War I destroyers; and the president sold the deal to Americans as a self-interested act that did not tie the United States to the fate of Britain. Even fervent anti-interventionists were persuaded that FDR had executed a shrewd Yankee horse trade that shored up the country's hemispheric defenses. Colonel Robert McCormick, editor and publisher of the virulently isolationist *Chicago Daily Tribune*, expressed his satisfaction that the Caribbean had become "an American lake."[48]

Churchill, who had counted on a gift from the United States rather than a trade, was less satisfied. When Attorney General

Robert Jackson explained to him that federal statutes prevented the president from simply giving the destroyers to the British, an angry Churchill replied, "Empires just don't bargain." "Well," Jackson countered, "republics do." Later, as historian Robert Shogan recounts, Roosevelt tried to soothe an exasperated Churchill by noting, "The trouble is I have an Attorney General and he says I have got to bargain." Churchill groused, "Maybe you ought to trade these destroyers for a new Attorney General."[49]

Even so, Churchill expressed satisfaction that, as he wrote, "the transfer to Great Britain of fifty American warships was a decidedly unneutral act," and he advised his staff against "making any complaints about the condition of these vessels" or their small number. Addressing Parliament, the prime minister portrayed the exchange as representing the bond between the two countries. Britain and the United States, he said, would henceforth "be somewhat mixed up together in some of their affairs for mutual and general advantage. . . . I do not view the process with any misgivings. No one can stop it. Like the Mississippi, it just keeps rolling along. Let it roll. Let it roll on in full flood, inexorable, irresistible, to broader lands and better days."[50]

The inexorability was not so evident to Roosevelt. Not until mid-November did he finally cut through the Gordian knot that had blocked delivery of a handful of B-17 bombers—called Flying Fortresses—that the Royal Air Force desperately needed. A few weeks earlier, General Marshall had informed the commander in chief that he had only forty-nine bombers fit for duty. "The President's head snapped back as if someone had hit him in the chest," wrote Stimson, who was present at that meeting. But despite Marshall's certainty that the United States did not have nearly enough bombers for its own defense, FDR was determined to give Britain the B-17s it needed.[51]

At his November 12 meeting with the president, Stimson, who had just discussed the matter with Marshall, explained that the United States had no problem sending lighter B-24s to Britain because British factories had manufactured the engines, but legal issues had arisen with the heavier four-engine B-17s. A proven expert in finding loopholes in congressional regulations, FDR had a few suggestions, and by the end of their luncheon, they had come up with the idea of providing the B-17s for the purpose of testing them under combat conditions. Fortunately, Attorney General Jackson gave a favorable opinion as to the legality of testing out the B-17 bombers in Britain. That was "the only peg on which we could hang the proposition legally," Stimson noted afterward.[52]

Marshall didn't like sharing scarce American bombers, or circumventing Congress to do so, but he was even more reluctant to fight the president on the issue. And as a military commander, Marshall was open to being proved wrong, an invaluable trait. He soon realized that by furnishing Britain with the B-17s, Roosevelt had done the right thing—and the important thing. Sending the Flying Fortresses to Britain and testing them in real battles, Marshall wrote, "will be a great advantage to us in that it will give us an actual service test of this particular type of heavy bomber prior to final commitments by us for the manufacture of more of this type." He ultimately came to believe that they should have done it far earlier because, as he later commented, "we found difficulties with the planes that the Air Corps had not perceived at all and they could hardly be used."[53]

That was a win-win for the United States, but FDR knew that such improvisations were tricky to achieve and limited in their usefulness. How could the spigot of aid be opened wide? How could American assistance to Britain—all aid short of war—roll on without charades or crippling quid pro quos?

In 1939, when FDR proposed changing the date of Thanksgiving in order to extend the pre-Christmas shopping season, the six New England states plus eleven others refused to go along. "We here in Plymouth consider the day sacred," announced the head of the board of selectmen in Plymouth, Massachusetts, where Pilgrims had celebrated the first Thanksgiving in 1621. So on November 28, 1940, another Thanksgiving took place. In Plymouth, covered in white from a heavy snowstorm, three thousand men, women, and children, many of them descended from Pilgrims, crowded into Memorial Hall to commemorate the first Thanksgiving in the New World. In the meeting house, filled with fir and pine branches, local citizens in period costumes played the parts of

Governor William Bradford, Myles Standish, and Indian chiefs as they reenacted three scenes from the past: the signing of the "Mayflower Compact," the first written expression of democratic self-government in the New World; the landing at Plymouth Rock; and the first Thanksgiving.[54]

In the early evening, as spectators streamed out of Memorial Hall into the crisp, wintry stillness of the November dusk, they heard the shouts of newsboys. "Germans bomb Plymouth! Two hundred tons of bombs fall on Plymouth!" For eight hours, the English Channel port city of Plymouth quaked under the barrage of Nazi aerial bombs. One hundred and fifty German planes battered the old town and harbor with high explosives, destroying docks, warehouses, navy supply depots, freight yards, and railway lines. In a nearby town, hundreds of people refused shelter and stood instead at high lookout points to witness the terrible spectacle. Quickly sending a radio message across the sea, the Reverend Alfred Hussey, minister emeritus of Plymouth's First Church in Massachusetts, told his English brethren, "We are not strangers, but neighbors . . . and no distance breaks the ties of blood. Your sorrows are our sorrows. Your battles are our battles. . . . From Plymouth, Mass., to Plymouth, England, fight on, Godspeed."[55]

Later that night, more Luftwaffe bombs rained down on the Channel port of Southampton and the western ports of Bristol and Liverpool. "RAID ON PORT HEAVY; NAZIS BOMB LIVERPOOL; CITY AFIRE," shouted the eight-column front-page headline of the *New York Times*. Having already crippled British industrial centers, the Luftwaffe was now targeting harbors, especially those where American ships could unload supplies, machinery, and armaments.[56]

Two weeks after that second Thanksgiving, President Roosevelt passed through Warm Springs, Georgia, and jokingly suggested to reporters that since he was a fan of compromise, he would be happy to designate a third Thanksgiving. The newsmen laughed. The president's decision to move up the date of Thanksgiving had brought record sales in department and chain stores.[57]

Otherwise, November was a lousy month.

CHAPTER THREE

Plan Dog

THE PRESIDENT OF THE United States was acting neither rationally nor strategically to ensure America's security. That was the opinion in the autumn of 1940 of Admiral James Otto Richardson, the commander of the U.S. Fleet based at Pearl Harbor. Not only did the admiral believe it unwise and impractical for the president to insist on basing the fleet at Pearl Harbor rather than on the Pacific Coast, he had heard talk of dispersing it further, sending ships to the Philippines and the British colony of Singapore as a show of force to deter Japan from attack.[1]

Although Roosevelt was certain that Germany represented a far greater threat, Japan posed an extremely difficult problem. Japanese militarists were targeting Indochina, Thailand, Malaya, Burma, the Dutch East Indies, and even Australia and India, and they were intent on toppling the government of Chiang Kai-shek and consolidating their hold on China. On September 12, the U.S. ambassador to Tokyo, Joseph Grew, sent an alarming cable describing Japan as "one of the predatory powers," adding that it had "submerged all moral and ethical sense." He concluded that Japan's "policy of southward expansion definitely threatens American interests in the Pacific."[2]

How could the United States, across the vast Pacific, constrain this bellicose, expansionist power? In September, FDR tested the island nation's vulnerability by imposing an embargo on iron and steel scrap. But the administration was sharply divided over the next step: embargoing the even more essential commodity of oil. The president and many of his advisors worried that such an aggressive move would cause Japan to strike out at its adversaries, dragging the United States into a Pacific war.

The dilemma was further sharpened on September 27, 1940, when Germany, Italy, and Japan signed the Tripartite Pact, an agreement among the three powers to come to one another's defense and "stand by and cooperate with one another" in their military efforts. The pact was specifically aimed at the United States. It was designed to stop American assistance to Britain and China by threatening the country with a two-front war, against Japan to the west and Germany to the east. For the United States, a two-ocean war represented the worst of all worlds, and Washington saw the pact for the direct threat it was.[3]

That summer Congress had approved an unprecedented expansion of American naval power. When it reached its target of 750 fighting ships, the United States would have the largest navy any power had ever possessed—a two-ocean navy, large enough to defend the country in both the Atlantic and the Pacific. But how much of it would be ready in the near future? The current fleet was not yet prepared for battles on the seas. And though the appropriations for naval expansion also provided that personnel would be increased from 145,000 to 224,000, Admiral Richardson believed the navy realistically needed 370,000.

On October 7, 1940, Richardson lunched with FDR at the White House. He had already decided, he later wrote, that it was his "personal responsibility" to "state the facts frankly" to the president. And the primary fact was that he had lost confidence in the president's ability to fulfill the role of commander in chief.[4]

The luncheon discussion "waxed hot and heavy," the admiral reported. It became apparent to Richardson that Roosevelt had no intention of accepting his recommendations, especially the suggestion that the fleet be returned from Hawaii to the West Coast, a move that FDR regarded as a retreat from Japanese aggression.

The admiral decided it was time to utter words to which he had given long and deliberate thought. "Mr. President," he said, "I feel that I must tell you that the senior officers of the Navy do not have the trust and confidence in the civilian leadership of this country that is essential for the successful prosecution of a war in the Pacific."[5]

Roosevelt's response apparently confirmed the admiral's belief that FDR was motivated more by politics than by policy and strategy. "Joe," he reported the president saying, "you just don't understand that this is an election year and there are certain things that can't be done, no matter what, until the election is over and won." Roosevelt was candid and calm, Richardson wrote, as he explained to the navy man that, election or not, a president could never be apolitical—these were simply the realities as FDR saw them. The next day, FDR placed a terse phone call to the chief of naval operations, Admiral Harold Stark. "I want Richardson relieved."[6]

Admiral Stark sympathized with Richardson's concerns about Pacific strategy, although he understood better than most of his naval colleagues that Japan and the Pacific were just half of the global crisis Roosevelt confronted. But Stark worried that the president was confronting the crisis erratically, with no clear strategy or even an effective structure for decision making. And Stark was not alone. In the fall of 1940, Army Chief of Staff George Marshall, Secretary of War Henry Stimson, and Secretary of the Navy Frank Knox were all concerned their commander in chief was evading the tough strategic decisions that only he could make and that would, in turn, commit the nation's military, industrial, and political resources to a certain set of priorities. Amid mounting signs that the United States might soon be at war, they longed to see Roosevelt articulate a plan of action, a plan for victory.[7]

General Marshall expected order in the planning and execution of military action, and as a cautious man, he was often baffled by FDR's bent for improvisation and troubled by the president's reliance on public opinion and amateur advice. Worse, Roosevelt's final decisions too often were ambiguous—or not actually final. "He wasn't always clear-cut in his decisions," Marshall recalled. "He could be swayed."[8]

A few days after Richardson's showdown with FDR, Secretary of War Stimson also tried—more diplomatically—to prod the president to action. "We have reached one of those crises of history," he wrote to FDR, "when the fate of the world depends upon a grave decision." After laying out several strategies the United States could adopt in the Pacific Ocean, he concluded by saying that "it is a time when you should study these possibilities thoroughly." But nothing happened.[9]

Stimson, who had served as secretary of war under William Howard Taft and as secretary of state under Herbert Hoover, was as ill prepared as Marshall for FDR's ad hoc style. Two days after Roosevelt's election victory on November 5, Stimson complained to his diary, not for the first time, that the president tended to act "so hurriedly and on the spur of the moment" that "it literally is government on the jump." The president's mind, he remarked a little later, "does not follow easily a consecutive chain of thought." Instead, the garrulous and charming Roosevelt "hops about in his discussions from suggestion to suggestion and it is very much like chasing a vagrant beam of sunshine around a vacant room."[10]

For all their disagreements and disappointments with FDR, Stark, Stimson, Marshall, and Knox were Roosevelt's hand-selected, trusted men. The president had not hired them as yes men; he wanted his close advisors to challenge him, to urge him in directions he needed to move, even though he might seem unappreciative or slow to follow.

Stark had been named chief of naval operations in March 1939. A fifty-nine-year-old bespectacled, scholarly-looking rear admiral, he had been astonished to receive such a prestigious appointment. Fifty admirals were senior to him—though none had his memorable nickname of Betty. He had met FDR in 1914 when, on the eve of World War I, Lieutenant Stark had transported Assistant Secretary of the Navy Roosevelt to his family's summer home on Campobello Island aboard the destroyer USS *Patterson*. At one point during the voyage, FDR asked if he could steer the ship. "No sir," Stark crisply replied. "This ship is my command, and I doubt your authority to relieve me." Roosevelt was impressed—and remembered. "You and I talk the same language," FDR wrote to

Stark in 1939 at the time of his appointment. But even when they didn't talk the same language, they typically were comfortable enough with their differences and with continuing the argument.[11]

George Marshall had served in World War I and seen the senseless bloodshed often caused by military officers' incompetence. In the 1930s, he rose through the ranks. His first meeting with FDR took place on November 14, 1938, when he accompanied the army chief of staff, General Malin Craig, to a meeting with the president. The subject was the president's plan to ask Congress for funds to build ten thousand airplanes—but not funds to provide crews for those planes or for weapons and infrastructure such as airfields. Though the proposal made little sense, when the president asked for opinions around the table the military personnel all went along with it—except for the silent George Marshall. "Don't you think so, George?" Roosevelt asked. "Mr. President, I am sorry," Marshall replied, "but I don't agree with that at all." Marshall later commented that his remark "ended the conference. The president gave me a very startled look, and when I went out they all bade me good-bye and said that my tour in Washington was over."[12]

Instead, five months later, FDR appointed him the chief of the army. Marshall pointedly told the president that he "wanted the right to say what I think and it would often be unpleasing." Roosevelt already knew that and agreed. Otherwise, General Marshall appeared to be a standard-issue military officer—formal; insistent upon order, logic, and hierarchy; poker-faced as the president indulged in his meandering stories and musty jokes—the opposite of the good-humored men Roosevelt was most comfortable with. The president respected and needed Marshall on the general's own terms, for the soundness of his military advice, his skill as a military strategist, and his brilliance in managing the sudden expansion of the army in an atmosphere of uncertainty and crisis. Marshall's reputation for frankness would make him the administration's most effective advocate before Congress in military matters. As House Speaker Sam Rayburn said, when Marshall "takes the witness stand we forget we are Republicans or Democrats. We just remember that we are in the presence of a man who is telling the truth."[13]

Stimson and Knox, the president's key civilian advisors, were both Republicans who were outspoken in their contempt for isolationism and in their advocacy for war preparedness and even intervention. Stimson had long believed that American defense and security required the nation to accept a global role and the responsibilities it entailed. Even before the United States entered the First World War, Stimson, who considered military service one of the "fundamental duties of citizenship," had called for a "citizen army." In a speech in early 1916, he declared that "every citizen should be trained and prepared to defend his country." True to his words, he enrolled at the Business Men's Military Training Camp in Plattsburgh, New York, part of a volunteer movement committed to military preparedness. Though he was fifty years old in 1917 and partially blind in one eye, he served with an army artillery unit in France, reaching the rank of colonel.[14]

By the early 1930s, as Hoover's secretary of state, Stimson worried that Europe was in worse condition than before the war and that the economic depression there would lead to serious political upheaval. Visiting Mussolini's Italy in 1931, he found "a form of government foreign to the American spirit," containing the "seeds of grave danger."[15]

Then came Hitler. In 1932, the National Socialists doubled their seats in the Reichstag. The next year, Hitler became chancellor, and German democracy plunged with shocking speed into militaristic super-nationalism and dictatorship. Stimson feared that the continent, not yet healed from the Great War, was marching toward a "grim conclusion." Distressed by the "moral abdication" and "extraordinary weakness and cowardice" he found in western Europe and by growing isolationism in the United States, he waited in vain for someone, as he wrote, "to show some guts." When Japan invaded China in 1937, Stimson published a long letter in the *New York Times* assailing "the wave of ostrich-like isolationism which has swept over us." Neutrality laws, he wrote, imposed a "dead level of neutral conduct" on the United States, leaving it with a "policy of amoral drift." The outbreak of war in Europe in September 1939 came almost as a relief; it was, Stimson commented, the end of "hopeless years of concession and appeasement." In his stern view, Europe's democracies were forced to come to grips with the consequences of their failure to recognize reality before it overwhelmed them with crushing force.[16]

On Wednesday, June 19, 1940, the phone rang in Henry Stimson's office in New York. It was President Roosevelt with a question. Seven years earlier, President-elect Roosevelt had held two long tête-à-têtes with Stimson discussing foreign policy. "We are getting so that we do pretty good teamwork, don't we?" he said after their second meeting. Now, in 1940, Stimson's interventionism had attracted the president's attention. Would he accept the position of secretary of war? As Stimson wrote in his diary, Roosevelt "was very anxious to have me accept because everybody was running around at loose ends in Washington and he thought I would be a stabilizing factor." He had already run the War Department, and he had both the stature and the experience to direct a complex mobilization.[17]

Stimson had heard that his name had been mentioned for the post, but he nevertheless asked FDR for a few hours to mull it over. In the early evening, he telephoned the president with a few pointed questions. Did Mr. Roosevelt know about the speech he had given at the Yale commencement two days earlier, in which he told graduating seniors and fellow alumni that the United States was facing the greatest crisis in its history and called for the first peacetime draft in American history? Yes, FDR said; he had read the text of Stimson's speech—and he agreed with it. Stimson had followed up his remarks at Yale with a muscular radio speech on national defense, demanding an immediate end to "our ill-starred so-called neutrality venture" and urging that the United States "accelerate by every means in our power the sending of planes and other munitions to Britain ... sending them if necessary in our own ships and under convoy." The aggressive foreign policy he advocated was made necessary, he forcefully declared, by the international emergency that threatened "the very existence of all that our country has cherished and fought for, for over 160 years."[18]

Though Stimson's interventionist views were strong and steadfast in contrast to the president's ambivalence, Roosevelt nevertheless welcomed into his circle of advisors a powerful figure who would push him toward a path he was reluctant to take.

Also in June 1940, FDR invited another interventionist—and Republican—to join his Cabinet as secretary of the navy. Frank Knox, then sixty-six years old, had been a Rough Rider who fought beside Theodore Roosevelt in the battle of San Juan Hill and then served as an army colonel in France during World War I. Knox later bought two newspapers, the *Chicago Daily News* and the *Manchester* (NH) *Union-Leader.* As Alf Landon's running mate on the GOP ticket in 1936, Knox had hammered the New Deal's "crackpot ideas," which, he jibed, contained "something of Karl Marx" but "equally as much of Groucho Marx."[19]

FDR held no grudge; he believed in having a short political memory. Besides, the Landon-Knox ticket had won only two states, Maine and Vermont; and right after the election Knox publicized his own unflinching internationalist and interventionist principles. In October 1937, he published an editorial in his *Daily News* that not only praised the president's "quarantine" speech but called for immediate repeal of the neutrality acts, which, he wrote, tied the president's hands "in advance in his momentous task of guiding the nation at a time of international turmoil." The day after German forces invaded Poland in September 1939, he editorialized that Americans should put politics aside and rally behind their president. A few days later, calling for national unity, he suggested that FDR name a bipartisan Cabinet. And in May 1940, he warned in his newspaper of the dangers of a combined German and Japanese attack on an unprepared United States and urged Americans to "hasten the tempo" of arms production, equip both naval and army air fleets, and repeal the arms embargo. He advocated extending every form of help, short of war itself, to the nations that "are now fighting the bestial monster that is making a shambles of Europe."[20]

After he entered Roosevelt's bipartisan Cabinet, Knox would outdo the rest of the administration with his public demands for action against the "alien dogs of war that snarl and fight in murdering packs." He liked to emphasize that it was not "what we *say* but what we *do* that counts." On that point, as well as on the grim necessity of America's eventual armed intervention in the war, FDR's quartet of advisors—Knox, Stimson, Marshall, and Stark— all agreed.[21]

But in the autumn of 1940, a majority of Americans were not convinced that there was no alternative to war, against either the Japanese or the Germans. The country, Stimson reflected, was "still asleep." Something had to stir it to face the situation squarely.[22]

But in a democratic nation bitterly divided over the question of war and peace, truth telling was not an easy matter. In the fall of 1941, Winston Churchill grumbled that "nothing is more dangerous in wartime than to live in the temperamental atmosphere of a Gallup poll." Henry Stimson, too, believed that the president's role, as he wrote, "centered on his obligation to act as the leader, and not merely the representative, of public opinion." But FDR felt quite differently—and not only because it was an election year. His close aide Sam Rosenman quoted him as once saying, "It's a terrible thing to look over your shoulder when you are trying to lead and find no one there." Roosevelt appreciated the importance of public opinion in matters as grave and communal as war and peace. "Governments such as ours," he wrote to a friend in June 1940, "can only move with the thought and will of the great majority of the people. . . . Were it otherwise the very fabric of our democracy—which after all is government by public opinion—would be in danger of disintegrating."[23]

Unlike the European dictators whose prime tool was compulsion, FDR had to rely on education and persuasion. In a campaign speech in 1932, he had noted that the art of leadership consisted in "persuading, leading, sacrificing, teaching always, because the greatest duty of a statesman is to educate." Now he would have to educate Americans and convince them and Congress that the nation must prepare for war. The Latin root of the verb *educate* is "ducere"—to lead—and "ex"—out of; the root of *convince* is "vincere"—to conquer—and "con"—with. The president would educate his fellow citizens, lead them out of the darkness of isolationism, and then they would conquer together.[24]

In 1940, FDR did not seek to persuade Americans with grim predictions of war's inevitability. He played a far more cautious game, frequently emphasizing the Monroe Doctrine of 1823, the mantra of defense of the Western Hemisphere that most Americans found uncontroversial. That principle seemed to represent a safe middle ground between war and isolation—one that was unlikely to infuriate the internationalists or alienate the isolationists. Even the über-isolationist Charles Lindbergh, while insisting that the rest of the world must fend for itself, embraced strong hemispheric defense.

"This western hemisphere is our domain. . . . We must allow no invading army to set foot," he had declared in the fall of 1939. "If it is challenged by any nation, the answer must be war."[25]

But where exactly did the "Western Hemisphere" begin and end? "Mr. President, on the record, is there any way, for practical purposes, that you could define the Western Hemisphere?" a reporter asked at a press conference. That was "too difficult on the record," FDR replied. But off the record, he drew a line through the middle of the Atlantic Ocean, about halfway between "the sticky-out point of Brazil" and the "sticky-out point of Africa." In the Pacific, "except for a funny little jog at the top," he extended the Western Hemisphere to the International Date Line, west of the Hawaiian Islands. He called this improvisation a "normal, common-sense definition."[26]

In the fall of 1940, FDR deftly used the concept of "defense of the Western Hemisphere" to pitch two crucial policies: the destroyers-for-bases deal with Britain and the peacetime draft. In promoting the destroyers deal, he proudly told Congress that "the value to the *Western Hemisphere* of these outposts of security is *beyond calculation*." The Selective Service legislation, meanwhile, provided that the young men drafted into the army would "*not* be employed beyond the limits of the *Western Hemisphere* except in the Territories and possessions of the United States including the Philippine Islands."[27]

The president elaborated on hemispheric defense in an October 12 Columbus Day radio address that reached listeners in Central and South America as well as across the United States. The threat of German infiltration of the Americas, he explained, justified invoking the Monroe Doctrine. "We shall be all for one and one for all," he declared, repeating d'Artagnan's famous toast to the Three Musketeers. He assured his international audience that if they all worked together, the Western Hemisphere would be able to withstand attacks from both the Pacific and the Atlantic. "This hemisphere wants no war with any nation," he said, underlining that peace was "the objective for which I hope and work and pray."[28]

But it wasn't all about peace—or the Western Hemisphere. Roosevelt threw some red meat into that Columbus Day talk. The signing of the Tripartite Pact two weeks earlier, as historian Warren Kimball wrote, provided "a convincing argument that the United States was truly threatened with encirclement." In a defiant conclusion, the president stated that "no combination of dictator countries of Europe and Asia will halt us in the path we see ahead for ourselves and for democracy. No combination of dictator countries of Europe and Asia will stop the help we are giving to almost the last free people now fighting to hold them at bay. Our course is clear. Our decision is made."[29]

A few days later, in a public letter to Frank Knox in observance of Navy Day, Roosevelt struck another militant note of realism. Acknowledging that the nation was "entering new rapidly changing and unpredictable world conditions," he expressed confidence that the Navy was preparing for the "successful prosecution of war, should war unfortunately come."[30]

Where exactly did the president's hesitation, caution, and pragmatism, his steps forward and back, leave him and the country? In fact, Roosevelt had cobbled together a foreign policy of motley ingredients: defense of the Western Hemisphere; buildup of the Army and Navy; universal compulsory military service; optimism about British survival and thus all-out materiel aid to Britain; no appeasement of the fascists; a desire to avoid war; the prospect that war might come; and absolutely no American boys sent to fight in wars outside the Western Hemisphere. It was the agenda of a commander in chief whose responsibility was to defend the country and prepare for war, of a president who desired peace but grasped the evils of Nazism, of an opportunistic candidate hungering for an election victory in November, and, finally, of a many-minded man whose capacity to keep examining options was virtually inexhaustible.[31]

Yet only the president could resolve the contradictions that left even his inner circle perplexed.

In the cheerless fall of 1940, no one knew if Hitler could be stopped or how long British cities and ports could continue to withstand night after night of Nazi bombing raids. Would Germany eventually take over Britain's fleet? What if Hitler successfully infiltrated South America? What if Japan continued to extend its reach in Asia? How much time was left before the United States itself would be attacked or forced to enter the war?

Facing this dangerous uncertainty, Stark, Marshall, Stimson, and Knox decided they had to have an overarching strategic plan. The military had developed a series of options and directives keyed to different contingencies, the so-called RAINBOW plans. Outlined in June 1939, before the outbreak of war, the four RAINBOW plans, which soon became five, had offered possible strategic responses to a combined Axis attack: defense of North America; defense of the Western Hemisphere; control of the western Pacific; and concerted offensive action with Britain and France to defeat Germany while maintaining a defensive posture in the Pacific against Japan.

By the fall of 1940, circumstances had radically changed around the globe while American capabilities themselves were fitfully improving. Though the RAINBOW plans were continually updated, the quartet felt they still lacked a forward-looking "grand strategy," as Stimson called it. Most urgent, they agreed, was to determine the nation's priorities in broad terms—Atlantic or Pacific, Germany or Japan—as well as the specific goals and commitments those priorities entailed. In late November, Stimson and Marshall discussed the need for a more "systematized basis" for formulating defense policy than "the present happy-go-lucky snap-of-the-moment method" that the president seemed to prefer.[32]

Time was of the essence. General Marshall estimated that the American military needed eighteen more months to prepare fully, but war could break out in the Pacific at any moment, while war in the Atlantic hinged on how long Britain could hold out under the Nazi onslaught. In the event of war, the military would execute one of the RAINBOW plans, whose origins lay in a world that had vanished.[33]

"If we lose in the Atlantic, we lose everywhere," General Marshall said in the fall of 1940. A few weeks later, in November, he wrote to Admiral Stark that "our national interests require that we resist proposals that *do not have* for their immediate goal the *survival of the British Empire* and the *defeat of Germany*, and 2. that we avoid dispersions that might lessen our power to operate effectively, decisively if possible, in the principal theatre, the Atlantic." Marshall's clear statement of strategic priorities tracked the president's views, and most Americans shared this Europe-facing perspective.[34]

Marshall also thought the United States was overextended in the Pacific. "A serious commitment in the Pacific," he told Stark in his November memo, "is just what Germany would like to see us undertake." But while he recognized the necessity of maintaining Great Britain as a bastion against Germany, he insisted that aid to Britain not compromise American preparedness. Both Marshall and Stark, as historian Kimball noted, "looked on support for England not as a solution to American national defense problems but as a temporary stopgap until the United States was rearmed."[35]

And what if American aid failed to sustain the British, and the planes, ships, and armaments fell into Nazi hands? In that case, as an army planner said at the time, anyone who had favored selling planes and other munitions to Britain "might hope to be found hanging from a lamp post."[36]

Before the spring of 1940, RAINBOW 1—continental defense—had been the top priority. But in May 1940, when Hitler's planes, tanks, guns, and soldiers were swiftly and brutally crushing the European democracies one by one, RAINBOW 4 moved to the top of the list. That plan assumed that Britain too would be defeated and the Royal Navy destroyed or captured, and that the United States alone would have to defend the Atlantic front of the Western Hemisphere. "We have to be prepared," Marshall had told his military colleagues on June 17, a few tense days before France's surrender, "to meet the worst situation that may develop, that is, if we do not have the Allied fleet in the Atlantic." But by fall, Marshall was more optimistic about Britain's future and convinced that its survival was of paramount strategic importance. "As long as the British fleet remains undefeated and England holds out," he said, "the Western Hemisphere is in little danger of direct attack." Nothing else mattered as much.[37]

Secretary of the Navy Knox agreed completely. Though more publicly outspoken than the discreet general, he kept private his opinion that Germany would soon declare war on the United States and that such a declaration would be "one of the *best things* that could happen" to defeat the Nazis. But he pulled few punches in a speech he gave on November 14 in Boston to a conference of

New England businessmen and governors, broadcast on national and international radio. He painted the pathetic picture of "an entire continental Europe enslaved," about to enter a desperate winter of "black starvation for helpless, innocent people, the victims of a thoroughly unwarranted war conducted by a fanatic, greedy for world domination." He outlined a sharp six-point program:

1. "We are going to give Great Britain *every possible degree* of aid we can—short of leaving ourselves defenseless."
2. "We will have concern for the Chinese people."
3. "We will pile up our armaments, whatever the cost."
4. "We won't appease anybody on earth."
5. "We won't talk about what we're going to do, but *do* it."
6. "We're going to harden our muscle and our will because self-preservation is possible only by self-sacrifice."[38]

Neither Roosevelt nor the rest of the quartet would disagree with this mix of policy and attitude. And Knox clearly expressed the consensus for a Europe-first policy; the United States would merely have "concern" for China. The naval secretary scored a hit with his tough, forthright talk. "His audience warmed to his conclusions," wrote the *New York Times*. "Many of his hearers, commenting later on the speech asserted that it was 'time that some one spoke out.' "[39]

Still, the secretary of the Navy had not advanced beyond "all aid short of war," even though he believed that "all aid" would not be enough.[40]

Roosevelt's speechwriter Robert Sherwood, with a vantage point inside the White House, believed that whatever the peril, the president "was not going to lead the country into war—he was going to wait to be pushed in." But there was no waiting, for the president or the country, if the United States hoped to be ready for the fight that would follow an attack or major provocation. With much of the world aflame and with strategic plans that were outdated and incomplete, the quartet, led by Admiral Stark, would formulate a new strategic framework for America's taking up arms in the global conflict.[41]

So in late October, Admiral Stark, haunted by "the possibility that we may at any moment become involved in war," set out to compose an analysis of the situation to present to his colleagues and to the president. In the quiet of his home, he worked on a draft of his memorandum for eighteen hours straight. With military concision, he methodically assessed the world situation, laid out likely scenarios, articulated what he considered America's prime objective, and weighed the country's priorities, capabilities, and options, while also taking into account "the political realities in our own country." He ended with his personal recommendation for a logical, deliberate course of action that would serve as a solid basis for coordinated military and naval planning. His aim, he unpretentiously told Frank Knox, was to shed "some light upon the major decisions which the president may make for guiding our future naval effort in the event of war, and in further immediate preparation for war."[42]

It was a humble goal for a document that outlined the course the United States would follow for the next five years—through the utterly unforeseeable events of the worst war in human history.

In an earlier discussion with the secretary of the navy, Stark had explained his outlook, which echoed Marshall's. "If Britain wins decisively against Germany," the admiral told Knox, "we could win everywhere; but if she loses, the problem confronting us would be very great; and while we might not *lose everywhere*, we might, possibly, not *win anywhere*." If Britain fell, "we would find ourselves acting alone and at war with the world."[43]

And Britain might well fall, Stark thought, its collapse aided by the incompetence of its military leaders. "I believe it easily possible, lacking active American military assistance," he wrote, "for that empire to lose this war." He considered the British "overly optimistic" about their chances for victory. When he learned that some Britons actually expected the United States to enter the war after the November election, he scoffed at their "non-realistic views of international political conditions" and their "slack ways of thought." General Marshall shared Stark's disappointment with British military leadership. They were "very poorly prepared," Marshall later recalled, "except as to their naval strength," adding, "I think the word 'poorly' hardly describes it." Ironically, the American officers' low opinion of British fitness for battle served Churchill's purposes. The more inept Britain appeared, he reasoned, the more likely it was that the United States would rush to its aid. "I am much encouraged by the American naval view" of British prospects, Churchill wrote to Royal Navy captain Arthur Clarke in November. It was *"particularly helpful"* that American military leaders considered Britain *"incapable of winning alone."*[44]

Stark's report, covering twenty-six double-spaced pages, was composed in nonaggressive, unpretentious language. On the first page, he explained that his goal was to present his "views concerning steps we might take to meet the situation that will exist should the United States enter war either alone or with allies." The report posed the crucial question—"Where should we fight the war, and for what objective?"—and then proceeded to offer four scenarios.[45]

Plan A proposed that the United States maintain a purely defensive posture in the Western Hemisphere and avoid any involvement in the war for as long as possible. Neither in the East nor in the West would the country provide more than material help to its allies and "minor" assistance in their defense. It was a plan that might have pleased American isolationists.

Plan B laid out a strictly defensive posture in the Atlantic but a full offensive against Japan in the Pacific. This plan offered no direct aid to Britain, on the assumption that the United States could place "full trust in the British to hold their own indefinitely in the Atlantic"—or at least hold their own until the United States decisively defeated Japan. But if America entered the war against Japan and Britain then lost to Germany, the United States would "reorient" toward the Atlantic. "There is no dissenting view on this point," Stark noted.

Plan C envisaged a two-front war, with the United States sending "the strongest possible military assistance" to the British in Europe and to the British, Dutch, and Chinese in the Far East. The burden of fighting major wars in two theaters at the same time was a grievous one, Stark acknowledged, that would so disperse U.S. forces as to preclude the concentration necessary for successful offensive operations in either theater. "Strategically, the situation might become disastrous should our effort on either front fail."

The last scenario, Plan D, foresaw the United States mounting a strong offensive in the Atlantic as an ally of the British while maintaining only a defensive position in the Pacific. Even if the United States were "forced into" a war with Japan, it would avoid major operations in the Pacific until Britain was secure.[46]

Of course, circumstances and contingencies would shape American actions. But taking all probable factors into account, Stark strongly recommended that the Roosevelt administration adopt Plan D. The other options he rejected as simply counterproductive. In Stark's analysis, it was the continued existence of Britain and its global empire that would best ensure the security of the United States and of the Western Hemisphere. And since it was Germany, not Japan, that most seriously threatened Britain's security and even survival, it followed that Germany also posed the greatest danger to the security of the United States. Thus, Stark concluded, "the full national offensive strength" must "be exerted in a single direction"—toward an Atlantic-first strategy with the defeat of Germany as the ultimate goal.[47]

The adoption of Plan D—Plan Dog, in naval parlance—would mean that the fate of the United States was inextricably bound to that of Britain, that the United States would do everything it could to meet Britain's "vital needs," and that American soldiers might have to fight in a land war in Europe. "Your boys are not going to be sent into any foreign wars," Roosevelt had promised a Boston crowd during the last week of October. That same week, Stark was envisioning American participation in a full-scale land offensive in Europe.[48]

American soldiers would eventually have to fight, the admiral argued, because the navy alone could not defend Britain against the Germans and certainly could not defeat them. Victory would "probably depend" upon an American land offensive. "I believe that the United States, in addition to sending naval assistance," Stark wrote, "would also need to send large air and land forces to Europe or Africa, or both, and to *participate strongly* in this land offensive."[49]

Stark harbored no doubt that his Plan D was "likely to be the most fruitful for the United States, particularly if we enter the war at an early date." But he recognized that in the short term, while the United States was still building up its military strength, it was not yet ready to engage in offensive actions. So he advised that for

the very near future, the nation "adopt Alternative (A) without hostilities"—hemispheric defense and only material aid to the Allies.
Plan A promised to "most rapidly increase the military strength of
both the Army and the Navy."[50]

Stark's last crucial recommendation was that members of the
American military senior staff hold secret talks that winter in
Washington with their British counterparts to "lay down plans for
promoting unity of allied effort" as "a preliminary to possible entry
of the United States into the conflict." It would be an exercise in
joint planning, and he hoped that Plan Dog would represent the
American position.[51]

For about ten days, Admiral Stark discussed his draft memorandum
with members of his staff and made the revisions they suggested.
Then he showed the paper to General Marshall, who readily
agreed that Plan Dog was the necessary strategy. Only American
boots on the ground would secure Britain and defeat Germany.
"You've got to get down and hold things," Marshall would later
explain. "You can destroy plants. You can destroy cities . . . but that
doesn't win." To "hold things" in Europe required, for Marshall, a
low American profile in the Pacific and nothing that would lessen
"our power to operate effectively, decisively if possible, in the principal theatre—the Atlantic." The strength of Plan Dog was its deci-
siveness in making Britain and the Atlantic the unquestioned
American priority and the most likely front for American military
intervention, while it minimized the Japanese threat.[52]

On November 12, Admiral Stark officially submitted the pol-
ished memorandum to his superior, Frank Knox, who forwarded it
right away to the president. For ten days, Stark anxiously awaited
the commander in chief's reaction.[53]

That reaction was something of a mystery. After reading the
memorandum, Roosevelt told Stark that he "would like War, State
and Navy to draw up a joint estimate." That bland, noncommittal
statement came as a disappointment. It was hardly, Stark wrote to
Marshall, the "definite pronouncement" he had hoped for. But
while the president withheld formal approval, he hadn't shot down
the plan either. On the contrary, he ordered that civilian and military departments study, discuss, amend, and refine it. The Atlantic-

first strategy of Plan Dog was adopted because the president did not say no. It was decision making by inferred acquiescence. Whatever else Roosevelt relayed to Stark remained between him, Stark, and Marshall. "I am holding the Presidential comment on my memorandum very tight," Stark wrote to Marshall, "but will tell you when I see you."[54]

Roosevelt did, however, quickly accept the proposal for joint staff conversations. That unambiguous acceptance, concluded historian Mark Lowenthal, "should be seen as a decision taken not only on its own, but also as a token of Roosevelt's tacit approval of the [Plan Dog] memorandum without committing himself to it as a guideline for future policy. . . . He was not willing to be prodded where he would not yet go himself."[55]

The final report reflected the views of the army, navy, State Department, and, however cryptically, the White House. But it was Admiral Stark, the naval chief of operations, who had seized the initiative. It was he who fought to bring coherence to what had been a muddle; it was he who, above all, drafted a plan that was true to the world crisis and to America's potential leadership role in that crisis.

Plan Dog did not answer all questions. It offered no blueprints for actual battles. It did not clarify how a battered Britain would pay for life-supporting military aid. It did not address America's economic and industrial mobilization for war, the conversion of peacetime industry to wartime production, the enlistment of workers, or the importance of a supremely cooperative and productive partnership between industry and labor. Yet even though, in 1942 and most of 1943, more American forces would be deployed against Japan than against Germany, Plan Dog would define America's paramount wartime strategy and goals. As historian Louis Morton wrote, it was "perhaps the most important single document in the development of World War II strategy." Not once during the entire war, Morton added, "was this decision successfully challenged."[56]

CHAPTER FOUR

Cruising in December

A CCORDING TO ROBERT SHERWOOD, the president's main business in early December on board the USS *Tuscaloosa* was fishing, basking in the Caribbean sun, and kidding around with his cronies. He was, Sherwood noted, "as carefree as you please."[1]

The banter began on the president's train en route from Washington to Miami. "Couldn't you tell us where you are going?" asked one reporter who accompanied the president.

> FDR: I wish I knew. Well, I'll tell you. . . . I won't deceive you at all. We are going to Christmas Island to buy Christmas cards and then we are going on to Easter Island to buy Easter Eggs.
>
> Q. Are you going to arrive there on Christmas Day?
>
> FDR: We have to get there before then to get the cards off.
>
> Q. Is the dog going aboard?
>
> FDR: Yes, and he is very good too. We had him on the *Potomac* the other day and he was just as good as gold. The chief trouble was to keep the crew from feeding him.
>
> Q. You have the same trouble with your aide Pa Watson, don't you? [Laughter][2]

A *New York Times* reporter noted that the president "loves to twit the newspaper men who cover the White House and if he succeeds in 'putting one over on them' he is as happy as a child who has perpetrated a successful April Fool's joke on his playmate." Such a scene, he added, "is impossible to imagine in Downing Street."[3]

A few hours later, shortly after noon on December 3, Roosevelt arrived in Miami to begin the eleven-day cruise. His entourage included only immediate staff—Pa Watson, his personal physician Dr. Ross McIntire, naval aide Captain Daniel Callaghan, Harry Hopkins—and Fala, FDR's black Scottish terrier pup, named after the Scotland home of some of the president's ancestors. As they boarded the *Tuscaloosa*, a band played and a twenty-one-gun salute rang out as sailors in crisp white uniforms stood at attention. Just as record cold temperatures, snow, and near-gale-force winds were lashing the Midwest and the Northeast, FDR and his companions happily sailed for Jamaica.[4]

That same afternoon, all the key players in the administration, including war production officials, were meeting in Henry Morgenthau's office. On the agenda was Britain's latest order for $2 billion worth of munitions, everything from thousands of aircraft engines to a million rifles. FDR had already given the go-ahead for the order; the question was how it would be paid for. Experts from the Treasury Department covered a blackboard with a forest of bewildering numbers. The bottom line was simple: Britain was $1 billion short. Prime Minister Churchill himself had recognized the brutal truth. "Even if we divested ourselves of all our gold and foreign assets," he wrote, "we could not pay for half we had ordered."[5]

The Neutrality Act of 1939 had lifted the arms embargo imposed by the Neutrality Act of 1935 and permitted the sale of weapons to belligerents. But it placed the burden of cash-and-carry on orders of war materiel. If the British didn't produce the cash, they didn't get the goods, and by the way, shipping was their problem. Newspaper editor James Pope, writing in the *Louisville Courier*, scoffed at American hypocrisy. "In heaven's name, how have we aided England? . . . We have sold England an indeterminate number of military airplanes. She has paid cash. She has come and got them. We have sold England, I understand, some old rifles. . . . She paid cash. She came and got them. . . . What an inspiration we are to the suffering humanity of older, more benighted lands. We are opening our hearts. We are opening our order books."[6]

On the subject of British finances, the president appeared to be of two minds. Just before leaving on his cruise, he said carelessly to Morgenthau that the English weren't "bust"—"there's lots of money there." This put him in the camp of Americans who were, as Lord Lothian put it, "saturated with illusions to the effect that we have vast resources available" and who believed those resources should be spent down before other sources of funding were explored. But Roosevelt had a more realistic view, too. For months, he had said repeatedly that the United States would soon be obliged to help Britain with loans and credit. It was in that direction that the administration had been drifting since the election.[7]

The president's advice to the men attending the meeting in his office, Morgenthau told his colleagues, was contained in an ambiguous note FDR wrote before leaving for Miami. He encouraged them to "use your imaginations" in finding a solution to financing British military needs. The men did so, and a consensus formed overwhelmingly around an alternative to cash-and-carry that could open the floodgates of aid to the British. It was put in a nutshell by the secretary of the navy. "We are going to pay for the war from now on, are we?" Frank Knox asked. "Got to," he said, answering his own question. "No choice about it."[8]

But giving away military property to the British on so massive a scale, they knew, could spark all kinds of legal and political issues. The sums involved were "enormous," noted Stimson, who expressed concern that America might be drawn into war "just to save our investment, or to save the purpose for which we made the investment." The group agreed that the president "should not go ahead on such an huge project alone" but must have congressional authorization for new lines of credit to Britain. But they were aware that the persistent power of isolationism meant that no less than a masterpiece of persuasion was needed to bring both the public and Congress along in a radical new program of aid.[9]

No such weighty meetings were taking place aboard the *Tuscaloosa* in early December. Only Harry Hopkins among the president's guests was qualified to discuss the world crisis, if FDR had been so inclined. "I am off for sunshine and a little rest which I much need," Roosevelt had written to two cousins. The Caribbean was a place for fishing, card games, martinis, and movies shown on the deck in the evenings—*North West Mounted Police*, starring Gary Cooper; *I Love You Again*, with William Powell and Myrna Loy; and *Tin Pan Alley*, with Betty Grable.[10]

And no harm was done in combining a little business with pleasure. The president answered batches of mail delivered to the ship by navy planes and toured defense sites the United States had acquired from the British in the destroyers-for-bases deal, tours that Robert Sherwood suspected were organized so as not to impede the president's goal of relaxation.

Under sunny skies and with smooth seas, pleasant salt air, and temperatures in the eighties, FDR visited Cuba, where he discussed plans for developing the Guantánamo naval base and loaded up on Cuban cigars. In Jamaica, he looked over possible sites for new anchorage and dockyard facilities and entertained British colonial officials and their ladies at lunch. Anchored off Eleuthera Island in the Bahamas, the *Tuscaloosa* welcomed aboard the Duke of Windsor, who as King Edward VIII had abdicated the British throne in 1936. Exiled by Churchill in the summer of 1940 because of his pro-Nazi and anti-Semitic views—and on the specific condition that he not visit the United States and spread defeatism there—the grossly ignorant duke was serving as wartime governor of the Bahamas, where he transformed Government House gardens in Nassau with "some imaginative touches" as well as the labor of local prisoners. Asked by reporters about his three-hour conference with the president, the former king was more effusive in describing the luncheon menu of mushroom soup and kingfish than in discussing defense of the Western Hemisphere.[11]

On Sunday, December 8, Roosevelt met with naval and diplomatic officials on the French island of Martinique. Because France had surrendered to Germany that past spring, FDR's administration feared that French ships and planes based on Martinique—including a hundred American-made fighting planes nesting on a French aircraft carrier—could fall into Nazi hands. Secretary Knox had pushed for U.S. forces to occupy the island, an idea Stimson and Marshall had rejected as likely to trigger a German takeover of all other French colonies.[12]

On the other side of the Atlantic, from dusk that Sunday until midmorning on Monday, wave after wave of Nazi bombers dropped their lethal cargo over London, ending a weeklong lull. It was the most concentrated raid since the Blitz had begun that past summer. While Roosevelt was fishing and relaxing, reading and working, German pilots targeted Birmingham, Greenwich, Southampton, Liverpool, Bristol, and Portsmouth, destroying what remained of their port facilities and war factories. But the high explosives and incendiary bombs also fell on schools, hospitals, churches, the famous Greenwich Observatory, theaters, shops, and entire working-class neighborhoods, reducing them to smoldering ruins.[13]

That same Monday morning, a naval plane delivered a special letter to President Roosevelt off Antigua. "This letter was one of the most important I ever wrote," Churchill later remarked. The desperation of Britain's plight burst onto the deck of the *Tuscaloosa* and catapulted Roosevelt from calm, sun-studded seas back into a dark, war-torn world.[14]

Churchill began with the solemnity of which he was a master. "The future of our two democracies and the kind of civilisation for which they stand," he wrote FDR, "are bound up with the survival and independence of the British Commonwealth of Nations." The future of the whole world now depended on relations between the British Empire and its former colonies in the New World, the privileged inheritors of Anglo-Saxon democracy. The prime minister accepted that it was "our British duty" to hold the front and "grapple with Nazi power" until the United States was prepared militarily to intervene. But because of the "solid identity of interest" between the two nations, Churchill, whose mother was American, ventured to ask Roosevelt to become his partner in war.[15]

"We think in English," Alexander Hamilton had said in 1789, encapsulating the profound intellectual and cultural ties and Enlightenment values binding the United States and Great Britain. A hundred and fifty years later, in the winter of 1940–41, Frank Knox reconfirmed that the roots of American freedom under law lay in British soil. "From a cultural standpoint it would be a calamity for us," Knox said, "if British life were uprooted and replaced by a Nazi growth. Even those of our citizens whose lineage leads back to parts of the world other than Britain must feel that their greatest benefits from life in this country are connected with stability of the institutions which Britain originated and which we have adapted to our own form of civilization."[16]

Britain and America were linked, as Robert Sherwood remarked, by a "common law" marriage. Even so, given the volatility of American opinion and British desperation, partnership between the two nations would be a dynamic, occasionally clashing combination of common and separate interests, driven by changing power relations and, above all, by the ascension of the United States to world leadership.[17]

Churchill's letter to Roosevelt reflected the depths of British dependence on American support to bring the "agony of civilisation," as he aptly termed the international crisis, to a positive conclusion. Winston Churchill, proud leader of the world's greatest empire, whose defiance of the Nazis had inspired resistance movements all over Europe and beyond, was begging the American president for help.[18]

Churchill's nation was besieged in almost every respect. So far Britain was standing up to the destruction and slaughter inflicted almost nightly by the Luftwaffe. But Churchill also confronted another threat, to which he devoted over half his letter. It was "less sudden and less spectacular, but equally deadly," he wrote FDR. "This mortal danger is the steady and increasing diminution of sea tonnage." Britain had lost 250,000 tons of shipping to German U-boat attacks in September, over 300,000 tons in October, and almost 376,000 tons in November. To Churchill, the conclusion was clear. The decision for 1941, he wrote Roosevelt, "lies upon the seas. Unless we can establish our ability to feed this island, to import the munitions of all kinds which we need, unless we can move our armies to the various theatres where Hitler and his confederate Mussolini must be met . . . we may fall by the way."[19]

Adding to Churchill's challenges, Britain was faced not only with Ireland's refusal to let the Royal Navy use its ports but also with Nazi control of France's northern and western coasts. And the

prime minister had to consider the possibility that the collabora-
tionist Vichy government, "by joining Hitler's New Order," would
"find an excuse for ranging with the Axis Powers the very considerable undamaged naval forces still under its control." In Asia, Japan
was "thrusting southward," threatening British air and naval bases.
"We have today no forces in the Far East capable of dealing with
this situation." These threats left Churchill with no choice but to
seek from the United States "supreme and decisive help" in "what
is, in certain aspects, our common cause."[20]

That supreme help pointedly did not include American soldiers. Although the prime minister believed their involvement was
both inevitable and essential to victory, he could not say so to the
American cousins. "Even if the United States were our ally instead
of our friend and indispensable partner," Churchill wrote in his letter to the president, "we should not ask for a large American expeditionary army."[21]

The prime minister expressed gratitude for the armaments that
had already been placed at Britain's disposal "by the great Republic
of which you are for the third time chosen Chief." But he needed
more, especially to overcome the shipping crisis: a reassertion from
the United States of the doctrine of the freedom of the seas from
barbarous warfare; naval escorts as well as air support for British
battleships, cruisers, and destroyers; more assertive American control over the western half of the Atlantic; and help in persuading
Ireland to let Britain use its ports. Above all, he asked for the "gift,
loan or supply" of a large number of American vessels of war as
well as increased American production—and sharing—of planes
and other munitions. "We look to the industrial energy of the
Republic," Churchill wrote. "May I invite you then, Mr. President,
to give earnest consideration to an immediate order on joint account for a further 2,000 combat aircraft a month?"[22]

After four thousand painful and troubling words, Churchill
finally reached the bottom line: the inescapable subject of money.
This was not the first time he communicated to the American president his anxiety about Britain's ability to pay for weapons. Just two
weeks into his premiership, in May 1940, he had written to FDR,
"We shall go on paying dollars for as long as we can, but I should
like to feel reasonably sure that when we can pay no more, you will

give us the stuff all the same." Now, in December, he informed Roosevelt that "the moment approaches when we shall no longer be able to pay cash for shipping and other supplies."[23]

Britain was not exactly broke, but the prime minister nevertheless pleaded with the American president not to force it to divest itself of all its saleable assets. It would be "mutually disadvantageous," he reasoned, "that after victory was won with our blood, civilisation saved and time gained for the United States to be fully armed against all eventualities, we should stand stripped to the bone. Such a course would not be in the moral or economic interests of either of our countries." He expressed faith that America would not "confine the help which they have so generously promised only to such munitions of war and commodities as could be immediately paid for." After promising that the British people would prove themselves "ready to suffer and sacrifice to the utmost for the Cause," he added a remarkable final line: "The rest we leave with confidence to you and to our people." As historian Warren Kimball noted, " 'The rest' was what really mattered." It was a recognition that the future of Britain and its empire would be ultimately at the mercy of the rising power of the United States, with the hope, Churchill wrote, that "ways and means will be found which future generations on both sides of the Atlantic will approve and admire."[24]

This extraordinary letter had been inspired by Lord Lothian, who on his return to Britain in November 1940 had told the prime minister that "there was an opinion in Washington that we were inclined to ask for more than was necessary. The only answer to this is a ruthless exposé of the strategic dangers." Lothian had long believed, as had Morgenthau, that such a full and frank report from London would have the greatest impact on the Roosevelt administration as well as the American public. Years later, Churchill recalled that Lothian had urged him "to write a full statement of our position to the President." But the prime minister was slow to embrace the idea. In fact, it was Lothian who wrote a first draft of the letter when he visited Churchill for two days in mid-November at Ditchley Park, an Oxfordshire country home that a friend had put at Churchill's disposal. Prime minister and ambassador exchanged revisions, and then Churchill sent the draft for comment to the relevant ministries, especially the Foreign Office, the Treasury, and the Admiralty. But he took his time before returning to the letter. Not until the end of November did he finally dictate a thorough redraft and send it out again to the ministries.[25]

The letter may have been the work of many hands, but it was the product, finally, of the prime minister. It bore the sounds and cadences of his voice, the timbre of his thought. His labors over successive drafts reveal how seriously, carefully, and sensitively he weighed his words, his points, his tone. The first draft of the letter had ended with a somber warning to Roosevelt that if the United States was unable to resolve the financing issues and provide Britain the aid it needed, "1941 may bring irreparable disaster to both of us and to mankind." But he judged that conclusion overly pessimistic. Instead the final version ended with expressions of "confidence" in the "achievement of our common purpose." And he decided to conceal any trace of resentment at being forced, as he had written in his first draft, into the role of "suppliant client" obliged to come "week by week to ask the United States for the means by which to carry on for another few days." In fact, Churchill remarked to a colleague, he would like to have told Roosevelt tartly, "If you want to watch us fighting for your liberties, you must pay for the performance."[26]

On the essential question of money, the prime minister had also harbored second thoughts. The original draft had requested that Britain be given all the munitions it needed "without payment now, leaving the question of repayment to be discussed and settled after the war"—a proposal strikingly close to the president's eventual policy. But in the letter he sent Roosevelt, Churchill chose to skip over the subject of repayment and emphasize instead the sacrifices Britain was making in the vital struggle to preserve civilization, with reminders of the all-too-real fighting and dying done by the British that were not—at least not yet—shared by the Americans.[27]

Returning to the United States on November 23, Lord Lothian held the informal press conference in which he offhandedly admitted Britain's need for "perhaps a little financial help." While that might have been a modest attempt to educate the American public, Lothian understood that only Churchill could awaken the American president to Britain's plight. When he met with Roosevelt a few days later, Lothian found him fatigued and depressed, unmoved by pleas for action.[28]

The British Cabinet approved the final draft of Churchill's letter on December 2, but Lothian, who was growing more optimistic, cabled a last set of revisions to London on the night of December 4–5. The American public, he wrote, "is being familiarised with the fact that before long we shall need both ships and financial assistance." He saw Roosevelt's Caribbean cruise as a harbinger. A sea voyage, he remarked on December 5, was the president's "customary prelude to evolving some stroke of policy." A new policy might not come forth until after the January inauguration, Lothian guessed, but he nevertheless felt confident that Roosevelt and the American public would respond positively to Britain's need for ships and money. "The general conviction is that we shall get both," he encouragingly wired the Foreign Office in London. "American opinion is beginning to doubt if we can inflict a decisive defeat on Germany without their active participation in the war."[29]

On Saturday, December 7, Lord Lothian played golf. The following morning, he had a long conversation with Secretary of State Hull, but that afternoon, he fainted. For the next few days he was in and out of consciousness, seized with internal pains and having difficulty breathing. A devout Christian Scientist, he refused conventional medical treatment, instead summoning a Christian Science practitioner from Boston. On December 11, with the ambassador unable to deliver a scheduled talk in Baltimore, Neville Butler, his deputy and a fellow Christian Scientist, gave it for him. "We think this is a situation which concerns you almost as much as it concerns us," read the statement. "It is for you to decide whether it is to your interest to give us whatever assistance may be necessary in order to make certain that Britain shall not fall." He asked Americans to understand that, though Britain stood alone against Hitler, "there is no challenge we have evaded, no challenge we have refused. If you back us you won't be backing a quitter."[30]

That was his final plea to Americans for aid to his country. The next day, the 58-year-old Philip Kerr, eleventh Marquess of Lothian, died of a uremic infection. "I am shocked beyond measure," President Roosevelt wired King George from the *Tuscaloosa*, "to hear of the sudden passing of my old friend and your

Ambassador, the Marquess of Lothian. I am very certain that if he had been allowed by Providence to leave us a last message he would have told us that the greatest of all efforts to retain democracy in the world must and will succeed."[31]

On December 16, the day after a funeral service attended by Eleanor Roosevelt, Cordell Hull, all of the justices of the Supreme Court, and envoys from virtually everywhere but Germany and Italy, Lord Lothian's ashes were laid to rest in Arlington National Cemetery. A dismal rain beat down while a U.S. Army band played Chopin's funeral march and then "Nearer, My God, to Thee." The ambassador received full military honors and a nineteen-gun salute. In London, he was eulogized in Parliament by Winston Churchill. "To die at the height of a man's career, at the highest moment of his efforts, universally honored and admired—to die while great issues are still commanding the whole of his interests, to be taken from us at the moment when he could already see ultimate success in view," the prime minister concluded almost wistfully, "is not the most unenviable of fates."[32]

The last paragraph of Churchill's letter beseeched the American president to regard his request "not as an appeal for aid, but as a statement of the minimum *action* necessary to the achievement of our common purpose." But was the White House, temporarily relocated to the Caribbean, ready for action?[33]

Back in the wintry capital, short days and gray, cold weather darkened people's spirits. The town was sinking into a "swamp," one reporter fretted in mid-December. Washington seemed to be lying inert—floundering, leaderless. Was the Roosevelt administration empty of the ideas and energy needed for the crises that flared around the globe and that increasingly threatened the United States?[34]

From Europe and Asia came pungent reminders of what was at stake. On December 10, Hitler harangued German workers for ninety minutes in a heavily guarded munitions plant in Berlin. Working men throughout the Reich listened on radios in their factories as he once more described the clash of two irreconcilable visions, two mortally opposed political and economic systems. "We find ourselves in the midst of a conflict in which more is at stake than the victory of one or another land," the Führer exclaimed. "It is truly a battle of two worlds against each other." Asserting that the word *capitulation* was not in his vocabulary, he promised that Germany would arm itself with the "fanaticism" needed to realize "the great German Reich of which great poets have dreamed."[35]

On the other side of the world, Japanese foreign minister Yosuke Matsuoka had spoken to the press the day before. He made it clear that under the Tripartite Pact, Japan would enter the fight if the United States attacked Germany. Asked about Japan's aims, Matsuoka replied that his country had "no territorial ambitions" and stood opposed to "conquest, oppression and exploitation." He was walking a strange tightrope. "We are not conquering China," he told reporters, then conceded, "What we are doing may look like a war of conquest, I admit." But in truth, he said, "We are traveling toward perfect equality between Japan and China." As for growing tension with the United States, the foreign minister said that all depended on the Americans' minding their own business. "We may have differences, even serious differences, but if both of us attend to our own business I cannot think there will be any serious clash." Matsuoka was as crooked as a basket of fish hooks, the secretary of state remarked. Roosevelt wasn't buying it either. The following day, December 10, from the *Tuscaloosa*, he announced an embargo on American exports to Japan of steel, iron, and iron alloys, a severe blow to that country's war production.[36]

The president was not yet ready to admit, even privately, the strong likelihood or inevitability of war, but perhaps he was beginning to provide leadership after all. Columnist Frank Kent wrote in the *Wall Street Journal* on December 6 that although it seemed "an unfortunate time for him to take a sea voyage," there were rumors that the president "has gone away to 'think things through' and 'clarify his mind,' which might, of course, turn out to be a good thing."[37]

Time magazine's reporter imagined the president aboard the *Tuscaloosa*, "spending quiet hours outlining a clear-cut pattern of action, . . . legislation, acts, appointments, policies: perhaps even a program as packed with dramatic action as the 100 days of 1933," the months "when the vitality of democracy was seriously questioned." *Time* confidently predicted that when the president returned to Washington, his "red-tanned face would shine through the gloomy fog of Washington's Union Station, and the answers might begin."[38]

Cautious optimism stole over Britain, too. Most important, the country's democracy was still strong. In early December, a small group of pacifist members of Parliament submitted a motion to the House of Commons. Fellow MPs listened respectfully if restlessly to their proposal for peace talks with Hitler and then rejected it by a vote of 341 to 4. The House of Commons, the *New York Times'* Raymond Daniell wrote approvingly, provided a "striking demonstration of the vitality of the democratic processes in this country engaged in a death struggle against the totalitarian States."[39]

That month, the Greeks drove Mussolini out of their country, inflicting the first serious military setback for the Axis in Europe. Turkey was standing firm against Axis pressure, and even France seemed to be causing problems for Germany. Signs of strain appeared in the alliance between Germany and the Soviet Union, a pact of breathtaking cynicism agreed to in late in August 1939, just before Hitler invaded Poland and Stalin began to tear away pieces of its eastern territories. It would not be long before the German dictator turned his malign attention from Britain to his erstwhile ally.

The people of Britain remained steadfast in the sixth month of the Nazi Blitz, which continued as relentlessly as ever—even though Operation Sea Lion, the plan to invade the British Isles that had provided Hitler's original motive for the bombing campaign, had lapsed into desuetude. The Führer could not afford a failed invasion; his charismatic grip on the German people depended on an unbroken streak of victories. His Luftwaffe simply had not achieved the air supremacy needed for invasion.

The Royal Air Force was increasingly able to answer the Luftwaffe punch for punch. British planes, Churchill announced to Parliament in mid-November, had raided the southern Italian port of Taranto, destroying half of Italy's battleships. As a result, commented a reporter in London, "there is a rising market in British stock." Still, Britain was barely hanging on, and in order to capitalize on these small advances, the reporter wrote, it needed more and speedier aid from the United States. The *Christian Science Monitor* wrote on December 10 that while a new plan for aid was in the works, "Britain is said to feel very strongly that it is fighting America's war almost as much as it is fighting its own." The British people and government felt it was fair to ask the United States, the article continued, to "assume some of the financial burden of the conflict and not demand that Britain exhaust all its world-wide resources."[40]

When Churchill's letter landed on the *Tuscaloosa*, throwing all the British cards on the table, it required a decisive reply from the United States. The president sat alone in his deck chair, reading and rereading the prime minister's words. Harry Hopkins observed him brooding silently, plunged in intense thought. "I didn't know for quite a while what he was thinking about, if anything," Hopkins later said. "But then I began to get the idea that he was refueling, the way he so often does when he seems to be resting and carefree. ... Then, one evening, he suddenly came out with it—the whole program. He didn't seem to have any clear idea how it could be done legally. But there wasn't a doubt in his mind that he'd find a way to do it."[41]

In a matter of days, sailing in the pure Caribbean light, the president considered, weighed, and, with an alacrity that had been missing of late, decided upon one of the most consequential policies of the entire war: a commitment to arm the British entirely at American expense. It would be the most open and resolute statement yet of where the United States stood—a statement that would bind the nation to Britain's fate. If the president's plan was approved by Congress, the Roosevelt administration, after months of indecision, halfway measures, and confusing signals, would finally assume leadership of the democratic forces in the war of two worlds. Over the next three months, the president would extend and deepen that role, creating the groundwork for an unprecedented expansion of American power and enduring global leadership.

"Roosevelt, a creative artist in politics," remarked Robert Sherwood, "had put in his time on this cruise evolving the pattern of a masterpiece, and once he could see it clearly in his own mind's eye, he made it quickly and very simply clear to all." Yet as the *Tuscaloosa*'s journey drew to a close, the president had discussed his masterpiece with no one but Harry Hopkins. He had come up with a lion-hearted policy, but he understood that in order to persuade the members of his administration, the members of Congress, and the American people to support it, he would need the skills of the fox.[42]

After eleven days at sea, fanned by salty breezes under a tropical sun, Roosevelt arrived in Charleston, South Carolina, on Saturday, December 14. From there, he and his companions traveled south by train to Warm Springs. The next day FDR drove himself in his light blue open-top car—the Georgia license plate bearing only the letters FDR—from the train station to the Warm Springs Foundation he had created in 1927 for his fellow polio sufferers. In cool and foggy weather, he spoke briefly to the patients. "I hope to be down here next March without any question *if the world survives* for the usual two weeks next Spring." Sherwood later wrote that Roosevelt seemed "exuberant and jaunty" after the cruise, but it is hard to discern any exuberance in that unsettling remark.[43]

Others quickly picked up on the president's words. "Of course the world will survive," snapped Pat McCarran, the isolationist senator from Nevada. "The United States will survive—if it keeps out of war—and it's going to keep out of war." But others commended the president's sober realism. He "has more fully sensed the dangers that menace all democratic nations, including the United States, than any other person in this country," said Democratic senator William King of Utah. The *Atlanta Constitution* agreed that "no one need think the President was speaking facetiously or that there is not very real danger that the world, as we desire it, may not survive."[44]

Just before boarding his private train for the trip back to Washington, Roosevelt repeated the disquieting message, telling the little crowd of villagers at the station that he planned to return in the spring "if things go all right."[45]

"The president is returning today from his cruise," wrote Henry Stimson in his diary on December 16. "I hope he will be well freshened up to meet his responsibilities." That day, Roosevelt's quartet of leading military advisors—Knox, Stark, Marshall, and Stimson—who knew nothing of the president's new thinking, met to discuss again the implications of inevitable American involvement in the war. Stimson noted that, keeping faith with Plan Dog, they agreed that "the eventual big act will have to be to save the life line of Great Britain on the North Atlantic."[46]

The next day, Roosevelt had lunch with Treasury Secretary Morgenthau, his longtime friend and Hudson Valley neighbor who had consistently advocated tough anti-Nazi measures. Morgenthau noted in his diary that FDR was "in a very good humor, very quiet and self-possessed and very proud of the fact that he didn't look at a single report that he had taken with him from Washington."[47]

Quickly, the two men got down to the business of Churchill's letter. "I have been thinking very hard on this trip about what we should do for England," FDR said, "and it seems to me that the thing to do is to get away from a dollar sign. . . . I don't want to put the thing in terms of dollars or loans, and I think the thing to do is to say that we will manufacture what we need, and the first thing we will do is to increase our productivity, and then we will say to England, 'we will give you the guns and ships that you need, provided that when the war is over you will return to us in kind the guns and the ships that we have loaned to you, or you will return to us the ships repaired and pay us, always in kind, to make up for the depreciation.' What do you think of it?"[48]

Morgenthau loved it. "I think it is the best idea yet!" He admired the cunning in FDR's condition that Britain would return ships and other war materiel to the United States after the war. It would certainly help get legislation passed, he reasoned, if Congress thought the United States was driving a hard bargain. "If I followed my own heart," he told Roosevelt, "I would say, let's give it to them; but I think it would be much better for you to be in the position that you are insisting before Congress and the people of the United States to get ship for ship when the war is over, and have Congress say that you are tough, and say, 'well, let's give it to them,' than to have the reverse true and have Congress say you are too easy." Roosevelt's new plan would be, as historian Kimball put it, a "give-away program that did not look like one."[49]

Finally, after more back-and-forth, FDR asked, "What would you think if I made a statement like this at my press conference this afternoon?" "Fine," Morgenthau said, catching Roosevelt's mood and that of the American public. "The sooner the better because the people are waiting for you to show them the way." And FDR indeed wanted to show them the way. He had no interest in the statements laying out British assets that Morgenthau had pre-pared—they had become irrelevant.[50]

The treasury secretary grasped the change that FDR's new idea represented and felt it offered a perfect solution. Roosevelt's "sense of trading and intuition," Morgenthau commented, was "absolutely amazing," and he reckoned that the startling new plan would take even the British—focused as they were on traditional forms of financing—by surprise.[51]

December 17 was chilly and wet. "Men and women sloshed up and down Pennsylvania Avenue," wrote *Time* magazine, "now and then looking curiously at the White House. There rested their hopes, their problems, perhaps the shape of their fate." And those men and women had questions, too. How grave the peril? How heavy the burden?[52]

That afternoon, Roosevelt spoke to reporters.

"I don't think there is any particular news," FDR casually said as he began his press conference. He faced a larger than usual crowd of newspapermen, drawn by the expectation of some big announce-ment, though they didn't know what sort. Before they could ex-press disappointment or incredulity, Roosevelt added that, well, maybe there was one small item that he could possibly mention, "one thing that I think is worth my talking about from—what will I call it?—the background method."[53]

First, he laid out his theme: the "best immediate defense of the United States is the success of Great Britain in defending itself." In other words, American self-interest was tied to aid to Britain. "Quite aside from our historic and current interest in the survival of democracy as a whole in the world," FDR told the reporters, "it is equally important from a selfish point of view of American de-fense that we should do everything to help the British Empire to defend itself."

The president's tone was serious, his tanned face solemn. He stressed that he was "just talking background, informally; I haven't prepared any of this—I go back to the idea that the one thing necessary for American national defense is additional productive facilities; and the more we increase those facilities—factories, shipbuilding ways, munitions plants, et cetera, and so on—the stronger American national defense is." Moreover, "orders from Great Britain" were "a tremendous asset to American national defense; because they automatically create additional facilities. I am talking *selfishly*, from the American point of view—nothing else. Therefore, from the *selfish point of view*, that production must be encouraged by us."

The president insisted that he was not interested in repealing the Neutrality Act or the Johnson Act, which prohibited loans to countries still in default on their World War I debts. Nor was he interested in lending money to the British government. That, he said, was "banal." Also "somewhat banal," though "we may come to it, I don't know," was the idea that the United States would pay for armaments and "make a gift of them" to Great Britain, which he didn't think "would care to have a gift from the taxpayers of the United States." He didn't say whether those taxpayers would care to make a gift to Britain.

After dismissing conventional approaches to the problem of aid, Roosevelt explained that it was hard to be more precise about what exactly he was aiming for because a variety of possibilities were being explored and he could speak only "in very general terms." Still, he said, increased American production, stimulated by British orders, meant that there would be more arms than the United States could itself immediately employ. If "the best defense of Great Britain is the best defense of the United States," he reasoned, then "these materials would be more useful to the defense of the United States if they were used in Great Britain, than if they were kept in storage here."

What about payment? "Now, what I am trying to do," he said, "is to eliminate the dollar sign. That is something brand new in the thoughts of practically everybody in this room, I think—get rid of the silly, foolish old dollar sign. Well, let me give you an illustration: Suppose my neighbor's home catches fire, and I have a length of garden hose four or five hundred feet away. If he can take my garden hose and connect it up with his hydrant, I may help him to put out his fire. Now, what do I do? I don't say to him before that operation, 'Neighbor, my garden hose cost me $15; you have to pay me $15 for it.' ... I don't want $15—I want my garden hose back after the fire is over. ... But suppose it gets smashed up. ... He says, 'All right, I will replace it.' Now, if I get a nice garden hose back, I am in pretty good shape."

As for legal questions, he couldn't go into details. But there would be "some kind of arrangement" so that "when the show was over we would get repaid sometime in kind, thereby leaving out the dollar mark in the form of dollar debt and substituting it for a gentlemen's obligation to pay in kind. I think you all get it."

The plan was completely new to the reporters, and while it sounded appealingly and suitably audacious, what would be buried in the fine print? One reporter interrupted with a question: Would the title to the garden hose—the ships, the planes, the munitions— still be in our name?

The president showed annoyance at the suggestion that such haggling might be involved when the fate of the world was at stake. Suppose it was the question of a ship, he said. "I haven't got the faintest idea, in whom the legal title would be of that particular ship. I don't think that makes any difference in the transaction. ... I don't know and I don't care."

Roosevelt had claimed to reporters that the idea of removing money from the equation was "brand new," and to the American public, it was. But in 1917, Assistant Secretary of the Navy Franklin Roosevelt had also wanted to eliminate the dollar sign: he had been unwilling to quibble over money with the owners of private vessels the government wanted to acquire for coastal defense. "The country must have the services of the vessels," he wrote, "and it should not ... be placed in a position where it would have to bargain and haggle over the price to be paid."

Twenty-three years later, in early November 1940, FDR told the Cabinet that "the time would surely come when Great Britain would need loans or credits," and he suggested that the United States could simply lease or lend ships or any other property to England and let England return the materiel after the war. "It seems to me that this was a very good suggestion," wrote Secretary of the Interior Harold Ickes in his diary. At the same time, FDR asked Arthur Purvis, the head of the British Purchasing Commission, if it was possible for the United States to build cargo vessels and lease them to Britain. It was an idea the president kept in mind—a way to aid Britain without demanding immediate payment and without threatening to liquidate its every asset. Ickes was furious at people so "ungenerous" that they "wanted to be perfectly sure that England was fighting naked, with bare hands, before they would be willing to go to her aid."[54]

As for the garden hose metaphor, Ickes himself had spoken in similar terms in August 1940. Grumbling that the United States wasn't doing enough to save England, he told the president that "we Americans are like the householder who refuses to lend or sell his fire extinguishers to help put out the fire in the house that is right next door, although that house is all ablaze and the wind is blowing from that direction." A few days later, FDR repeated Ickes's comment to Ambassador William Bullitt and said, according to Bullitt, "How do you think the country and the Congress would react if I should put aid to the British in the form of lending them my garden hose?" But it was Roosevelt, meditating on Churchill's letter aboard the *Tuscaloosa*, who brought these threads together in an entirely original plan that had a fighting chance of winning acceptance from the American people and Congress.[55]

At the end of the president's remarks, which went on for longer than the reporters had expected, one of them posed a straightforward question: Did Roosevelt think that his new plan "takes us any more into the war than we are?" The president's reply: "No, not a bit." A follow-up query: "Even though goods we own are being used?" FDR: "I don't think you go into a war for legalistic reasons; in other words, we are doing all we can at the present time."[56]

The crisis that could have been crippling and paralyzing turned out to be catalytic. Roosevelt had given a master class in high-intensity salesmanship to the reporters gathered around his desk; he had framed his surprising new policy in moral as well as practical terms. He purported to follow the golden rule by generously offering neighborly assistance to England. And as a pragmatic politician, he had conceived his help as a loan, to be repaid somehow in kind after the war. He did not divulge, however, that he was also maneuvering and even exploiting Britain to ensure the security of the United States. After all, the fire in his neighbor's house could easily spread to his own. He would arm British soldiers so that, like a mercenary army, they could do the fighting for him. This quid pro quo would have been rejected by any country less desperate for survival than Britain was. The United States was in a position to dictate terms—Churchill's letter had acknowledged as much.[57]

The president could not dictate terms to the American people or to Congress, but he had tilted the odds in his favor. Much of the press, which dubbed his proposal the "Lease-Lend Plan," was already won over. Walter Lippmann was in full agreement; the supply of arms to Great Britain, he wrote, "cannot be allowed to depend upon Great Britain's capacity to pay." The *New York Times* showered approval on the plan, expressing relief that "never will there be a cessation of that steady flow to Britain of the war materials which are needed to smash Hitler's system and save democracy for all of us." *Time* praised the president's removal of the dollar sign from the aid equation, crediting him with splitting the "indivisible atom" of money, power, and freedom. Columnist Dorothy Thompson, who two weeks earlier had reported that the country was in a "slump" and FDR in a "down" mood, now asserted that Roosevelt was "perhaps the only democratic statesman" able to recognize "the epochal and revolutionary nature" of the struggle against Nazi Germany, a fight to defend "an order ideologically true to the deepest Anglo-Saxon traditions" of freedom, individual rights, and democracy. The *Atlanta Constitution* editorialized that if the United States did not provide at once "every dollar, every gun, every ship, every plane that Britain needs," making it "an impregnable shield for our own country," then "there is a dreadful danger that before long we can sadly say to ourselves, as a nation, in the words of Homer:

> Thou wilt lament
> Hereafter, when the evil shall be done
> And shall admit no cure."[58]

The isolationist press preferred to believe that there was only an invented evil. The *Chicago Daily Tribune* scoffed that the president's press conference was "probably the strangest ever held in the White House" and attacked Roosevelt for cooking up a phony crisis "*which does not exist.*" The cure was to stop "Mr. Roosevelt and his war party" from bringing "precipitate action here."[59]

The German embassy was more sanguine than the *Tribune*. The German chargé d'affaires in Washington, Hans Thomsen, assured Berlin that the plan brought the United States no nearer to immediate war but was rather a long-term scheme by FDR to create so deep an American investment in Britain that the United States would, in time, be forced into the war to protect that investment. This analysis recalled, though with entirely different premises, Stimson's remark at the December 3 meeting in Morgenthau's office that the amounts of money involved were "enormous" and that America might be drawn into war "just to save our investment, or to save the purpose for which we made the investment."[60]

Hitler's naval chief, Admiral Erich Raeder, was less optimistic for the short term than Thomsen. Raeder foresaw that under Roosevelt's new program, American convoys would soon replace British patrol and escort ships in the North Atlantic, challenging Germany's growing mastery of the seas and ensuring a vital lifeline to the British Isles. The convoys would also increase the opportunity for dangerous clashes, intended or not, between the United States and Germany, possibly triggering war between them. Moreover, Britain's armaments industry, which the Luftwaffe had so painstakingly ravaged, would effectively be "shifted to America," out of the German bombers' reach. Raeder would prove prophetic, and the Führer seemed to realize it. So concerned was he about FDR's new initiative that he violated his own rule to avoid speaking provocatively in public against the United States. He unleashed a Foreign Ministry spokesman to complain bitterly that while the United States had shown "only restraint and friendliness" toward Britain, toward Germany it had adopted a policy of "pinpricks, challenges, insults, and moral aggression." Now, he warned darkly, that behavior "has reached a point at which it is insupportable."[61]

If Germany hoped that its threats would turn Americans against the president's new policy, the intervention backfired. Even an extreme isolationist like Hamilton Fish, a New York congressman who represented FDR's Dutchess County and who in the past had collaborated with the German embassy in Washington to promote their common anti-intervention agenda, declared that the U.S. government would "decide on what action to take to protect American interests regardless of complaints emanating from Berlin."[62]

Such breaks in anti-Roosevelt solidarity added to the elation of the men and women in the British embassy in Washington, who had worked long and fervently to secure a commitment of the kind the president announced on December 17. The day after Roosevelt's press conference, a greatly relieved Neville Butler, the embassy's first secretary, wrote happily to the Foreign Office in London that "it looks as if . . . the post election hangover" was over and that the administration "had at last decided to go full steam ahead with its plan for helping Britain."[63]

But in London, exhilaration was tempered by caution and worry. America had frustrated Britain before. For Winston Churchill it was an especially sobering time, for his country remained alone and was not in control of its destiny. He had bent his knee to Roosevelt with no assurance that his submission would be rewarded. From the draft of a telegram to FDR at the close of a shattering year, the prime minister deleted the following sentence: "Remember, Mr. President, we do not know what you have in mind, or exactly what the United States is going to do, and we are fighting for our lives."[64]

CHAPTER FIVE

The Arsenal of Ideas

N O BOMBS FELL ON England on Christmas Eve. No air-raid sirens sounded. An unwritten truce in the Battle of Britain brought quiet, if not peace, for one precious night and day. On the radio, members of the choir of Coventry Cathedral stood among the ruins of their bombed church and sang an ancient carol. Then—not from Buckingham Palace, whose shattered windows were boarded up like those of thousands of other London homes, but from somewhere in the countryside—King George delivered a short Yuletide message. The British people had surmounted a grave crisis and had their feet "planted on the path of victory," he said hearteningly, but he warned that more danger and suffering lay ahead.[1]

While the king spoke, crowds of Londoners—a million in all—were trudging toward underground subway stations, basements, sub-basements of warehouses and office buildings, and other shelters. Carrying, along with their bedding, satchels full of gifts for the children, they expected to find, as *New York Times* correspondent Raymond Daniell wrote, "a greater prospect of cheer there than in their windowless, heatless and sometimes lightless homes." The spirit of camaraderie in war-ravaged London was "such as seldom has been seen in big cities." People who before the war would not have thought of speaking to one another were now combining resources for their Christmas celebration. "One will bring Christmas pudding. Another will bring roast chicken or turkey if she can afford it." There was among Londoners, Daniell found, "a sincere desire to be kind to one's fellow-sufferers." As George Orwell observed, Britain was a society both individualistic and class-ridden, but "in moments of supreme crisis the whole nation can suddenly draw together and act upon a species of instinct, really a code of conduct which is understood by almost everyone, though never formulated."[2]

That code of conduct included the true Christmas spirit, and it had prevailed since that past summer when Hitler launched his merciless bombing campaign. Friends of the royal family received Christmas cards showing King George and Queen Elizabeth standing in front of the bombed section of Buckingham Palace. The greeting read, "There'll always be an England." Many people, according to *Time* magazine, cheerfully called it a "Blitzmas card."[3]

Amid the singing of carols on Christmas Eve, President Roosevelt lit a giant festive tree on the ellipse behind the White House. Afterward, he spoke informally with reporters. Was it possible, he wondered aloud, to make the ceremony more "homelike" in the future? Perhaps the tree lighting and carol singing could be held inside the White House instead of outdoors, he said, adding soberly, "*if* we are all here." Ten days earlier, he had told the patients at Warm Springs that he would be back in March "*if* the world survives." Now, on Christmas Eve, the future still hinged sadly on that conditional word. Roosevelt may have been thinking of his own mortality, but likely also of the death of peoples and nations, even of the civilized world.[4]

Later that evening, though, he put aside such thoughts and addressed the nation on the radio, asking Americans to "strive forward in Faith and in Hope and in Love." His talk resembled a sermon—one that embraced Christians and non-Christians because, as he said, "the spirit of unselfish service personified by the life and the teachings of Christ appeals to the inner conscience and hope of every man and every woman in every part of the earth. It transcends in the ultimate all lines of race, of habitat, of nation." While carefree children would have a merry Christmas, he suggested, adult

Americans in the midst of a world crisis could have a happy one "if by happiness we mean that we have done with doubts, that we have set our hearts against fear, that we still believe in the Golden Rule for all mankind, that we intend to live more purely in the spirit of Christ."[5]

With the falling snow, the quiet streets, the ringing of bells, and the bustle of family gatherings, Christmas offered moments for reflection. There were prayers for peace and also for victory, compassionate prayers for the victims of war, for the fathers, brothers, and sons who might be asked to fight. But Hitler was also thinking of victory; the Christmas cards he sent to Mussolini, Francisco Franco, and a host of other dictators contained only the words "Our Winged Victory" and showed German bombers and the Winged Victory of Samothrace, a Hellenistic statue that German troops had looted from the Louvre.[6]

In churches across the United States, parishioners listened on Christmas Eve and Christmas morning to ardent sermons teaching that there could be no peace of Christ with such evil abroad in the world. At the Cathedral of St. John the Divine, William Manning, an Episcopal bishop, asked, "What shall we say of Christmas this year, in the midst of a world at war, in the midst of aggressors, barbarities, tyrannies, and iniquities such as the world has scarcely ever seen before? We cannot forget, we have no right to forget the terrible events now taking place." At Temple Rodeph Sholom, Rabbi Louis Newman, lighting the first Chanukah candle on Christmas Eve, reflected, "If there were more emphasis on the moral message of the Christmas season, there would be no bombardments of non-combatants in London, there would be no preachment of hatred against unoffending minorities, no cruelties inflicted on those imprisoned in concentration camps, no refusal of asylum to homeless and tempest-tossed refugees."[7]

At Midnight Mass in St. Patrick's Cathedral, Archbishop Francis Spellman exhorted his six-thousand-strong Catholic congregation to use the values of Christian life "to attain a triumph over destruction, a triumph over the principle that might makes right, a triumph over economic conditions that deny men the means to live." But in Rome, where the Catholic faithful trudged through slush and snow to Mass at St. Peter's, Spellman's master, Pope Pius XII, pronounced himself unable to choose between "the contrasting systems which are part of our times." Other than praying for a "triumph over hate," the pope chose neutrality between the two sides, declaring that "the church cannot be called upon to favor one more than another."[8]

Few American clergymen of any denomination clung to such bankrupt moral relativism, and a growing number were convinced that merely sermonizing about Christian values and ideals was no longer sufficient. Franklin and Eleanor Roosevelt, attending a Christmas morning interdenominational service at the First Congregational Church in Washington, listened to William Banhart, an evangelical minister, demand "a holy blitzkrieg" to save civilization. Only all-out opposition to Hitler—including military force—could, he argued, restore peace, kindness, and justice to the world.[9]

One group embracing that view, led by the theologian Reinhold Niebuhr, would launch the periodical *Christianity and Crisis* in February 1941 as an internationalist response to the pacifist *Christian Century*, which condemned Lend-Lease as a "blueprint for dictatorship."[10]

In the 1920s, Niebuhr had been an ardent pacifist, as had millions of other Christians in the wake of World War I. Now, however, he saw only "confused religious absolutism" in pacifism. Boundless Nazi aggression had awakened most churches and most congregants to pacifism's futility. Nevertheless, the Selective Service Act granted conscientious objector status to draft-eligible young men who, for reasons of religious training and belief, opposed military service. The Roosevelt administration had set up Civilian Conservation Corps–type work camps for conscientious objectors who were willing to make a constructive contribution, though some—including ministers, lawyers, and students—were tried, convicted, and jailed for refusing to register for the draft.[11]

For Niebuhr, pacifism had it all wrong. The pacifists, he wrote, praised "the peace of tyranny as if it were nearer to the peace of the Kingdom of God than war." How could a true Christian conscience not recoil from Hitler's tyranny, which aimed "to annihilate the Jewish race, to subject the nations of Europe to the dominion of a 'master' race, to extirpate the Christian religion, to annul the liberties and legal standards which are the priceless heritage of ages of Christian and humanistic culture?" The immediate task, Niebuhr held, was not to be more loving or retreat to a sentimentalized form of Christianity, but to become "fully alive" to Nazi cruelty and fully committed to the just war needed to defeat it. Christians who failed to understand the urgency and necessity of such a just war should "have the decency and consistency to retire to the monastery, where medieval perfectionists found their asylum."[12]

More and more Christians were coming to share Niebuhr's view. Bishop Henry St. George Tucker, head of the American Episcopal Church, told *Time* that "we should give as much aid to the British as they need, and if it is necessary to take that last step and go to war we should do it." A Congregationalist minister was certain that before long, "even the more pacifistic in the church would favor our entering the war." Methodists, according to a church official, now "believe the future of Christianity itself is related to the defeat of this new religion of totalitarian force."[13]

The National Lutheran Council put it most starkly, passing a resolution saying that in order to protect American liberties and privileges, "men again may need to die."[14]

New York Times theater critic Brooks Atkinson, who wrote an annual Christmas column, cheerlessly remarked that in 1940 "the spirit of peace and joy seems hard to reconcile with the agonizing realities of these times."[15]

Among those realities were anti-interventionist movements in the United States. At one extreme was the pro-Nazi German-American Bund, whose Christmas message praised Hitler for helping the German people realize their full potential of power and prestige and for providing German Americans with a model of "courage and faith."[16]

Then there were the American isolationists who, in the Christmas spirit, spearheaded the project of feeding the hungry in occupied Europe. Their spokeswoman was Anne Morrow Lindbergh, author of *The Wave of the Future*. In a Christmas Eve radio broadcast sponsored by the American Friends Service

Committee, Mrs. Lindbergh took aim at the British naval blockade of Germany and its occupied European countries. With the British controlling Gibraltar and Suez and dominating the open sea, the blockade was about 90 percent effective in preventing overseas supplies—from raw materials to food—from reaching the continent. The British people, wrote the foreign correspondent Raymond Daniell, felt "that any soft-hearted weakening of the blockade for humanitarian reasons would be the result of muddled thinking, as it would lead inevitably to a strengthening of Germany, prolongation of the war and more casualties on both sides." But Mrs. Lindbergh proposed that the United States distribute food to the Nazi-occupied nations of "starving Europe." Americans had already "given much aid to England," she said with an edge of resentment, quickly adding that "we are not criticizing England." Still, despite Germany's indiscriminate sinking of Allied and neutral merchant ships, she argued that it was time for Britain to lift its naval blockade and allow food and medical supplies to reach Hitler's victims.[17]

The suggestion of sending food shipments to occupied Europe had been made a few weeks earlier in a nationwide radio address by former president Herbert Hoover, who organized the National Committee on Food for the Small Democracies. During the First World War, Hoover had been an acclaimed administrator of food relief for Europe, though in 1931, when hungry Americans waited numbly in breadlines, he limited his aid and compassion to a statement that "nobody is actually starving."[18]

Petitions opposing the new Hoover plan were sent to President Roosevelt. In one, Protestant theologians and ministers asserted that "the American people have been driven to recognize that their own security is intimately involved in the success of Great Britain's heroic defense. They are unwilling to take any action which would compromise that defense." Forty-four Catholic laymen released a statement declaring that "any attempt to force the British blockade and feed the conquered populations of Europe is contrary to the best interests of Christianity and of America." And thirty-five prominent physicians wrote, "We believe that the Hoover Plan would prolong, rather than cure, the suffering of the conquered peoples of Europe; that it would give aid and comfort to the Nazis in their task of keeping these people in subjection. . . . We believe, above all, that it is unfair and dangerous to ask the pinched and rationed British to give up one of their effective weapons—the blockade."[19]

The Hoover-Lindbergh plan was dead on arrival. The British adamantly rejected it, and with the sole exception of Poland, the governments-in-exile of the occupied European nations all joined Britain in repudiating the plan. As Lord Lothian had explained before his death, Britain itself was risking starvation and "undergoing every conceivable hardship in the fight for freedom not only for herself but for all freedom-loving peoples." In these circumstances, loosening the blockade would "endanger our existence and imperil our cause."[20]

It was a quiet holiday week in the White House. A ten-foot Norwegian spruce, glistening with artificial snow and icicles, stood in the East Room. Bright poinsettias had replaced ferns in the hallways, and wreaths of spruce and pine cones decorated the windows. Someone had remembered the mistletoe. In the past, Christmas in the Roosevelt White House had been a bustling, noisy time filled with children, grandchildren, toys, big family dinners, joyful unwrapping of presents, and Franklin reading Dickens's *A Christmas Carol* to the family. But this year all of the Roosevelt children but Franklin Jr. were scattered around the country. Late on Christmas Eve, after the tree lighting on the ellipse, the president dictated a rough draft of a talk he intended to give on December 29. It was to be a fireside chat, a method of communication with the American people that FDR had perfected early in his presidency.[21]

Radio broadcasting was still in its early days when Roosevelt gave his first fireside chats, and none of his predecessors (including Hoover, who as secretary of commerce in 1927 had spearheaded the creation of the Federal Radio Commission, later renamed the Federal Communications Commission, or FCC) had used the medium as he did. For Americans sitting around their big wooden boxes packed with vacuum tubes and circuitry, hearing the voice of the president in their kitchens and living rooms was a wondrous event. And Roosevelt was no thumping, stumping politician; his voice was beautifully modulated, almost intimate, his tone that of a

neighbor explaining important matters clearly and without conde-
scension.

The fireside chat was so powerful a tool of persuasion that
Roosevelt rationed its use. He had last given one on May 26, when
he talked to Americans about national defense. Many saw the
interval since then as a time of drift and indecision. Harold Ickes
had been urging FDR to speak to Americans—they needed "to be
aroused to the danger that the country is in," he wrote on
December 1, advising the president to stir up "their patriotism and
willingness to sacrifice themselves." Roosevelt replied that he
might do just that, noting that he had gathered a lot of material for
such a talk.[22]

Roosevelt might have done well to speak earlier, but the timing
on December 29 was good. Having announced his Lend-Lease
plan at his December 17 press conference, he now needed to
explain to Americans the background to this dramatic move, the
world situation as it now stood, and the American role in the global
crisis. He needed to secure strong support for Lend-Lease from
the American people as well as from Congress. Would he be able
to bring the country behind the means and the ends he proposed?

After the president and his wife returned from church on
Christmas morning, the White House kitchen prepared a holiday
dinner for a small gathering that included the president's mother,
Sara; Franklin Jr., his wife, and their two-year-old son; Harry
Hopkins and his eight-year-old daughter; and of course Fala.
There were also five last-minute guests: Crown Prince Olaf of
Norway, his wife Princess Martha, and their three children. The
family had recently fled their Nazi-occupied country.[23]

At dinner, the president carved the turkey for his guests.
Turkey and trimmings were also enjoyed at nearby army camps;
less fortunate people in Washington were served Christmas dinner
by the Central Union Mission and the Salvation Army, while prisoners in the District Jail received a special meal of roast pork and
pumpkin pie.[24]

The president, anxious to return to work on his talk, asked
Missy LeHand to summon Sam Rosenman and Robert Sherwood
to join him and Hopkins the next day. Sherwood remembered
FDR working at the long table in the Cabinet room and looking

up from time to time at a portrait of Woodrow Wilson. "Peace without victory" had been Wilson's aim in the First World War, and the painting was a reminder that, with the Nazis, peace was no substitute for victory.[25]

On evenings when Roosevelt and his team worked on speeches, they all first gathered for cocktails in the Oval Study and then had dinner. "The White House cuisine did not enjoy a very high reputation," Sherwood commented. Salads, for example, were mountains "of mayonnaise, slices of canned pineapple, carved radishes, etc." Roosevelt would look at the salad and murmur sadly, "No, thank you." After dinner, the president usually sat on the couch near the fireplace, his feet up on a stool specially designed for him, and started reading the latest draft. Drinks were brought in at 10:00. "During these evening sessions," Sherwood wrote, "the telephone almost never rang. ... One would have thought this house the most peaceful, remote retreat in a war-wracked world."[26]

On December 28, the day before the fireside chat, the president and his speechwriters gathered for an all-day working session in the spacious Cabinet room. The weather was gloomy, and Henry Stimson had plans to attend a funeral. But FDR asked the war secretary to stay in Washington to go over the talk. Stimson read the speech the next morning and took the draft to the War Department, where he read it aloud to his aides. "We were all delighted with his forthright and outright analysis of the situation and characterization of the Nazis' bid for world power," Stimson wrote in his diary, though he added that he had just received "startling and serious figures" from the Intelligence Department revealing the "enormous" disparity in airplane production in Britain and in Germany. "It shows that in building our arsenal, we have got a big job."[27]

The final speechwriting session took place that afternoon, just hours before the broadcast. "Mr. President," asked Hopkins, "do you feel that you could include in this speech some kind of optimistic statement that will hearten the people who are doing the fighting—the British, the Greeks and the Chinese?" Sherwood remembered Roosevelt mulling that idea over for a long time, "tilting his head back, puffing out his cheeks as was his habit." Finally he dictated two additional sentences: "I believe that the Axis powers are not going to win this war. I base that belief on the latest and best information." Rosenman and Sherwood, wondering what that information could possibly be, concluded that it was only Roosevelt's personal confidence that his proposal for Lend-Lease would pass Congress and make an Axis victory impossible.[28]

At 9:00 p.m. on Sunday, December 29, the small group of nervous guests assembled in the diplomatic reception room of the White House. Up front sat the tall Hollywood star Clark Gable; his wife, actress Carole Lombard; a somber Cordell Hull and other Cabinet members; the president's mother, Sara; Senate Majority Leader Alben Barkley of Kentucky; and a few others. On the president's desk stood seven microphones, two glasses of water, two new sharp pencils, a notepad, and an open package of Camel cigarettes. Five minutes before the broadcast began, the president entered the room in his wheelchair. Dressed in a dark blue suit and bow tie, he seemed, one of the reporters present wrote, in high good humor.[29]

More than five hundred radio stations across the country were tuned to his microphones. Roosevelt had "probably the largest American audience ever reached by radio," according to the *New York Times*; and with his talk beamed around the world by short-wave, he would reach one hundred million listeners. From New York to California, the country came to a standstill. Attendance at movie theaters that evening dropped sharply. In bars, city apartments, and country homes, people waited. Expectations were sky-high for a speech that officials and the press had been suggesting would be FDR's most important since the beginning of the war.[30]

The president spoke in simple terms, clearly, gravely. After reminding Americans that they had met the ruinous banking crisis of 1933 "with courage and realism," he came to the present situation. "Never before since Jamestown and Plymouth Rock," he solemnly said, "has our American civilization been in such danger as now."[31]

"The Nazi masters of Germany have made it clear," he continued, "that they intend not only to dominate all life and thought in their own country, but also to enslave the whole of Europe, and then to use the resources of Europe to dominate the rest of the world." Hitler wanted to revive the oldest and worst form of tyranny, he said, one in which there is "no liberty, no religion, no hope." If Nazi Germany succeeded, all Americans "would be living at the point of a gun. . . . We know now that a nation can have peace with the Axis only at the price of total surrender."

Roosevelt wanted to persuade his fellow citizens of their peril: "Frankly and definitely there is danger ahead—danger against which we must prepare." But some Americans had apparently learned nothing from the events of 1940. They included the isolationists, whom the president described as a "small minority who want to see no evil and hear no evil, even though they know in their hearts that evil exists." The gist of their stance, he said, was, "Please, don't frighten us by telling us the facts." Roosevelt also condemned appeasers who believed that "the Axis powers are going to win anyway" and that the United States should try to get the best deal it could. A negotiated peace! he scoffed. "Is it a negotiated peace if a gang of outlaws surrounds your community and on threat of extermination makes you pay tribute to save your own skins?"

If that was not enough to alarm Americans, FDR had more. In May, in his fireside chat on national defense, he had asserted that a fifth column of enemy agents—"spies, saboteurs and traitors"—had infiltrated the United States with the aim of disrupting "the entire pattern of life of a people." Now he elaborated on those claims: "Evil forces" from fascist Europe "are already within our own gates." These "secret emissaries" were "trouble-breeders" whose goal was to destroy the nation's unity and "shatter our will to defend ourselves." The government was working to ferret them out. But there were also American citizens, "*many of them in high places*, who, unwittingly in most cases, are aiding and abetting the work of these agents . . . [and] doing exactly the kind of work that the dictators want done in the United States." State Department officials had objected to including the reference to Americans "in high places" among the fifth columnists, but FDR had overruled them. He was determined to raise his allegations to the highest pitch.

On the other side were the British, who represented "the spearhead of resistance to world conquest." The United States was determined to send "every ounce and every ton of munitions and supplies that we can possibly spare to help the defenders who are in the front lines." Although the State Department had suggested he say that Britain's war needs "must be treated as an integral part of our own defense needs," instead FDR said, more vaguely, "We must integrate the war needs of Britain and the other free nations which are resisting aggression."

Not a word was uttered about dollars, pounds, or garden hoses—there was no mention of Lend-Lease at all. Instead Roosevelt wanted to emphasize that American generosity was for the country's own protection. The British, after all, were not asking American boys to do their fighting; they were asking only for the "implements of war, the planes, the tanks, the guns, the freighters which will enable them to fight for their liberty and for *our* security." American boys were less likely to have to fight, he said, "if we do all we can now to support the nations defending themselves against attack by the Axis than if we acquiesce in their defeat . . . and wait our turn to be the object of attack in another war later on."

Then Roosevelt offered some reassurance: "Our national policy is not directed toward war. Its sole purpose is to keep war away from our country and our people." Perhaps that was true, or perhaps he wanted it to be true. But his closest advisors didn't believe Hitler could be defeated without American intervention, and Plan Dog was drafted on the assumption that its implementation was all but inevitable—perhaps sooner rather than later.

If the British were to insulate the United States from active participation in war, the president went on, American defense industries needed to operate continuously without strikes or lockouts. Differences between management and labor had to be reconciled "by voluntary or legal means." Emphasizing how much he counted on the skill and stamina of American workers, who "provide the human power that turns out the destroyers, the airplanes, and the tanks," he promised to protect their labor rights, and in return he expected them to "discharge their full responsibilities to the urgent needs of defense." The challenge was steep, but there was no reason why America would not succeed. "We have the men—the skill—the wealth—and above all, the will."

Building up to his finale, the president spoke of the "arsenals of America" where "guns, planes and ships" would be built "with all possible speed." This was now the "purpose of the Nation." And then he uttered the words that would go down in history: "*We must be the great arsenal of democracy.*"[32]

When he was finished, a radio announcer stepped in, declaring, "Ladies and Gentlemen, you have heard a profound pronouncement by the President of the United States." After the fireside chat, wrote a reporter for *Time*, "around the radios of the world people relaxed; some lit cigarettes and had a highball; some prayed and went to bed."[33]

According to Sam Rosenman, the phrase "arsenal of democracy" had come from Jean Monnet, a French businessman who was in Washington to negotiate arms purchases for the British government. Monnet had supposedly spoken the words to Justice Frankfurter to describe what he saw as America's role in the war. Frankfurter asked Monnet not to use the phrase again—so that the president might. It found its way to a War Department official and then appeared in a draft the War Department sent to the White House. When FDR saw it, he said, "I *love* it."[34]

That is a plausible story. Robert Sherwood, who was also present at the speech's creation, related a simpler version of the term's origin. Harry Hopkins provided it, Sherwood said, having come across it in a newspaper article. But Sherwood himself had used a similar phrase in an interview that past May with the *New York Times* drama critic Jack Gould. He told Gould that the United States was "already, in effect, an *arsenal* for the democratic Allies. Let it be *proclaimed* as such, as an expression of our national policy."[35]

Whatever the source of the phrase, once the president of the United States voiced it at such a consequential moment, it belonged to him; and through him, it rang out throughout the world. For tens of millions of victims of Axis aggression, the words "arsenal of democracy" held a wealth of promise. Since industrial output was likely to prove as crucial to the outcome of this war as it had been for all military conflicts stretching back at least to the American Civil War, the United States was claiming preeminence, assuming leadership of the democracies even while its mobilization was stumbling, with demand outpacing supply as far as the eye could see, and without an American soldier having set foot on any battlefield.[36]

Roosevelt's December 29 fireside chat was surely one of his most transformational speeches. He made as powerful a case for aiding Britain as had yet been made, drawing on the strongest of people's self-interested motives—to avoid death or oppression—but also on the kinship and empathy most Americans felt for the British. And for the first time, he realistically acknowledged that his policies might lead the United States to war. "If we are to be completely honest with ourselves," he stated, "we must admit that there is risk in any course we may take."

While Roosevelt was delivering his talk, German bombers descended on London, delivering the worst incendiary attack since the start of the Blitz, dropping ten thousand bombs in an effort to reduce the city to a flaming skeleton. Did the Nazis, Sherwood wondered, hope that the new wave of violence would quash the coverage of the president's talk? "They needed far more bombs and bombers than they possessed," he wrote, "to nullify the lasting effect of those words, 'the arsenal of democracy.' "[37]

In London, thousands of English firemen and volunteers joined the battle, desperately struggling to control the flames that lighted the way for more raiders. Raymond Daniell described that terrifying night for *New York Times* readers. "People who were in the East End said it was like being trapped in a forest fire. The streets there are narrow and the blaze leaped across from roof to roof. Pedestrians trying to get out of that blazing, doomed part of London found themselves constantly hemmed in and cut off by new fires and toppling buildings." No casualty figures were available, Daniell wrote, but "it is inconceivable that so much damage could be done to steel and mortar without harm to flesh and blood."[38]

The famous war correspondent Ernie Pyle heard the wail of sirens in his flat in east London. From a high, darkened balcony, he and a couple of friends watched the spectacle of London on fire. In seconds, they saw two dozen incendiary bombs go off. "They flashed terrifically, then quickly simmered down to pinpoints of dazzling white, burning ferociously." He described "the whole horizon of a city lined with great fires—scores of them, perhaps hundreds." It was a "dreadful masterpiece" that he would remember as "the most beautiful sight I have ever seen. It was a night when London was ringed and stabbed with fire."[39]

In the morning, wearing his usual black Homburg hat and puffing a cigar, Prime Minister Churchill trudged through the remains of the city, through its smoldering, muddy streets, surveying the devastation, the destroyed homes, the wreckage of a seventeenth-century church designed by Christopher Wren and the massive stone fifteenth-century Guildhall that housed Roman, Saxon, and medieval antiquities. "What about peace?" a woman shouted at the prime minister. He stared hard at her. "Peace?" he snarled. "When we shall have beaten them!"[40]

Yet the barbarity of the attacks shook Churchill, and his deep gratitude for Roosevelt's arsenal speech was overwhelmed by the gnawing anxiety that Congress might not act quickly enough on Lend-Lease to spare Britain from having, as he telegrammed the president, either "to default or be stripped bare of our last resources." He also labored under uncertainty about Lend-Lease's scope: that, too, would be in the hands of Congress. And what about the raw materials and oil that Britain needed as urgently as weapons? His message ended with forced cheer and rightful foreboding: "All my heartiest good wishes to you in the New Year of storm that is opening upon us."[41]

"Truly exciting and just the invigoration and call to action that the country needs," Felix Frankfurter wrote to Sam Rosenman immediately after the president's speech. Telegrams and letters poured into the White House from across the country—by a hundred to one, Americans expressed enthusiasm for the president's address.[42]

The *Washington Post* conducted "man in the street" interviews. In a deli, a reporter asked a customer if he agreed with the president's denunciations of the Axis. "Agree? Sure I agree. Hitler has ruined everything over there, hasn't he? Are we going to let him do it over here?" The counter man in a drugstore on 14th Street NW said, "We've got to get ready. Get behind the President, and I mean everybody!" "That goes double," interjected a coffee drinker seated at the counter. "He can have my boy if he wants him. Yes, if they give him a gun now he won't need it later." "Boy is he right," a cab driver chimed in. "What guy that calls himself an

American is going to sit around until they come over here and push us around."[43]

Except for a few isolationist newspapers like the *Chicago Daily Tribune*, which accused Roosevelt of yet another attempt "to destroy the republic," most of the American press celebrated his fireside chat. The *Cleveland News* judged that the president delivered "the kind of message most Americans were anxious to hear. It breathed confidence. It breathed determination to put national defense ahead of all else." The *Richmond Times-Dispatch* editorialized, "Never until last night had a responsible official of our government defined the issues of this war so unmistakably and spoken out so categorically in denunciation of the totalitarians." The *New York Herald Tribune* called it one of the greatest talks of Roosevelt's career, "superb in its directness, its realism, its courage and its purpose." In an editorial entitled "An American Doctrine," the *New York Times* praised the fireside chat as "one of the historical landmarks of American foreign policy.... With extraordinary eloquence and deep sincerity, it affirmed a doctrine intrinsically as old as the Republic."[44]

But *Times* columnist Arthur Krock, while commending the speech, pointed out that because FDR had equivocated in the presidential campaign, six to eight crucial months of building that arsenal of democracy had been lost. The *Christian Science Monitor* and *Denver Post* lamented that had the head of a major democratic state decidedly rejected appeasement five years ago, war might have been avoided.[45]

On Capitol Hill, interventionists applauded. Sol Bloom, a New York Democrat and chair of the House Foreign Affairs Committee, took away from the speech the clear message that if the nations fighting for liberty and self-government won, the United States would also win. But if they lost, "we face war in defense of our life and liberty." FDR's address even won plaudits from many congressional non-interventionists who approved of a strong American defense as well as aid to England under some circumstances. Michigan senator Arthur Vandenberg said he agreed with the president's "denunciation of an appeasement peace. ... There is clear need for all possible aid to England. ... The grave question remains whether we shall stay short of war." In the House, Hamilton

Prime Minister Winston Churchill views the bombed-out ruins of Coventry Cathedral in November 1940.

U.S. Army Chief of Staff General George C. Marshall (left) confers with Secretary of War Henry L. Stimson.

The first is freedom of speech and expression everywhere in the world.

The second is freedom of every person to worship God in his own way everywhere in the world.

The third is freedom from want — which translated into _world_ ~~international~~ terms means economic understandings which will secure to every nation ~~everywhere~~ a healthy peace time life for its inhabitants __ _everywhere in the world_

The fourth is freedom from fear — which translated into _world_ ~~international~~ terms means a world-wide reduction of armaments to such a point and in such a thorough fashion that no nation ~~anywhere~~ will be in a position to commit an act of physical aggression against any neighbor __ _Anywhere in the world._

_17A_ That kind of a world is the very antithesis of the so-called "new order" which the dictators seek to create ~~at the point of a gun~~ _with the crash of a bomb_ in Europe and in Asia.

To that "new order" we oppose the greater conception, the moral order. A good society is able to face schemes of world domination and foreign revolutions alike without fear. It has no need either for the one or for the other.

Above: A page from FDR's draft of his January 1941 Four Freedoms speech.

Left: Four Freedoms poster, Federal Art Project.

*General George C. Marshall leads the inauguration day
parade on January 20, 1941, on his bay gelding, King Story.*

The military extravaganza at President Roosevelt's inauguration day parade.

Above: 1940 GOP presidential candidate Wendell Willkie views the damage to the Guildhall in London in January 1941.

Left: Cartoonist Fred Seibel makes the point that aid to Britain serves American self-interest and protects America too.

Isolationists Burton Wheeler, Charles Lindbergh, Kathleen Norris, and Norman Thomas at an America First rally in 1941 in Madison Square Garden in New York City.

Cartoon by Dr. Seuss. 1941.

*This cartoon by Clifford Kennedy Berryman lampoons former
ambassador to Great Britain Joseph Kennedy's tendency to take
contradictory positions, sometimes supporting Roosevelt for reelection
and endorsing his policies and sometimes favoring isolationism.*

President Roosevelt signs the Lend-Lease Act on March 11, 1941.

*At the York Safe and Lock Company in York, Pennsylvania,
workers assemble guns and gun mounts.*

*Ford Motor Company workers and their children picket at the company's River
Rouge plant in April 1941, carrying signs comparing Henry Ford to Hitler.*

Ford Motor Company's hired thugs beat up striking employees at the company's River Rouge plant in April 1941. This photograph by Milton Brooks won the first Pulitzer Prize for photography.

President Roosevelt and Prime Minister Churchill aboard the HMS Prince of Wales *during the Atlantic Conference in Placentia Bay, Newfoundland, in August 1941.*

Fish also agreed with much of the president's talk, though he insisted that the United States was not "in any danger of attack, as apparently the Nazis are unable to cross twenty miles of the Channel to land troops in Great Britain."[46]

But the president's fireside chat only gave new wind to the hardcore isolationist bloc in Congress, led by Montana's Democratic senator Burton Wheeler. Gearing up for the coming battle over Lend-Lease, the tall, gangly Wheeler, whose steel spectacles gave him an appropriately menacing expression, delivered his reply to the president's speech by radio the following evening. "We do not believe that the preservation of the American people or our democracy depends upon any foreign nation," he declared. Whereas the president's policies had "only one ending, total, complete and futile war," an American offer of a "just, reasonable and generous peace" to the German people "would crumble Hitlerism" more quickly and effectively than "all the bombers that could be dispatched over Berlin." General Robert Wood, the chairman of Sears Roebuck and head of the America First Committee, described Roosevelt's speech as "virtually a personal declaration of undeclared war on Germany." He berated the president for "his flat rejection of the idea of a negotiated peace" and for creating instead "a false sense of insecurity." The United States, he insisted, was not "facing the fate of Belgium."[47]

The impact of Roosevelt's address on the fate of Lend-Lease in Congress remained to be seen, but the president appeared to be winning the battle of public opinion. In November 1939, only 20 percent of Americans had favored aiding the democracies even if it involved no danger of U.S. entry into the war. But in 1940, the country's willingness to risk war on behalf of Britain began to rise steadily. At the end of the year, the numbers spiked upward, with more than two-thirds of Americans agreeing that it was more important to help England win "even at the risk of getting into the war" than to "concentrate entirely on keeping out."[48]

A few days after the president's fireside chat, Gallup's researchers asked a question that went to its heart: "Do you think our country's future safety depends on England winning this war?" The results were overwhelming: yes: 68 percent; no: 26 percent; undecided: 6 percent. In the inland, insulated Midwest and the Plains states, where the impact of the America First Committee was strongest, 55 percent answered yes. In the South, which had long been pro-British, internationalist, and militarist, 76 percent agreed. Politicians in the uniformly Democratic South, moreover, were well known for their anti–New Deal and interventionist stances. Though Roosevelt had vainly sought to purge them from the Democratic Party in 1938, by 1940 they had become his most loyal and fervent supporters. Gallup concluded that it was not for "sentimental reasons" or because of blood ties and a common language that Americans believed the two nations' fates were tied together. "It is for the much more *selfish* reason that Americans believe their own future safety as well as the American economic system depended on a British victory." Americans feared that if Britain lost, "Germany would be free to come after the United States."[49]

On December 31, Roosevelt held a press conference at which a reporter noted that "the press in Germany this afternoon charges that your speech was . . . stale, spiteful, and filled with monumental untruths. I think they are questioning your veracity." Everyone in the room laughed. "Would you like to comment?" "I don't think so," FDR replied with a grin. "Mr. President," asked another reporter, "are you making any New Year resolutions?" "I will make the usual one—make a resolution to try to be on time at press conferences—and it never works!" Everyone laughed again. "Happy New Year to you all," FDR said at the end of the meeting.[50]

That day, Adolf Hitler gave his own response. In a defiant New Year's Eve proclamation to his soldiers, he vowed that after having avenged in 1940 Germany's defeat in World War I, "the year 1941 will bring consummation of the greatest victory in our history." The Führer boasted that the successes of German armed forces had been more than triumphs of blood and iron—the occupied countries and their people had been "*morally conquered* through our noble conduct and exemplary discipline." He promised more of the same, until the "democratic warmongers and Jewish capitalists" were permanently crushed.[51]

That day, in a separate New Year's message to the German people, Hitler derided the "stupid and infamous lie" that he intended to conquer the world; on the contrary, he declared, he was a peacemaker.

His offer of an accord with Britain in May had been rejected by "capitalistic war profiteers" whose "only god is money." Blame for the war lay with "the stupidity of the rulers in these plutocratic democracies" who failed to "put brakes on the limitless egoism of the individual" and recognize that fascist collectivism—the "happiness of peoples"—was the wave of the future. As benediction, Hitler employed the phrase used by belligerent fanatics through the ages, "God has given our battle His approbation."[52]

"Is he trying to delude himself?" asked the editorial board of the *New York Times*. A year earlier, Hitler had promised that 1940 would be the year of victory—"everything would be over by Christmas." He boasted that his armies had conquered morally; in reality, the *Times* wrote, "Hitler has turned Europe into a prison house and filled it to the farthest corners with fear and hate, hunger and hopelessness." His precarious grip on the continent was maintained not by German virtue but by "force alone." Hitler said he was standing "at the door of a new year," but the British stood there too, "and behind them the United States."[53]

Yet as the new year dawned, much remained uncertain. In 1940, the president had made the destroyers-for-bases deal, instituted compulsory universal military service, tacitly agreed to Plan Dog, and committed the United States to supplying Britain with the tools of victory. Could Roosevelt sustain the momentum of leadership through the coming months? Would Congress approve Lend-Lease? How would the United States bring about the destruction of the aggressive fascist regimes and renewal of the democratic faith—without direct participation in the conflict?

Crowds jammed into Times Square to celebrate New Year's Eve. But the *Times* wrote that "even in the most hectic whirlpools of the downtown throng, there hovered the realization that London, Rome, Berlin were blacked out; that smoke still rose from the ruins of British buildings; that there were more dark days ahead for countless human beings in other countries."[54]

At midnight in the White House, the president, in the company of his wife, mother, and a few close friends, offered a toast: "To the United States of America." Three miles away from the White House, at their Woodley estate, Secretary of War Henry Stimson recorded in his diary that he and his wife "did not sit up to see the Old Year go out last night but went to bed early. There seemed to be no occasion for jubilation over the coming in of the New Year, for it is fraught with all kinds of ominous forebodings to both Mabel and me."[55]

There was indeed little to be lighthearted about as 1941 began. "We can but hope," Eleanor Roosevelt wrote in her "My Day" column on January 2, "that a better world will rise from the ashes of the present one."[56]

"This Annual Message is unique in our history," President Roosevelt told the members of Congress gathered in the House chamber on January 6, as he began a State of the Union address that he hoped would convey his determination to fight for the Lease-Lend plan he had unveiled in December. Cabinet members and diplomats were also present, as was Eleanor Roosevelt. The moment, the president went on, was "unprecedented" because "at no previous time has American security been as seriously threatened from without as it is today."[57]

Roosevelt spoke as clearly as ever, but reporters remarked that his voice had no lightness, no touch of humor. His speech contained the grim truths he believed Americans needed to hear; its keynote was realism. "Every realist knows," he said, "that the democratic way of life is at this moment being directly assailed in every part of the world. . . . I find it, unhappily, necessary to report that the future and the safety of our country and of our democracy are overwhelmingly involved in events far beyond our borders."[58]

Americans could not afford to be "soft-headed" in these circumstances. It was "immature" to "brag that an unprepared America, single-handed, and with one hand tied behind its back, can hold off the whole world." And it was unrealistic to think that a "dictator's peace" could return true independence or restore freedoms—or even be "good business." Since the aggressor nations remained on the offense, the administration had no choice but to devote itself "almost exclusively" to meeting the foreign peril, to ensuring that "the justice of morality . . . will win in the end."[59]

The immediate task was a determined increase in armament production with the paramount goal of speed. But though leaders of industry and labor had come on board, Roosevelt confessed himself unsatisfied with the progress so far, explaining that the greatest difficulty in mobilizing wartime production came at the beginning, with the immense complexities of the initial transition. Still, he had no doubt that Americans would join him in putting forth "our energies, our resources and our organizing powers" to guarantee that democracy's defenders had all the ships, tanks, planes, guns, and armaments they needed. "This is our purpose and our pledge."

Roosevelt and his speechwriters had produced seven drafts of his address. Though the crucial issues were aid to Britain and war production, at one point in their work on the fourth draft, the president began to think about taking a new turn, pushing the speech's horizon out to a vision of the postwar world. That vision emerged from intense engagement with the war's core issues, especially its moral dimensions—the unfathomable evil and cruelty of the Nazis, their rejection of all civilized values, and the precious Anglo-Saxon principle of freedom under law. And there was the impact of all this on people's lives in times of crisis—the war, yes, but also the Depression, economic breakdown, and social dislocation, and the impact of such crises on rights and freedoms, including the most fundamental of all, the right to life. There was overwhelming insecurity in the world, ranging from people's elemental safety and need for shelter and food to jobs and income, access to medical care, and help for the vulnerable.

Roosevelt remembered something he had said in a press conference that July during a discussion of long-term peace objectives. Perhaps it would make a good conclusion, he mused. He leaned far back in his swivel chair "with his gaze on the ceiling," Sam Rosenman would later recall. "It was a long pause—so long that it began to become uncomfortable." Then the president leaned forward again and dictated slowly and carefully. Here he needed no speechwriters—the ideas and words were his.[60]

He decided to end his speech with a hopeful picture of the world after the war. It would be more than a restoration of the prewar situation, and more than a victory over the gangster Nazi regime. Implicitly blaming the punitive Treaty of Versailles for decimating the German economy and fostering the rise of the Nazi Party, he proposed instead a postwar world that drew on the

American model, including his own New Deal. He imagined modern democracy spreading throughout the world, promising social justice and economic opportunity along with the full engagement of citizens in choosing and directing their own governments. This future had nothing in common with the fascist collectivism Hitler had offered the German people in his New Year's proclamation.

"There is nothing mysterious about the foundations of a healthy and strong democracy," FDR told Congress. "The basic things expected by our people of their political and economic systems are simple." The postwar world, he said, would be "founded upon four *essential* universal human freedoms": "The first is freedom of speech and expression—*everywhere in the world.* The second is freedom of every person to worship God in his own way—*everywhere in the world.* The third is freedom from want—which, translated into world terms, means economic understandings which will secure to every nation a healthy peacetime life for its inhabitants—*everywhere in the world.* The fourth is freedom from fear—which, translated into world terms, means a world-wide reduction of armaments to such a point and in such a thorough fashion that no nation will be in a position to commit an act of physical aggression against any neighbor—*anywhere in the world.*"

The first two freedoms were well-known parts of America's British inheritance. They were citizens' First Amendment rights of freedom of speech, press, conscience, and belief, inalienable rights that were essential to their liberty and humanity. Those rights expressed the inherent freedom of the individual *against* government interference.

Freedom from want belonged to the twentieth century, not the eighteenth. This freedom reflected the New Deal philosophy of rights not *against* government but rights *through* government, through the Roosevelt administration's unprecedented use of government powers to promote an economic recovery, provide relief to those most damaged by the Depression, and also create structures that would guarantee economic security for Americans far into the future. Freedom from want meant rights to the basic requirements of modern life: food, shelter, health care, education, work, minimum wages, fair labor standards, workers' rights to collective bargaining, and security in old age.

The president's call for freedom from fear was potent and inspiring at a moment when millions were enslaved or threatened by lawless, violent dictatorships. Freedom from fear recalled Woodrow Wilson's League of Nations in suggesting that an international organization be established after the war to mediate disputes between nations before they escalated into armed conflict. If that mediation failed, the organization's member nations would unite to enforce its resolutions. Roosevelt didn't promise to end all wars, but such an organization would offer people around the world a chance for security against the mass murder, state terror, brutality, and oppression that Europeans were experiencing under Hitler's boot and citizens of the Soviet state under Stalin.

In Roosevelt's mind, freedom from want and freedom from fear were joined. Many of the roots of Nazism and the European war could be traced to the economic deprivation, societal disruptions, and hyper-nationalism spawned by the Treaty of Versailles and the Great Depression. If freedom from want could be secured in the postwar world, he reasoned, people would be less likely to succumb to demagogues or be driven to aggression and violence because their basic material needs went unfulfilled.

In fact, all of the Four Freedoms were interrelated. Together they gave a moral meaning and purpose to the war: they offered the basis for a postwar world order founded on individual freedom and prosperity, tolerance in every dimension, and international peace and security. Although Norman Rockwell's famous 1943 illustrations of the Four Freedoms portrayed them in an exclusively American context, FDR had stressed that not just Americans but all human beings were entitled to those four essential human freedoms.[61]

Henry Luce, the publisher of *Time*, *Life*, and *Fortune*, warmly applauded FDR's important talk. In his article "The American Century," which appeared in *Life* magazine in February 1941, Luce asked whether the president's ideas were too abstract, too optimistic, too far from realizable in the world as it was. "Shall we use some big words like Democracy and Freedom and Justice? Yes, we can use the big words. The President has already used them. And perhaps we had better get used to using them again. Maybe they do mean something—about the future as well as the past." For

Luce, the future was not about American dominance but about a guiding American cause: a generous, moral commitment to the security and well-being of the world. "It must be a sharing with all peoples of our Bill of Rights, our Declaration of Independence, our Constitution, our magnificent industrial products, our technical skills," he fervently wrote. "It must be an internationalism of the people, by the people and for the people."[62]

That was Roosevelt's vision, too. Like Luce, he believed the United States was the necessary country, the nation whose ideals, as he expressed them in the Four Freedoms, would salvage and rebuild a war-torn world. Both he and Luce wanted nothing more than to extend American values "everywhere in the world."[63]

Robert Sherwood believed that Roosevelt's words about essential freedoms would resound throughout history. The president's voice, he wrote, was the "voice of liberation, the reassurance of the dignity of man. . . . Roosevelt seemed to take his speeches lightly, but no one knew better than he that, once he had the microphone before him, he was speaking for the eternal record—his words were, as [poet Carl] Sandburg said, 'throwing long shadows.' "[64]

Two weeks later, on the eve of Roosevelt's third inauguration, four thousand people, including the president's wife, sons James and Elliott, daughter Anna, mother Sara Delano Roosevelt, and a host of others luminaries, jammed into Constitution Hall in Washington, where they heard and watched performances by famous Hollywood stars and artists. Charlie Chaplin struck a solemn note when he delivered a dramatic speech from his new movie, *The Great Dictator*, one of the few incisive film satires of Hitler. "To those who can hear me," he said, "do not despair. . . . Let us fight for a world of reason, a world where science and progress will lead to all men's happiness. . . . We are coming out of the darkness into the light!"[65]

Irving Berlin, the Russian-born Jewish-American composer, sang his hymn "God Bless America," accompanied by thousands of audience members in a spontaneous chorus. Almost a second national anthem, it was, Berlin said, "not just a song but an expression of my feeling toward the country to which I owe what I have and what I am."[66]

Shortly after sunrise on January 20, hundreds of thousands of people began gathering along Pennsylvania Avenue. As if they were going to a football game, many wore extra overcoats and carried blankets and thermos bottles. They filled the sidewalks and perched in trees to watch the spectacle.[67]

"No, Fala, you can't go with me today," FDR told his black Scottie pup at the threshold of the White House. In high spirits, the president drove down Pennsylvania Avenue to the Capitol in an open car, chatting animatedly with House Speaker Sam Rayburn and waving his tall silk hat to the crowds. Physically, Roosevelt had scarcely changed since his first inauguration in 1933. His hair was grayer and a trifle thinner, his face and neck sagged a little, and the lines of his forehead and around his eyes were sharper. To close observers, though, he looked tired more often than he had in earlier years.[68] His hand on an opened page of an old family Bible, Roosevelt took, for the third time, the oath of office, intoned by Chief Justice Charles Evans Hughes. *Times* columnist Arthur Krock wrote that the oath "was more than a pact with his 130 millions of countrymen and countrywomen; it was a pact with mankind's ancient dream of freedom for the human spirit; it was a pact with free men everywhere."[69]

After sealing that pact, the president turned to the immense shivering crowd and addressed a nation not yet at war, but not at peace. It was a philosophical talk: unlike in 1933, when his subject was fiscal chaos, or 1937, when he stressed the importance of fulfilling the promises of the half-dealt New Deal, this time he reached for a higher, even spiritual plane. His theme was the survival of democracy in a world of violent totalitarian aggression "never before encountered."[70]

"Democracy is not dying," Roosevelt declared. Without naming her, he scorned Anne Morrow Lindbergh and her book *The Wave of the Future*, and said he refused to believe that "tyranny and slavery have become the surging wave of the future, and that freedom is an ebbing tide." The "prophets of the downfall of American democracy have seen their dire predictions come to naught." Democracy could not die, he said, because it was "the most humane, the most advanced and in the end the most unconquerable of all forms of human society."

Using one of the unpretentious, homespun analogies he liked to include in his talks, he explained that a nation was like a person; it had a physical, intellectual, and spiritual life. Its body must be clothed, fed, and housed and its mind kept informed and alert. But a nation, "like a person, has something deeper, something more permanent, something larger than the sum of all its parts." No single word could name it, "and yet we all understand what it is." For the United States it was something he called "the democratic aspiration," a living faith, a quasi-divine purpose in national life, an ongoing quest for freedom, justice, equality, happiness. If that "spirit of America" were killed, "even though the Nation's body and mind, constricted in an alien world, lived on, the America we know would have perished."

To keep that spirit alive, all citizens would be called upon to make countless sacrifices. That guiding light, he said, "does, and will, furnish the highest justification for every sacrifice that we may make in the cause of national defense." Ending his address with patriotic, fighting words, he declared that "we do not retreat. . . . As Americans, we go forward, in the service of our country, by the will of God."

The address won plaudits in the press—the *New York Times* called it "a straightforward and a deeply stirring reaffirmation of faith in democracy"—but FDR was disappointed, he told his speechwriter Sam Rosenman, "at its lack of impact." After such powerful addresses as the Arsenal of Democracy speech and the Four Freedoms State of the Union message—both delivered in the past three weeks—perhaps the Inaugural Address was destined to be anticlimactic. Yet it advanced the themes of those talks, describing in fresh terms the irreconcilable conflict between democracy and tyranny and capturing in a single phrase—"the democratic aspiration"—the central thrust of the American experiment. FDR's third inaugural speech yielded no memorable catchphrase, but it added to the arsenal of ideas that would guide Americans and people everywhere through the war and its aftermath.[71]

After his speech, Roosevelt went outside to watch the inaugural parade from a reviewing stand in front of the White House. First came a platoon of Washington motorcycle police, and behind them rode General Marshall, the army chief of staff, on his light bay horse King Story. Marshall saluted his commander in chief, then dismounted and joined Roosevelt on the reviewing stand. Marching to the tempo set by military bands, there followed units from the Army's cavalry and infantry, the Navy, Coast Guard, and Marines, with West Point cadets and Annapolis midshipmen in their wake. Airplanes in mass formation soared overhead. After a brief pause for the street to be cleared, twelve hundred soldiers from Fort Knox, Kentucky, swung into action; scout cars, motorcycles, trucks with anti-tank guns, anti-aircraft guns, field guns, and cannon sped past. Tanks, with throttles open, roared along at thirty miles per hour, their treads leaving deep indentations in the pavement. The Coast Defense branch of the Army followed with mobile cannons and searchlights.[72]

It was a staggeringly militaristic extravaganza. In his Inaugural Address, the president had largely skirted war talk or allusions to Lend-Lease, apart from the remark that "the Nation's hands must not be tied when the Nation's life is in danger." But the parade was a vivid display of the nation's willingness to fight to preserve its way of life. The soldiers, tanks, planes, and guns provided, one reporter noted, "a dramatic foretaste of things to come in the military program of the United States."[73]

Hitler was getting the message. He met with Mussolini the same day at his retreat atop the Obersalzberg mountain in the Bavarian Alps, where the "thorniest question" they faced, according to New York Times foreign correspondent Herbert Matthews, was the new stage the United States had entered. The Führer could assume that Lend-Lease aid was unlikely to be effective for some time, but his impatience with—and nervousness about—the United States was mounting. Matthews reported that Hitler thought "it may be considered advisable to make some move as a warning to the United States."[74]

America was clinging to its noncombatant role, still accepting the sacrifice of British lives for its own security. And yet the weeks following Roosevelt's return from the Caribbean had elevated the United States to a preeminent role in the world conflict. The president had firmly planted the Stars and Stripes next to the British Union Jack and had persuaded two-thirds of Americans to approve of aid to Britain, even if that meant war for their country. His three important statements—the Arsenal of Democracy fireside chat, the State of the Union message, the Inaugural Address and the military spectacle that followed it—established America's determination to lead the nations fighting the forces of tyranny.

The United States was leveraging its unparalleled industrial potential and the soft power of its ideas to battle Hitler for global leadership. But there remained a war to be won, and it was highly improbable that Americans could win the war without entering it. Though Henry Luce greatly admired FDR's Four Freedoms, he pointed out that they were not immortal. "Some amongst us are likely to be dying for them—on the fields and in the skies of battle. Either that or the words themselves and what they mean die with us—in our beds."[75]

CHAPTER SIX

Make the Army Roll

A COMPANY THAT CANNED citrus fruit began to make parts for merchant ships. Factories for lawnmowers, vacuum cleaners, textiles, adding machines, and mechanical pencils turned to making shrapnel, gas masks, mosquito netting, automatic pistols, and high-precision instruments. The country was mobilizing its industries for defense.[1]

Americans were participating in a remarkable transformation. The wheels of industry were turning from coast to coast, in some places around the clock, as the nation unleashed its resources and manpower on a vast scale. A *Time* magazine reporter who ventured out of the nation's capital into the rest of America wrote that leaving that enclave "was like leaving the quiet of an office to walk into the crashing roar of a factory."[2]

Industrial plants underutilized since the start of the Depression hummed again. Steel mills in Birmingham, Alabama, operated at 100 percent capacity. From the Texas Gulf Coast to Newport News, Virginia, shipyards received $1 billion in orders for destroyers, freighters, and cargo ships. Square footage devoted to manufacturing airplane engines increased in 1940 from 2 million to almost 5 million. Factories had to be converted or built from scratch. Companies invested in new facilities for mass production as they had not done in more than a decade. The Reynolds Metals

Company broke ground on a $23 million aluminum plant in Alabama and a $17 million rolling mill; in Grand Prairie, Texas, a $7 million airplane factory sprang up from bare earth, and in Freeport, Texas, Dow Chemical spent $15 million on a new plant for extracting magnesium from Gulf water. Textile mills in the South received $19 million in new orders. The agricultural South was industrializing.[3]

The labor force was booming. Millions of men and women of all ages—men in cuffless trousers and women wearing slacks for the first time—streamed into factories and worked on assembly lines. Vocational high schools were on overtime, training and re-training men and women for new roles in the workforce. And all the new workers needed someplace to live. They could not be expected to commute long distances to work, nor could they and their families live in tents, as Undersecretary of War Robert Patterson had recommended. Their morale was critical to the defense effort. So 2.5 million new homes would be built along with schools and recreational facilities. Roosevelt had anticipated this need: in July 1940 he appointed a real estate man named Charles Palmer to head a new Division of Defense Housing.[4]

The transition from a peacetime economy to all-out defense production transformed local communities. The powerful energy of the nation's industrial activity produced prosperity throughout the land, and that oceanic vitality, more than any of the social or economic programs of the 1930s, would fulfill the promises of the New Deal.

The manager of the State Employment Service in the small city of York, Pennsylvania (population fifty-six thousand), re-marked in early January 1941 that "our task a year ago was to find jobs for men; now it's to find men for jobs." The reason was defense work, with contracts worth an estimated $40 million pouring into the town. The search for workers was so thorough that employers were even checking old payrolls. By January 1941, York had become an "industrial beehive," reported the *New York Times*. Its industries were turning out tanks, tank guns, gun mounts, anti-aircraft guns, tool gauges, powder presses, machine gun cradles, shells, and trench mortars. "The casual eye can see everywhere," the *Times* wrote, "evidence of the change the defense preparations have brought into the lives of workers, employers, merchants, teachers, taxicab drivers, sales girls and clergymen." There was a new spirit of community and solidarity. In York, workers and employers alike "talk patriotism without getting pompous about it. Both sides speak realistically about the necessity of making sacrifices."[5]

"Labor is all for defense," declared the head of the local American Federation of Labor. "If it is shown that the defense program has absorbed all labor and it is necessary to increase hours, we will never flinch. The first to fall, if democracy falls, is labor." The AFL had long shown its commitment to democratic values. In 1933, its members voted to boycott German goods and services until Germany recognized the right of working people to organize in unions and until it ceased its persecution of the Jewish people.[6]

The U.S. military had suddenly become the biggest buyer and consumer of the nation's industrial production—and the biggest source of profits. And yet the industrial output was not enough to arm the United States for its own defense, and not enough to supply Britain with what it needed to defend itself against Germany. Production fell behind schedule. Some manufacturers, eager to exploit the new economy without converting their factories, refused or neglected War Department orders. And as demand exceeded supply and profits mounted, workers fought to win their fair share as well as to protect their labor rights against the push for production at all costs.

Mobilization was a massive and complex effort to achieve a goal that could be expressed in a single phrase—the defense of the United States. It was a goal for which the government was responsible, yet American government was not yet succeeding in that responsibility. It was not yet setting priorities or coordinating and maximizing the nation's production.

Not that the Roosevelt administration hadn't tried to harness industry's output. The landscape was littered with failed experiments to salvage the United States from the virtual disarmament that followed World War I. During the 1920s and the Depression, Americans largely carried on as though that war had indeed ended all wars—or at least ended U.S. participation in them.

While the Germans rearmed in the 1930s and built a modern military based on the freshest technology, the United States fell far behind, in quality, quantity, and innovation. In all the essentials of Blitz warfare, according to the official history of U.S. mobilization, Germany had "superior aircraft, superior tanks, mobile units, artillery, antitank and anti-aircraft guns." American stocks were "woefully deficient." In the spring of 1940, the German Luftwaffe could put 25,000 planes into action, compared with the U.S. Army Air Corps' 2,665. As Secretary Stimson put it, "In 1940 the only weapons available in the United States in any number were surplus stocks from the last war."[7]

Only in early August 1939, a month before Hitler's invasion of Poland, did President Roosevelt create the War Resources Board, a civilian advisory committee made up mainly of the chiefs of some of the largest corporations—and no representatives of labor. Edward Stettinius, chairman of U.S. Steel, was its head and filled its staff with more corporate executives.

Charged with helping the Army and Navy Munitions Boards formulate plans for putting industry on a wartime basis, the WRB promptly produced a secret Industrial Mobilization Plan that, if executed, would put the entire American economy on full war footing. But the board's recommendations and even its existence were a bridge too far at a time when the president appeared eager, as the *Washington Post* put it, "to negative any suggestion that the United States is preparing for war." Given the choice between increased industrial production and avoiding the appearance of war preparations, the administration chose the latter, and the War Resources Board was dissolved after only four months.[8]

But with German tanks and planes crushing the democracies of western Europe in the spring of 1940, and with the risk of American involvement mounting, the need to mobilize industry became urgent, as did the need for an authority to manage the transition to a war economy. By executive order, Roosevelt established the National Defense Advisory Commission in May. Basically a consulting agency, the NDAC was almost destined to fail because, as designed by a president determined to retain control of the mobilization, it lacked any authority to direct the effort. At its first meeting at the White House, the president explained how it would work: the commissioners would bring their recommendations to him and he would back them up—if he agreed.

The NDAC's responsibilities were spread out among seven different and largely autonomous sections, each with its own interests, staff, and even legal counsel. William Knudsen resigned from the presidency of General Motors to take charge of industrial manufacturing, exchanging his $300,000 salary for $1 a year—becoming the first of the war's "dollar-a-year" men, who were either rich enough to decline government pay or able to stay on their company's payroll. Sidney Hillman, the vice-president of the Congress of Industrial Organizations and a well-known labor activist, had the broad mandate of overseeing labor and its relations with management and government. Under the circumstances, he achieved wonders. U.S. Steel's Edward Stettinius was responsible for raw materials, especially critical strategic materials like aluminum and zinc. The others, a mix of New Dealers, businessmen, and academics, were charged with agricultural policy, transportation, purchasing and price stabilization, and consumer protection.[9]

The tasks of the NDAC were gigantic, vague, and virtually impossible to realize. There was no mechanism for coordination among its sections, and no channel for handling complex issues such as setting production priorities, awarding contracts, balancing domestic and foreign orders, or settling labor disputes. One of the NDAC's main defects was its inability to set priorities. Most industries marked their orders A-1 priority, placing 90 percent of all defense orders in that category, which effectively meant there were no priorities at all. Procurement posed another problem, for the army had no expertise in knowing what products to buy or how to buy them. For example, the army placed an order for the kind of underwear soldiers wore in 1917, unaware that it could not be produced on 1940 machines.[10]

By December 1940, the NDAC was under assault from all sides. The agency was the source of great confusion; according to Labor Secretary Frances Perkins, "Speed was so essential that people acted without sufficient reflection." With British needs mounting as the Battle of Britain intensified, the Roosevelt administration was faced with the challenge of stepping up the tempo of rearmament, which meant winning and keeping the cooperation of its two key players, industry and labor.[11]

In 1940, the house of labor was divided—and subdivided.

In the small hours of Thanksgiving Day, November 21, 1940, a fistfight broke out in the bar of the Hotel Roosevelt in New Orleans. A. H. Raskin, the *New York Times'* labor reporter, was there for the annual convention of the American Federation of Labor, the nation's largest union. He was having a quiet drink with David Dubinsky, the respected head of the International Ladies Garment Workers Union (ILGWU).[12]

Dubinsky and Sidney Hillman, his ally, mentor, and fellow immigrant from eastern Europe, were both founders of the Congress of Industrial Organizations. Its original incarnation was the Committee for Industrial Organization, formed in 1935 within the AFL by Hillman, Dubinsky, John L. Lewis, the head of the United Mine Workers, and others who believed that in mass-production industries such as aircraft, automobile, chemical, and steel, labor should be organized by industry-wide unions, not the small craft unions that dominated the AFL. In 1938, Dubinsky, Hillman, and Lewis decided to take the CIO out of the AFL and name it the Congress of Industrial Organizations. But by 1940, Dubinsky was upset with Lewis's militancy and dictatorial style, and he took the ILGWU out of the CIO and back to the AFL—on the condition that the AFL purge itself of racketeering, corruption, and gangsters.

As Raskin recounted, Joey Fay, the boss of the notoriously corrupt construction unions in New Jersey, drunkenly marched over to their table in the bar. In increasingly profane terms, Fay shouted at Dubinsky for proposing a tough anti-racketeering resolution to the AFL convention. It was "the dirtiest, lousiest resolution" he had ever seen anywhere, Fay yelled. Within seconds, the beefy Fay landed a punch that flattened Dubinsky's cigar against his face. Friends restored peace by dragging Fay back to his table. Dubinsky tried to capitalize on the brawl to drum up support for his resolution, but the convention approved only a toothless alternative; it merely recommended that unions take measures to expel corrupt leaders from their ranks.[13]

Whereas the AFL's internal conflict was over gangsters in its ranks, its rival organization, the CIO, holding its convention at the same time in Atlantic City, was even more bitterly fractured over the issue of Communists. From its founding, accusations of Communist infiltration, if not domination, had flowed freely from the organization's enemies in government and industry as well as from the AFL. All tried to plant the idea that the CIO was little more than an outpost of Stalinism. The question of how to respond to those allegations—and to the actual Communists who in fact did form an aggressive minority in its ranks—had tormented the CIO almost from its inception.

These in-house clashes over racketeers and Communists were costly distractions from the unions' main business of protecting their members' interests. But far costlier and more perilous to the nation's mobilization for defense was the venomous and untiring rancor between the AFL and the CIO. "Where, oh where is Dubinsky today?" John L. Lewis demanded in Atlantic City. "He is crying aloud now for the AFL to abandon the crooks and racketeers of the organization!" Lewis served notice that he had no interest in making peace with the AFL.[14]

The bitter enmity between the two organizations led to strikes in which the issue was not wages or working conditions but whether the AFL or the CIO would win the right to organize and represent workers in a particular plant or industry. These "jurisdictional" strikes dangerously halted critical work in defense factories.[15]

While the dramatic labor conventions were in session in Louisiana and New Jersey, President Roosevelt was spending Thanksgiving in Hyde Park. Along with Labor Secretary Perkins, he had tried repeatedly to narrow the rift between the antagonists. In March 1939 he hosted peace talks at the White House, which Lewis torpedoed; later that year he sent letters to the AFL and CIO conventions, asking for a new effort at conciliation—the CIO did not respond.[16]

Now, in late November 1940, Roosevelt addressed his plea for unity only to the AFL. He apologized for being unable to attend the convention in person, but "in these days of crisis" he could not travel far from the capital. He thanked the AFL unions and their leaders for their help in shaping the transformational labor and social legislation of the New Deal. But he had still more to ask. "Now we have come to a period which demands intense and sustained cooperation so that our beloved Republic can present, in any emergency which might be forced upon us, the solid, imposing front of a great and united democracy." Peace between the two labor giants might not be easy to achieve, but he expressed the hope that well-intentioned and honorable men could work out a solution to restore unity and harmony—or at least "a sensible working arrangement."[17]

As he had done in the past, AFL president William Green quickly declared his willingness to meet with CIO representatives "anywhere, any time, any place." But just as swiftly, the CIO slammed the door. Philip Murray, who had just taken over the presidency from the fiery Lewis, had a succinct message for FDR: thanks, but no thanks. Murray accused Roosevelt of trying "to force shotgun agreements" between the CIO and the AFL, and the CIO wasn't interested. There could be peace and unity in the labor movement, he wrote, only when the AFL effectively surrendered and accepted the CIO policy of single unions representing entire industries. Until then, the CIO would focus on a whirlwind campaign to organize labor in defense industries, unconcerned about conflict with the AFL or the federal government.[18]

In November 1940, as delegates were arriving in Atlantic City and New Orleans for the labor conventions, five thousand striking members of the United Auto Workers, a CIO affiliate, were picketing twenty-four hours a day outside the Downey, California, plant of the Vultee Aircraft Company, the leading producer of basic training planes for Army Air Corps cadets. In the past five months there had been hundreds of labor disputes, but the NDAC's Sidney Hillman had managed to settle almost all of them without work stoppages. The few that did occur—at aluminum, steel, and aircraft plants—lasted from a few hours to just three or four days. One of Hillman's great successes was averting a strike of 135,000 workers at General Motors.

But the Vultee strike had gone on for two weeks, the longest work stoppage since the rearmament program began. Carrying signs and banners demanding a 25¢ increase in the 50¢ hourly wage, the UAW workers had stopped production on $84 million in defense orders. Army pilots were crossing the picket line to ferry finished planes out of the idle factory.[19] "I submit to you," declared the West Coast UAW president Lou Michener, "that a 50-cent-an-hour minimum does not represent this American way of life." He was right. The nation's 225,000 aircraft workers received a lower hourly wage than employees doing similar work in auto factories. All that Vultee employees wanted was to make a decent living, have the protection of economic security, and enjoy some leisure time. Even Eleanor Roosevelt weighed in, noting in her "My Day" column that workers were expected to "make sacrifices of wages and hours because of the necessities of national defense." But why, she asked, wasn't management using its soaring profits to pay workers fairly and to reduce the bloated salaries of its executives? "Sacrifices," she concluded, "will have to be equal."[20]

Perhaps. But Americans were incensed that workers were blocking vital production. Charges flew that Communists in the CIO were sabotaging the nation's defense, and bills to curb or prevent strikes were proposed in Congress. Gallup reported that 60 percent of those polled wanted tight restrictions over labor. "I fear that the public will demand elimination of all strikes," said Representative John Costello of California. The *Atlanta Constitution* implored Americans to "stop placing the spotlight on the second and third letters only of the word 'America' and catch the vision of the complete word itself."[21]

No administration in American history had supported the rights of workers as vigorously and successfully as the Roosevelt administration, but in the crisis year of 1940, it viewed work stoppages in defense industries as threats to the nation's survival. War Department officials and Hillman's representative rushed to the Vultee plant in southern California to confer with management and union leaders. Finally, after days of tense negotiations, the strike was settled—despite the fact that the War Department negotiator, Major Sidney Simpson, showed up drunk and was fired immediately by Secretary Stimson. The break came when workers won an hourly pay raise, more paid vacation time, and an annual sick leave in exchange for accepting a no-strike clause in their contract and for agreeing that future labor grievances would be decided by an arbitration board.

In the end, the Vultee strike proved relatively easy to settle: workers had strong union representation, management agreed to negotiate, and government mediation succeeded. Many people were relieved that government coercion had been avoided, but others feared that the Vultee strike was only the opening gun. As the interests and rights of workers clashed with mounting demands for arms production, the Vultee strike highlighted the obstacles and challenges that lay ahead.[22]

As the Roosevelt administration shifted its priorities from advocacy for workers to the push for maximum industrial output, defense contracts became the flashpoint. The government had awarded important contracts to some large companies that not only resisted unionization but refused to abide by the standards for minimum wages and maximum hours, as well as for health and safety. Under the 1936 Walsh-Healy Public Contracts Act, these standards had to be part of all defense contracts.

Bethlehem Steel was one such company. Although it was a leading recipient of defense contracts, the National Labor Relations Board (NLRB) had found it guilty of violating the 1935 Wagner Act, which guaranteed the rights of workers to organize into unions and engage in collective bargaining. Not even Sidney Hillman could make headway to ban Bethlehem Steel from government work.

The most notorious and defiant industrialist was old Henry Ford, a pro-German and virulently anti-Semitic isolationist who refused to accept defense contracts that would help Britain, dismissing the British Empire as a lost cause. While Ford-Werke plants in Germany turned out military vehicles for the Nazi army, the Ford Motor Company in Michigan rejected a contract in June 1940 to manufacture nine thousand Rolls-Royce airplane engines, six thousand of which were destined for the Royal Air Force.[23]

But the Roosevelt administration wanted no feud with the cantankerous Ford: it needed his company's vast production capability. In November 1940, half a year after Ford turned away the Rolls-Royce contract, the War Department awarded, and Ford accepted, a $122 million order for more than four thousand Pratt and Whitney airplane engines—all for the American Army and Navy.[24]

The government's huge tender to Ford Motor surprised and angered many in the labor movement. For years, Ford had violated labor laws and resisted—often violently—the right of its workers to be represented by the UAW. Only a month before the War Department offered Ford this new contract, a federal appeals court had found the company responsible for igniting a riot in 1937 at its vast River Rouge plant in Detroit: thugs employed by Ford's "service department" had brutally beat up union organizers. On nine occasions, the NLRB had found Ford in violation of the Wagner Act. "Labor union organizers," Henry Ford growled, "are the worst thing that ever struck the earth." But the government nevertheless awarded the contract to Ford because no other equally large facilities were available.[25]

Assistant Secretary of War Robert Patterson defended his department's order, stressing that the paramount concern was fast production, not labor grievances. But an outraged Sidney Hillman lodged a protest with the NDAC and then appealed to President Roosevelt, from whom he received what seemed to be a sympathetic response. "I have had a great many complaints about the War Department contracts to the Ford Motor Company," the president wrote to the NDAC, pointing out that the company had been "judicially held to be in the wrong." He asked the commission to explain "what has been done to assure full compliance with Federal laws before these contracts were awarded."[26]

A month later, in December, the War Department awarded Ford Motor yet another defense contract, a modest $1.4 million assignment to produce fifteen hundred light reconnaissance scout cars for the army. Small as it was, the contract felt like a slap in the face to unionists. Hillman was furious. He pointed out that the job could easily have been handled by smaller companies that, unlike Ford, complied with labor laws. But even though the government could not argue that alternative facilities were unavailable, Hillman could not block the order.[27]

During the Great Depression, the nation's economic elite had lost not only much of its wealth, but also much of its prestige. In his first Inaugural Address in March 1933, FDR had branded the industrialists and financiers "unscrupulous money changers" and "economic royalists," offering only "outworn tradition" and "false leadership." They were, he charged, "rejected by the hearts and minds of men" and had "fled from their high seats in the temple of our civilization." The heroes of the Roaring '20s became the villains of the New Deal '30s.[28]

But in 1940 the tables were turning yet again. These men were now the producers, the can-doers. They knew how to make things—plans, budgets, factories, airplanes, hand grenades, woolen socks. As the government expanded to administer a wartime economy, the moneychangers streamed back to the temple. The industrialists were now patriots to be praised by government officials as essential to the defense of the United States. The captains of industry were riding what would become the greatest expansion of industrial capacity in history—but in 1940, their achievements were neither heroic nor adequate. Manufacturers and factory owners were often lackadaisical or careless in filling defense contracts. Some put more profitable consumer orders first; others sought guarantees against losses before they would invest in new facilities.

William Knudsen, the NDAC's man in charge of industrial manufacturing, understood production as well as anyone, all the pieces, materials, paperwork, and men that had to come together to produce, for example, a single plane. And he did not have to fight, like Hillman, to have his voice heard. But with only narrow authority, Knudsen was unable to gain control of the nation's wobbling industrial mobilization. How could anyone?

On the morning of December 20, after the "All in!" call, FDR greeted reporters warmly, then opened the press conference in typical form: "There isn't any news today—really, literally." No news? "Churchill Warns Anew on Invasion" read the front-page headline that day in the *New York Times*. Other stories included reports of German troop movements into southern Italy, German planes flying Italian reinforcements to Albania, German dive-bombers pummeling the Greeks, a $100 million contract signed by the British War Purchasing Commission with a New York shipbuilder for sixty new freighters, and the British Commission's negotiations with American manufacturers for other defense contracts to total $3 billion. Only three days before, Roosevelt had told the same crowd of reporters his plan for Lend-Lease, which was not irrelevant to the question asked by one intrepid reporter.[29]

Was there any truth to reports that a reorganization of the National Defense Advisory Commission was in the works? Newspaper articles had quoted an unnamed "high defense authority" who leaked word that a "czar" would soon be appointed to head all defense production. "No, no," Roosevelt replied dismissively. That was just a story. Nothing had been decided.[30]

By then, Henry Stimson, the head of the War Department and the man ultimately in charge of bringing industrial production into line with the needs of the American military, had no doubt that the NDAC was a failure the United States could not afford once Lend-Lease became law. He was especially concerned about the critical problem of bottlenecks in war production. Airplane manufacturers were slow to convert to a war footing, and some not only maintained their peacetime production level of commercial planes but planned to double it in 1941.[31]

Stimson had addressed this issue with the press on November 26. "Which is more vital to the Nation right now," he asked, "increased military and naval strength in the air, or increased business for the commercial airlines?" What could be more outrageous than army bombers grounded for lack of engines while manufacturers were furnishing similar engines for commercial planes? Stimson singled out the Douglas Aircraft Corporation in Santa Monica as one of the most egregious culprits. Douglas was turning out twelve big commercial planes a month but lagged two months behind schedule in filling the War Department's orders for bombers. "I think we put the fear of God into the Douglas Company," Stimson said afterward. FDR backed up his secretary of war, telling reporters later that day that the military program "ought to come first."[32]

But personal pleas and public shaming did not really put war production on an organized footing, even though Congress had given the administration the ultimate weapon in a section of the Selective Service Act passed in September 1940. The Russell-Overton amendment authorized the government to take over the factories of any company that refused to participate in national defense. If the government could draft young men to serve for $1 a day, reasoned its authors, Senators John Overton of Louisiana and Richard Russell of Georgia, it should also be able to draft industry. And public support for this option was not lacking: 70 percent of Americans favored seizing the plants of uncooperative companies.[33]

Across the Atlantic, the urgency of American arms production was even more obvious. The British people were profoundly worried— less about their inability to pay America for war materiel than about America's ability to produce it before their island was over- run by Nazis. As one reporter wrote, the British feared that be- cause they were not yet embroiled in the war, the Americans were not making "the maximum industrial effort or anything like it."[34]

All of British society, on the other hand, had become organized and disciplined for war. In December, Churchill appointed Minister of Labour Ernest Bevin, the firebrand trade unionist and Labour Party leader, to serve as the head of all defense production in Britain. Ultimately, remarked the British historian Daniel Todman, Bevin became "one of the most important figures on the home front." Taking the slogan "Work at War Speed," Bevin aimed to end what George Orwell called "the tug-of-war between private profit and public necessity." His goal was total mobilization: there would be no exception because of rank. "Everybody in this war," he demanded, "has to be a member of the working class or the army." All privileges formerly accepted in British society "must entirely disappear into the common pool." He would make strikes and lockouts illegal, though not in so many words, and workers in de- fense industries would be forbidden to leave their jobs without government permission. Employers, meanwhile, could not dismiss employees except for misconduct. Young British women as well as men too old for the military draft could be drafted for work in war industries. Bevin proposed a lengthening of the workweek along with an increase in wages. "Tell us what to do and we'll do it," was how Bevin characterized the British spirit. The result was a massive expansion of war production under the most difficult con- ditions.[35]

The Columbia University historian Allan Nevins, at Oxford University that winter, saw at close range the unprecedented centralization of government authority. "All wealth, all productive power, all activities," he wrote, "are being socialized or pooled in a way that would have seemed impossible three years ago." Reflecting on the preparedness campaign in the United States, Nevins wondered how Americans, who still felt safe in their homes, could be persuaded that they too must sacrifice many of the ordinary habits of ordinary times.[36]

For Roosevelt, the immense project of putting the whole nation on a wartime basis would turn on national unity. It was a fortunate coincidence that in early December, the theme at a black-tie dinner of the Economic Club of New York was "National Unity for Defense." Though he was cruising in the Caribbean and unable to attend the dinner, FDR sent a message to be read aloud to the eminent guests, the cream of the nation's financial and industrial elite.

The president framed his remarks under the democratic banner of individual rights and freedom, calling for unity by consent rather than by the coercion of a Führer state. "There can be no real unity," Roosevelt wrote, "where the people have no voice. In a democratic order, national unity is the *voluntary* expression of the mind and spirit of a *free* people." In other words, the national unity he envisaged was the one cherished by the founding fathers, Enlightenment men who placed priceless value on the freedom of the human mind, on open public debate and deliberation, on due process and individual rights. "The freedoms that we must and will protect in the United States are the freedoms which will make *the individual* paramount in a true democracy," the president said. Unity for the defense of American self-government, unity in opposition to the Nazi enemy, would expand, not diminish, individual freedom. One sure way to protect the individual was to respect not only labor rights but also the capitalist ethos. It was therefore imperative, FDR told the members of the Economic Club, to ensure "proper reward for labor, proper incentive for enterprise and a proper return on investment." The one thousand businessmen in attendance applauded enthusiastically.[37]

A few days later, William Knudsen addressed a similar gathering at the annual convention of the National Association of Manufacturers at the Waldorf-Astoria. No organization had been more fiercely opposed to Franklin Roosevelt or more determined to undermine the New Deal. The sixty-one-year-old Big Bill, who as a young man had immigrated to the United States from Denmark with $30 in his pocket, now called on both industry and labor to grasp the magnitude and urgency of the task ahead. With aircraft production 30 percent behind schedule, he warned the tuxedoed titans of industry, anything less than maximum output and total cooperation between labor and management would have disastrous consequences. "Let us work and work harder," he implored, so that Nazi barbarism "spreading to our shores will be an impossibility forever."[38]

Roosevelt and Knudsen were using a tool basic to leadership and democracy: persuasion. But the mediocre efforts of the NDAC had proven that talk was no substitute for action. Now, with the United States committed to supplying vast amounts of war materiel to American and British forces, the need for action became overwhelming.

In mid-December Henry Stimson was pushing for the NDAC to be replaced with a powerful new agency whose leaders would have the authority to settle disputes between industry and labor, cut red tape, award contracts, manage procurement, resolve internal conflicts, and thus achieve the goals set for them. Stimson thought that the new agency should have a single director, a man with the power to coordinate the different elements of the rearmament campaign—in short, a "czar" of production.[39]

Stimson met with the president on December 18, the day after the Lend-Lease press conference. To his surprise, he found that Roosevelt had also been thinking about the NDAC's ineffectiveness and quickly agreed to its replacement.

Then, in the late afternoon on December 20, a few hours after FDR had brushed aside reporters' queries about a possible reorganization of the NDAC—"No, no," he had said—the press was hastily called back to the president's office. He would, in fact, shake up the defense structure, he told them, but not by reorganizing the NDAC. He would issue an executive order to create a new Office of Production Management. Its goals would be similar to those of the NDAC—to raise production to the highest level possible—but, with a comprehensive mandate, it would be better equipped to achieve them. The OPM would have the authority, according to FDR's executive order, to "formulate and execute in the public interest all measures needful and appropriate" to "increase, accelerate, and regulate the production" of everything required for the national defense and to ensure effective coordination of government and industry.[40]

The NDAC's seven sections would be cut to just three. The first was that of "the buyer and the user" of defense materiel. That meant the War and Navy Departments, represented by Secretaries Stimson and Knox, whose charge was to "buy wisely." The other two sections were management and labor, which would also be headed by familiar faces: William Knudsen would command the division representing industrial management, while Sidney Hillman would run the labor section.[41]

Knudsen would also serve as the OPM's director-general, with Hillman as associate director-general, and Stimson and Knox as board members. There would be no single "Czar or Poobah," FDR explained to reporters, "who combines all three of those elements in his own person." No one person could fairly and knowledgeably represent labor, management, and the military services.[42]

But how would the Knudsen-Hillman leadership work? Who was the OPM's *real* head? Asked that question at a later press conference, Roosevelt paused, blew out a cloud of cigarette smoke, and, grinning, said the answer was both of them. Knudsen and Hillman would share their tasks with equal authority, like the partners in his old law firm of Roosevelt & O'Connor. But this time the firm was Knudsen & Hillman, and the head man was named Knudsenhillman. Hmm. Some reporters wondered, would Knudsenhillman get along with himself?[43]

Why had the president gone against Stimson's recommendation that the OPM have one head? Though he was delegating more authority to the OPM than he had to the NDAC, Roosevelt remained wary of creating an alternative power center. Stimson thought FDR had been influenced by advice that "to give it a Head would create a super-Government."[44]

"You cannot, under the Constitution, set up a second President of the United States," Roosevelt told reporters on December 20, nor could he delegate any part of his own "ultimate responsibility." Yet he did not consider himself "the top" of the OPM: Knudsen and Hillman would have wide latitude. "But believe me," he added, "if they make some kind of a decision which goes wrong and I say that it is contrary to the national interest, I will probably call them in and say, 'Here, here, what is this?' "[45]

Holding up a chart showing a web of interlocking missions nearly as complex as the manufacturing process itself, the president explained the different sub-offices of the OPM: one, headed by Edward Stettinius, would be responsible for raw materials; another would be headed by Donald Nelson, a former Sears Roebuck executive, in charge of defense purchasing for American and British forces; and another, composed of Knudsen, Hillman, Nelson, Stettinius, and others, would handle the all-important defense priorities. The new arrangement, sighed a relieved Henry Stimson, was less than he'd hoped for but "certainly an improvement." There were many ways, he wrote, "of skinning the cat."[46]

Some defense officials grumbled that labor should have been granted only an advisory role, and one journalist reported that a tense struggle had taken place behind the scenes. But Roosevelt and Stimson understood that the war would be won by workers in defense plants, and Stimson had a low opinion of the wealthy industrialists who, he thought, were "rather on the side of appeasement." Labor and the "common people," he remarked, "have been pretty strong on the moral issue." Workers would necessarily be "the *backbone* of defense," and that meant making labor an equal and respected partner with industry in order to prepare for and win the war.[47]

A reporter asked the president what would become of the National Advisory Defense Commission. "I am coming to that now," FDR said. The NDAC would continue to function as a subordinate body, its seven commissioners fulfilling their specialized tasks under the umbrella of the OPM. But, gutted of its major responsibilities, the NDAC merely lingered on into October 1941, when, according to the minutes of its last meeting, it was "suspended indefinitely."[48]

Just as Lend-Lease had come like a lightning stroke, divulged by the president at a press conference, so had the news of the new

Office of Production Management. Up to that point, mobilization had been unsteady at best, but now it was full speed ahead.

Americans were coming together as Roosevelt had challenged them to do. Big business was coming on board. Although FDR grumbled in March 1941 that "at least nine out of ten men being brought here by the Production people are not only Republicans but are mostly violent anti-Administration Republicans" and although he beseeched a friend to "dig out for me the names of twenty or thirty Democratic businessmen who have had successful experience," his veteran aides and officials were nevertheless finding common ground with the wealthy men who, indeed, had long regarded the Roosevelt administration as the arch-foe of American capitalism. After Pearl Harbor, of course, as OPM administrator Donald Nelson remarked, "the manufacturers, with sons, brothers, and employees in the armed services, gritted their teeth and hurried."[49]

The titans of industry had nothing to complain about. In 1940, about 170,000 companies accounted for 70 percent of the nation's manufacturing output; by 1943, just 100 companies held 70 percent of war and civilian contracts. Although Roosevelt had warned in 1936 that the dominance of the "economic royalists" had excluded "our many thousands of small business men and merchants who sought to make a worthy use of the American system of initiative and profit," the war mobilization set the stage for the comeback of the economic royalists and for the "unwarranted influence," in Eisenhower's words, of the "the military-industrial complex" of the postwar era. Greater democratization and more "far-reaching change in the economic order" could have taken place, remarked Bruce Catton, Nelson's close associate who served as the OPM's director of information, if the full energies of small businesses had been used and if labor had been allowed to "move up to partnership with ownership in the great war industries."[50]

In March 1941, Missouri's senator Harry Truman became chairman of a special Senate committee to act as a watchdog over the national defense program—from scrutinizing defense contracts and industry corruption to investigating government mismanagement and waste. Truman's mission had FDR's approval, though the president worried that probes into the administration's failures would be seized upon by enemies of the defense campaign. But the Truman Committee, as it became known, served as a welcome check on both industry and government; it reassured Americans that the defense buildup was not the riot of profiteering, corruption, and incompetence it had been in World War I. For example, looking into profligate government spending, Truman's investigation into the army camp construction program—"Anybody with horse sense could have picked out a site which would have cost half the present total," he said of one camp in Florida—led to an overhaul of all phases of the program.

As for industry, in addition to exposing companies that were selling defective material to the government, Truman also brought the hammer down on companies making excessive profits on defense contracts. The Ohio aircraft parts company Jack and Heintz, for example, won redemption by agreeing to cut executive salaries to near nothing, eliminate profit from production, and offer its workers attractive salaries and bonuses in the form of war bonds. Other large companies, such as General Electric and Eastman Kodak, recognizing that profiteering bred public resentment, voluntarily turned over a part of their profits to the government.[51]

Workers got even more scrutiny, from government, industry, and the press, all focused on labor disputes they labeled damaging to the defense effort.

Labor would play its part well, but workers, under stress because of the intense mobilization of industry, did not give up their right to strike. Between December 1940 and March 1941, more than three hundred strikes took place, some for higher wages; others, like the two-month strike that halted the testing of airplanes at Wright Air Field in Ohio, were jurisdictional disputes. If they did not cripple crucial defense programs, strikes did slow them down. So on March 19, 1941, President Roosevelt created the National Defense Mediation Board by executive order. Its mission was to settle labor disputes in defense industries, first by facilitating collective bargaining or, failing that, by mediating the dispute, and then, as a last resort, by proposing voluntary arbitration. The eleven-member board consisted of three "neutral" representatives from the public, four from industry, and four from labor, two each from the AFL and CIO. By May, the board was swamped with cases, including threatened strikes by hundreds of thousands of coal miners and West Coast shipyard workers. Labor disputes involving over six hundred thousand workers had come before the board in just its first two months; most were resolved successfully. By the end of 1941, the NDMB would settle over a thousand strikes and other disputes, and while conflict would persist throughout the war, the government's role in reducing the number and length of strikes was crucial to the building of the arsenal of democracy.[52]

Labor won significant concessions from industry, including the right to unionize in more companies. Holdout corporations like Bethlehem Steel, Westinghouse, International Harvester, Goodyear, and Ford Motor were unionized in 1941, a year in which total union membership grew by 1.5 million workers. Ford finally surrendered to the UAW that June, agreeing to pay a wage equal to the highest in the industry and abolishing its "service department" of thugs hired to beat up union organizers. "By going the whole way and giving the men everything they have asked for," commented one Ford official, "the company hopes it has eliminated every possible source of friction that can hamper or delay national defense production."[53]

Ultimately, labor-management cooperation worked remarkably well. Despite some strikes, which took place even though responsible union leaders had made a no-strike pledge to the president, and despite some cases of greedy management and outright fraud, the sheer might of American industry made the United States the greatest producer of armaments the world had ever known. In one wartime labor song, the Union Boys, including Pete Seeger and Burl Ives, sang, "It's that UAW-CIO makes that army roll and go." Together, labor and industry produced a vast flood of war materiel without compromising labor unions, workers' rights, or the free enterprise system.[54]

CHAPTER SEVEN

Have We the Vision?

O N JANUARY 10, 1941, Representative John McCormack of Massachusetts, the majority floor leader, and Senate Majority Leader Alben Barkley of Kentucky simultaneously introduced the Lend-Lease bill, blandly entitled "To Promote the Defense of the United States and for Other Purposes." Its colorless name contrasted with its revolutionary and patriotic number—deliberately assigned by McCormack: "House Resolution 1776." This, of course, was the tumultuous year when the thirteen colonies declared their independence from Great Britain because King George III had violated their long-established rights as Englishmen. Now the tables were turned, and a majority of Americans wanted to rescue and protect the mother country so that they themselves might continue to live governed by the ideals and institutions the British had bequeathed to them—the Enlightenment principles of freedom under the law, self-government, and the individual right of due process. In 1941 the number 1776 meant not a Declaration of Independence but a Declaration of *Interdependence*.[1]

That was not how the resourceful Congressman McCormack pitched Lend-Lease to his mostly Catholic constituents in South Boston. "Madam, do you realize that the Vatican is surrounded on all sides by totalitarianism?" he wrote to one resident.

"This is not a bill to save the English, this is a bill to save Catholicism."[2]

Eight days earlier, on January 2, Roosevelt had given the green light to Treasury Secretary Morgenthau to begin drafting the Lend-Lease bill. They had already heard from Arthur Purvis, the head of the British Purchasing Commission, that his country needed about $15 billion worth of war materiel. It was an immense sum—but the president scarcely blinked. For years his hands had been tied by laws and regulations that mandated neutrality, tied by public opinion, and tied also by himself. Now he wanted the authority to do what he believed needed to be done.[3]

Almost immediately, Morgenthau forwarded the president's instructions to the aides and advisors in the Treasury Department who would actually draft the legislation. When one treasury official suggested that the bill not be too sweeping, Morgenthau responded that it should be "as wide as the world, and then let somebody else tighten it up." By midnight, a first draft was written and circulating through the War, Navy, and State Departments, as well as to a few outsiders like Supreme Court justice Felix Frankfurter, whose advice that the legislation be even broader was incorporated into the revision. Roosevelt also wanted to involve the House in the drafting, and Speaker Rayburn assigned the Legislative Counsel of the House to work with the administration on the bill.[4]

On January 6 a new draft was submitted to the president, resulting in more changes. Three days later, after all the departments had weighed in, Roosevelt held a meeting at the White House that brought together leaders of the Senate and House. He read aloud sections of the bill and asked for comments and questions. Should there be an upper limit to the aid the United States would provide Britain? asked Luther Johnson of Texas, a member of the House Foreign Relations Committee. "Emphatically, no," FDR replied. He wanted as few limits as possible. As one of Morgenthau's aides put it, the administration would send Congress a "shoot the works" proposal.[5]

But Roosevelt's top priority was action. On the last day of the year, when Churchill had sent him the telegram outlining his anxieties about the Lend-Lease plan and the fierce urgency of British needs, the prime minister had warned that without a strong aid program, "Hitlerism cannot be extirpated from Europe, Africa, and Asia."[6]

On January 10, the day the legislation was introduced in Congress, Roosevelt held a press conference. "Mr. President, are you expecting—or hoping for—quick action on the British aid bill?" FDR explained that not only was speed "a great essential" but "the Government can't do a single thing until an appropriation goes through." Delays in authorization meant delays in appropriations; delays in appropriations meant delays in placing orders; and delays in placing orders meant delays in production. Back in September, Roosevelt had made the destroyers-for-bases deal by bypassing Congress. If he hadn't done so, as he wrote to King George VI that November, "the subject would still be in the tender care of the Committees of the Congress!" But Lend-Lease was a game-changer, and Congress's approval was indispensable. There could be no sleights of hand or obfuscations. "We don't want to fool the public," FDR said to Morgenthau. "We want to do this thing right out and out."[7]

Roosevelt would continue to discuss the bill at press conferences, but he did not lobby the public. He made no major radio address on its behalf, nor did he travel the country campaigning for it. Anxious to garner as many bipartisan votes as possible for the bill, he decided to stay above the fray and avoid "serious arm-twisting," as historian Warren Kimball put it. Behind the scenes, of course, he played a dominant role. He had overseen the bill's swift drafting and had set the strategy that he hoped would speed it through Congress. To make sure officials kept to the plan when they testified before congressional committees, he even vetted their opening statements.[8]

Only once did Roosevelt respond publicly to criticism of Lend-Lease. Senator Burton Wheeler, insisting again that Lend-Lease would propel the country into war, added the incendiary remark that the bill represented another "New Deal Triple A foreign policy—plow under every fourth American boy." That set the president off. At a January 14 press conference, he blasted Wheeler's ugly aspersion as "the most untruthful, as the most dastardly, unpatriotic thing that has ever been said." His voice rising in anger, he added, "Quote me on that. That really is the rottenest thing that has been said in public life in my generation."[9]

That day, Roosevelt received a wire from Harry Hopkins in London, who hoped for an update from the White House. "What is your best judgment as to when this Bill will pass?" Hopkins wrote, adding that the going in London "is pretty rough but all is well. I am seeing everything here from German bombs to some of your cousins."[10]

The House and Senate took up the Lend-Lease bill in mid-January. Both Sol Bloom of New York, chair of the House Foreign Affairs Committee, and Walter George of Georgia, chair of the Senate Foreign Relations Committee, wanted quick action, quick committee approval, and quick passage. Yet there were obstacles in their path. The House committee, with a membership of twenty-five, included isolationist and anti-administration Republicans led by its ranking member, Hamilton Fish. Among the sixteen members of George's Senate committee were strong advocates of the president's policies, Democrats like Tom Connally of Texas, Carter Glass of Virginia, and James Byrnes of South Carolina. But the committee also included some of the nation's most prominent isolationists: Republicans Hiram Johnson of California, Arthur Vandenberg of Michigan, and Gerald Nye of North Dakota, and Democrats Bennett Clark of Missouri and Guy Gillette of Iowa.

On January 15, under klieg lights in the spacious chamber of the House Ways and Means Committee, the members of the Foreign Affairs Committee heard their first witnesses—Secretary of State Cordell Hull and Treasury Secretary Henry Morgenthau. The room was so packed with onlookers that forty special police were brought in to supervise the crowd.[11]

Hull, the lead witness, made the broad case for the bill in an opening statement drafted in part by the president. He painted a picture of "an organized, ruthless and implacable movement of steadily expanding conquest." Against this fascist juggernaut, the United States had the right and the duty to actively assert the law "of self-preservation," and Lend-Lease was essential to that goal. A congressman asked, but what about neutrality? Neutrality, Hull answered, had done nothing for Hitler's victims and represented a "suicidal course" for the United States. "Now," he emphasized, "is the time for self-defense."[12]

The task for the second witness, Secretary Morgenthau, was to describe Britain's dire financial state. The president had been reluctant to authorize full disclosure, but Treasury officials insisted that Congress's first question would be "How much have they got?" Morgenthau had agreed with Purvis that Britain would sell $100 million of its assets in the United States as a gesture of good faith. But the bottom line, he told committee members, was that "when it comes to finding the dollars to pay for anything like what they need in the future, they just have not got it." Britain had completely opened its books to the Americans—"the first time in history," Morgenthau pointed out, "that one government has put at the disposal of another figures of this nature." He spoke in such detail about British finances, supported by even more detailed documents, that committee members were hard pressed to challenge them. Opponents took up blunter weapons. George Tinkham, a Republican from Massachusetts, called Lend-Lease a "blank check" and objected to Roosevelt's wide authority in the bill. "I don't have the same confidence in the President as you do," Tinkham told the treasury secretary. "And if you don't mind my saying so," Morgenthau shot back, "that's why you are in the minority."[13]

The next day it was Secretary of War Stimson's turn. The United States, he asserted, stood in "real and great danger of invasion" if the British Navy were destroyed. The emergency was far more acute than the one in 1917. In that crisis, he said, there was a "stable front line" in France, and Italy and Japan were allied with Britain and France against Germany. Now the situation was reversed: Italy and Japan were part of the German-dominated Axis; the arsenals of the conquered European countries had been taken over by the Axis; and Great Britain, which had had abundant munitions factories during the First World War, was now "compelled to enter our markets for a substantial quantity of weapons for her own use." The Lend-Lease legislation was "the best and simplest plan" to carry out a crucial national policy.[14]

Isolationists could hardly wait to pounce on Stimson, the rogue Republican who, complained the *Chicago Daily Tribune*, was "one of the most belligerent interventionists in the President's cabinet."

Stimson, in fact, had little patience for anti-interventionists and worried about the fate of the nation "if they represent any very large percentage of our population."[15]

When Hamilton Fish of New York said he doubted the United States was in danger of imminent invasion, Stimson rose dramatically to his feet and pointed his finger at the congressman. America, he said, was in "very great danger of invasion in the contingency the British navy is destroyed or surrendered." When Fish then made the preposterous claim that, under the broad powers of the bill, the president was free to give away the army and navy, Stimson called that notion "utterly fantastic." Finally, Fish demanded that the secretary of war disclose whether certain weapons had already been transferred to the British. Stimson stood up again and answered, in a voice clearly audible throughout the chamber, that he did not intend to make himself "the voluntary channel for conveying information to Mr. Hitler by making public statements on these matters." Later, in his diary, he fumed that Fish's questions were "puerile, silly and blinded by an intense hostility to the president."[16]

Stimson's brief was to advance one of the administration's most powerful arguments in favor of Lend-Lease: that by aiding Britain, as he told the committee, "we are *buying*—not lending. We are *buying* our own security while we prepare." The United States was also buying time—purchasing it, Stimson said, "from the only nation which can sell us that time." Far from bringing Americans closer to war, he maintained, the bill would keep the war away for as long as possible by giving Britain the survival tools it needed.[17]

The stark truth was that the United States was also buying the blood of British soldiers, who would be sacrificed in battle while the United States built its defenses. "If England is willing to furnish men to fly the planes, we should be willing to furnish the planes," remarked Oklahoma's Democratic senator Joshua Lee. "Suppose it does take our wealth. That is not as precious as the blood of our boys."[18]

Stimson was not opposed to shedding American blood; he considered it a sad necessity. "We cannot permanently be in a position of toolmakers for other nations which fight," he had written in his diary on the evening of FDR's Arsenal of Democracy fireside chat.

He was convinced that American men, aware of the difference between right and wrong, "will not be satisfied unless they are offering their own bodies to the flames and are willing to fight as well as make munitions." Fish, in fact, asked provocatively, "Is it not rather cowardly of us, if England is fighting our battle, not to go into the war?" The war secretary could only reply, "I am not going to pursue this line of argument. We are not concerned with it in this bill." Though he believed active involvement in the war was inevitable, he knew that with Lend-Lease the president had gone as far as he could. He left committee members with the disturbing thought that the United States might face a crisis within three months. Lend-Lease could not pass soon enough.[19]

"I resign this rather warm chair to you," Stimson said to the next witness, Frank Knox, after a day and a half of testimony. The secretary of the navy explained to the committee that because the British fleet had "always stood sentinel" in the Atlantic, the United States had been safe from attack from Europe. But now, with the United States still lacking a strong two-ocean navy, American security depended on the British Navy's ability to "prevent the establishment of any non-American aggressive military power in any part of the New World."[20]

Did the Axis, asked Fish, really have the naval might to attack the Western Hemisphere? Knox replied that the Axis nations, if they conquered all of Europe, would have seven times the strength of the United States. Returning to his pet idea, Fish then proposed an amendment to the bill that would prohibit the president from giving away the American Navy. His patience exhausted, Knox dryly said that he would accept such an amendment if Mr. Fish accepted one that prohibited the president "from walking down Pennsylvania Avenue standing on his head." Both amendments, he added, would be "equally pertinent." Asked what the United States should do if Britain were defeated, Knox replied, "I would put every able-bodied man in the country to building warships. I would enlist a huge standing army. I would build the biggest air force in the world."[21]

But it was essential that the British survive, at least until the United States could complete its preparations. Like Stimson, Knox emphasized that with Lend-Lease, the United States was buying time "to build ships and to train their crews. We need time to build up our outlying bases so that we can operate our fleets. . . . We need time to train our armies, to accumulate war stores, to gear our industry for defense. Only Great Britain and its fleet can give us that time. And they need our help to survive."[22]

The following day the committee heard from William Knudsen, the director general of the new Office of Production Management, whom the committee members handled more gently than his predecessors. With a slight Danish accent and a bashful smile, Knudsen explained that he was a production man, not a policy man, focused only on getting things done. Asked why the United States wasn't demanding collateral from the British for armaments received, Knudsen replied, "I'm not in the finance business." He urged the bill's speedy passage and pointed out that Britain could not benefit from its provisions until late in the year. Texas's Luther Johnson pitched a softball question, asking Knudsen why he had left his high-paying job at General Motors to accept a post in the OPM with no salary. Not wanting to "sound sentimental," Knudsen answered that the United States had been "pretty good" to him over the years. "I was in a position to work for nothing, and I felt that if I could do something for the country, I would like to do it. That's all." The audience and committee, including members on both sides, broke into applause. "Mr. Knudsen's face reddened," reported the New York Times, "and he appeared quite embarrassed."[23]

Now it was time to hear from the opposition's witnesses, the isolationists invited by Hamilton Fish to testify on "the President's dictator bill." No such "dictator bill" existed, objected Chairman Bloom. "Sure, it's a dictator bill," Fish shouted. "What else can you call it?"[24]

Fish's lead witness was Joseph P. Kennedy, FDR's former ambassador to Great Britain, a post for which Kennedy had turned out to be the wrong man in the wrong job at the wrong time. Appointed in 1938, he had developed a close relationship with Prime Minister Chamberlain while also gravitating toward the leading appeasers in Britain's high society, especially the Germanophile aristocrats in Lady Astor's so-called Cliveden set. Hitler's envoy to Britain, Herbert von Dirksen, effusively called Kennedy "Germany's best friend in London." In October 1938, just weeks after the debacle of the Munich conference, Kennedy spoke at a Trafalgar Day dinner in London and advocated British and American concessions to Hitler. The next day's *New York Times* headline read "Kennedy for Amity with Fascist Bloc."[25]

Kennedy "always has been an appeaser and always will be an appeaser," Roosevelt said disgustedly in October 1939, telling Henry Morgenthau that the ambassador was "just a pain in the neck to me." Yet the president was afraid to make a political enemy of Kennedy, who might lead a charge of Democratic isolationists against him in an election year. When the ambassador was in the United States for a preelection visit in the fall of 1940, FDR invited him to the White House and persuaded him to give a speech supporting his reelection. But a few days after the president's victory, Kennedy gave an injudicious interview to the *Boston Globe* in which he declared, "Democracy is finished in England. It may be here." Two short, indelible sentences and one prestigious career in ruins. The casual words could not be removed. "I never want to see that son of a bitch again as long as I live!" the president exploded. On December 1, Kennedy went to the White House to tender his resignation.[26]

Out of a job, Kennedy continued to peddle his isolationist views. A few days before his testimony to the House Foreign Affairs Committee, he gave a speech on nationwide radio. After denying at length that he was a defeatist or an appeaser, he scoffed at any danger to the United States from fascist aggression. "For the life of me," he said, "I cannot understand why the tale of a great military machine 3000 miles away should make us fear for our security." If the United States devoted its energy and resources to its own defense, "I have little doubt that we can be secure against any power or group of powers in the wide world." Perhaps anxious for his personal wealth, he warned that war would mean a tottering capitalist order: bankruptcy, an enormous national debt, and higher taxes. These would bring "ruin to our civilization and an end to our democratic form of life."[27]

On January 21, Fish introduced Kennedy to the House committee as the "one man who, above all others in America, has been striving to keep this country out of war." But Kennedy's tortured testimony disappointed his anti-interventionist friends. The former ambassador admitted that the situation in Britain was "very critical," that the Luftwaffe's night raids on cities and ports had intensified, and that England was struggling to wage war "against a force which seeks to destroy the rule of conscience and reason." Still, he maintained, helping the beleaguered British was not worth "exhausting our own resources so as to threaten our whole civilization." He supported all aid to Britain short of war, but in "less drastic ways" than the Lend-Lease bill "in its present form." While defending Roosevelt's competence and patriotism and even agreeing that the crisis required some concentration of power, he opposed the bill only because it granted too much authority to the president. Kennedy's testimony lasted five hours, after which Roosevelt commented that the former ambassador was "blowing hot and blowing cold at the same time."[28]

Charles Lindbergh, the charismatic aviator, was far less conflicted. Hours before the doors of the committee room opened at 10:00 a.m., a crowd of his admirers waited in line for seats in the visitors' galleries and the chance to see him in person.

Fourteen years earlier, Charles Lindbergh had been the fearless young man with the winsome smile who piloted the single-engine, single-seat *Spirit of St. Louis* in an unprecedented thirty-three-hour flight from New York to Paris—the first successful transatlantic flight. Lucky Lindy's solo journey had captured the world's imagination and brought Europe and the Americas symbolically closer, overcoming in one bound the great obstacle of the Atlantic Ocean. Now Lindbergh was the principal spokesman for the America First Committee, and for the notion that the United States was an impregnable fortress, safe behind its oceans. He had campaigned against Roosevelt in 1940, and in May had told a friend that the president's war aims were like Hitler's: to "impose his world order, in the guise of defending other peoples' freedom" even at the cost of the "ultimate destruction of millions of human beings." That same month, Roosevelt had confided to Morgenthau, "If I should die tomorrow, I want you to know this: I am absolutely convinced Lindbergh is a Nazi."[29]

To believers, Charles Lindbergh carried an aura of purity and righteousness. His fans, despite Chairman Bloom's admonitions, repeatedly broke into applause during his testimony; they also booed committee members who dared to ask critical questions. Jeers rang down from the galleries when William Courtney of Tennessee bluntly asked Lindbergh which side, Britain or Germany, he wanted to win. "I prefer to see neither side win," Lindbergh answered candidly. "There is not as much difference in philosophy as we have been led to believe," he said, dismissing Roosevelt's efforts to expose the fundamental chasm between fascism and democracy. How did he propose to resolve the violence in Europe? He preferred "a negotiated peace" since both sides were equally to blame for the war.[30]

Lindbergh was adamantly opposed to Lend-Lease. It would be a grave mistake, he insisted, for the United States to extend aid to Great Britain—for any reason, on any terms. First of all, no matter how much help it received from the United States, Britain could not possibly win the war. Since his first visit to Germany in 1936, Lindbergh had been intoxicated with the country's growing military strength, especially in aviation. Nazi officials had no trouble convincing him that Germany was far stronger than it actually was. He was America's leading defeatist.

Second, he was convinced that Britain's war with Nazi Germany was simply not an American affair. Lindbergh was blind to the contradiction between his unshakeable conviction that the United States could remain isolated from the rest of the world and his own experience in crossing the Atlantic. As Secretary Hull put it, "Oceans are barriers but they are also highways." Lindbergh, however, insisted that the country faced absolutely no danger of a foreign attack so long as it remained neutral and "so long as we keep a reasonable Army, Navy and Air force." As for "transoceanic bombing raids" launched from Europe, they were possible, he conceded, but he believed their effect would be "negligible." He had no doubt whatsoever, he assured the committee, "that we can endure in this hemisphere no matter what happens in the rest of the world." ("How did the Japs get close enough to attack us?" he would write in his diary on December 7, 1941.)[31]

Had he, asked an impatient Luther Johnson, "ever expressed any opposition to Hitler?" "Yes," Lindbergh responded, "but not publicly." In fact, he had often suggested publicly that Roosevelt posed more of a threat to the United States than Hitler. The real danger, he liked to say, "lies here at home in our own midst," not from "an invasion from abroad." The "trend" in the United States, he told the committee, "particularly as represented in this bill, has been away from democracy."[32]

It was left to Republican isolationist Karl Mundt of South Dakota to elicit the aviator's high motives, his self-sacrificing, inspirational patriotism. "Why," Mundt asked, "do you endanger your reputation by expressing these convictions? ... You're willing to risk rebuke if you can help avoid war for us?" "I'm ready to risk anything!" Lindbergh exclaimed. It was a bravura performance that thrilled his fans, including those in Berlin, where an official German spokesman rhapsodized that the aviator's candor was "courageous" and that it called for "hats off!"[33]

Yet even as he was applauded by Nazis, Lindbergh's intransigence alienated many Americans. He himself was starting to see the reality; after his testimony, he admitted in his diary that isolationists were "slowly losing ground." More and more Americans were rallying to President Roosevelt's leadership, persuaded by his view of the American role in the world crisis and of the actions the country needed to take, even at the risk of war. A headline in the *New York Times* in late January read "Few Voters Back Lindbergh Views." The *Times* reported that 79 percent of Americans and 93 percent of British opposed a negotiated peace between Germany and Britain because any pledge from Hitler was "worthless" and would at best be a pause in his march toward world domination.[34]

A panoply of other anti-interventionists followed Lindbergh to assail Lend-Lease before the committee. Norman Thomas, the perennial Socialist Party presidential candidate, said that to be drawn into the war would be the death of American democracy, especially if the president were granted authority that not even "an angel from heaven" should have. Hanford MacNider, a distinguished World War I veteran who had been Calvin Coolidge's assistant secretary of war and Hoover's ambassador to Canada, spoke for the America First Committee. Not only was he "unalterably opposed" to taking part in "the Old World's everlasting quarrels," but passage of the legislation would be "the beginning of the end of this republic." Robert Hutchins, the president of the University of

Chicago, judged that "we are morally and intellectually unprepared to execute the moral mission to which the President calls us."[35]

"The argument of the isolationists seems utter, arrant non-sense," wrote *Times* reporter Raymond Daniell when he returned from London in the middle of the Lend-Lease debates. The terrifying idea that the president's proposal might fail, thereby discrediting FDR's interventionist policy, led Daniell to imagine a path "for some demagogue, some American Quisling, to campaign and win on a platform of collaboration with Hitler's new order for the sake of trade, prosperity, and lower taxes."[36]

"I cannot say, as you can well understand, that this is for me a completely happy birthday," FDR admitted, with more than a touch of sadness in his voice, in a radio talk late in the evening of January 30, when he turned fifty-nine. "These are not happy days for any of us in the world." As had been his custom since 1934, he used his birthday to raise money for the March of Dimes, which funded research into a cure for polio. He told his listeners that although there was not much to celebrate in that dark winter, Americans were singularly fortunate to live "under a free people's philosophy" that led them to "believe in and insist on the right of the helpless and the weak and the crippled everywhere to play their part in life—and survive." It was because of that philosophy that "the lights of peace blaze in our great cities and glow in our towns and villages—that laughter and music still ring out from coast to coast—that we will return to safe beds tonight."[37]

Roosevelt was miserable with a bad cold and looked tired and drawn. But tens of thousands of other Americans, desperate for an excuse for laughter and play, responded to the call to "dance so that others might walk" by attending hundreds of March of Dimes fundraisers and birthday balls around the country. In Boston Garden, guests in glittering gowns, tuxedos, or formal military uniforms danced, watched military drills, listened to band concerts, and applauded vaudeville acts. In Warm Springs, patients enjoyed a birthday cake iced with silvered sugar in the shape of dimes. In Washington, five hotels were packed with partygoers, including famous Hollywood stars along with General Marshall, Admiral Stark, and their wives.[38]

Eleanor Roosevelt made the rounds of all five hotels, cutting the president's birthday cake at each celebration. But as she entered the ballroom of the Washington Hotel, words that Adolf Hitler had spoken earlier that day in the Berlin Sportspalast were accidentally piped into the public address system. The familiar jumble of threats and boasts echoed weirdly in a room crowded with Americans gathered for a celebration and charity event.[39]

That same day, January 30, Roosevelt's Lend-Lease proposal received two boosts, an auspicious one from the House Foreign Affairs Committee and an inadvertent one from Berlin. The House committee reported favorably on the bill by a vote of 17 to 8. Three days before, in an effort to win over committee members who were still wavering, especially those concerned about excessive presidential power, FDR had summoned a bipartisan congressional group to the White House to discuss amendments to the legislation. He agreed to some modest restraints on his power: that defense materiel could be sent to Allies only with the military's approval; that the president's authority under the new legislation was to end in 1943; that the bill did not "permit the authorization of convoying vessels by naval vessels of the United States"; and that the president must make reports to Congress at least every ninety days. When Roosevelt's team drafted the bill, they had anticipated the need for concessions—and also anticipated the praise the president would receive for his magnanimity in accepting them.[40]

Lend-Lease also received unintentional assistance from Berlin. Hitler's rambling speech that afternoon in the Sportspalast was full of the usual sulfuric anti-British and anti-Jewish invective, brutal threats, and smug wisecracks. And the crowd of Nazi followers obediently followed the script and cheered wildly as the Führer warned Americans against aiding Britain and promised that German U-boats would torpedo *every* ship "that comes before our torpedo tubes."[41]

"Hitler completely misunderstands American psychology," editorialized the *New York Times*, "if he imagines that this kind of talk will frighten us." The only effect his threats would have, the *Times* added, "would be to fire public opinion to dare greater risks in giving effective help to Britain."[42]

Floor debate in the House on Lend-Lease began on February 3. Passions ran highest among the anti-interventionists, who outdid themselves with warnings of the bill's calamitous consequences— the destruction of American democracy and the enslavement of free Americans in the name of national defense. There was also the familiar libel that the bill was designed by "Franklin Roosevelt Napoleon," as a Kansas congressman called him, to pull the United States into the war. The charge of treason was also hurled around the House chamber. Summing up opposition opinion, Republican Dewey Short of Missouri shouted that the bill "stinks."[43]

On February 8, after six days of floor debate, the House passed the amended Lend-Lease bill by a vote of 260 to 165. The tally ran along party lines, with Democrats providing 236 of the yes votes and Republicans 135 negatives. Speaker Sam Rayburn called the bill's passage by the House, just a month after it was introduced, "magnificent proof of the ability of our democracy not merely to debate fairly but to act timely."[44]

"It seems now to be certain," Prime Minister Churchill said in a radio address in response to the vote, "that the government and people of the United States intend to supply us with all that is necessary for victory. . . . We do not need the gallant armies which are forming throughout the American Union. . . . Give us the tools and we will finish the job." In fact he needed more than tools. He had diplomatically elided the truth that his ultimate goal was to get the American military directly involved in the war.[45]

Although the cards were now stacked against them, the anti-interventionists refused to give up. The nation's largest isolationist organization, the America First Committee, sounded the alarm about the "dictator bill."[46]

In mid-February, the AFC held a large rally at the Mecca Temple in midtown Manhattan, with an overflow crowd of thirty-five hundred people. The speakers included Senators Burton Wheeler and Gerald Nye, Norman Thomas, the fascist demagogue Joe McWilliams, and a host of other isolationists, pacifists, defeatists, and pro-fascists. Denouncing aid to Britain, Wheeler accused Roosevelt of seeking the power to wage war unilaterally, and with the anti-Semitic undertones that frequently colored isolationist oratory, he condemned America's "financial oligarchy" for driving the nation into war. "I am positive," he declared, "that the great mass of *real* Americans, whether they live in New York City or Butte, Montana, are opposed to our intervention in the war unless we are attacked." On the eve of George Washington's birthday, he asked whether Americans intended to follow the wisdom of the founding fathers who had freed the nation from its English captivity, or whether they would yield submissively to British propaganda. Describing what war would look like, he painted a picture of mothers sobbing, men dying, fatherless children, and crowded military hospitals.⁴⁷

The next speaker was Senator Nye, whom Roosevelt had called "unscrupulous," only to be topped by columnist Joseph Alsop, who described him as having "no principles whatsoever." Nye didn't hesitate to name the warmongers, foremost among them "the Roosevelts and the Knoxes and the Stimsons and the Morgenthaus." To give the president the power he asked for in the Lend-Lease bill, Nye said, would be "insanity, madness, suicide." Not only would it "bring submarine warfare to our very shores," it would end in death and heartbreak for millions of Americans and leave the country economically, socially, and politically a "shambles."⁴⁸

The zealous audience at the Mecca Temple booed every mention of Roosevelt and Churchill but remained silent on hearing the names Hitler and Mussolini. When John Flynn, the acting chair of the rally, took up a collection for the AFC and received thousands of dollars from the audience, someone stood up and shouted, "Who's giving the money, Hitler or Mussolini?" "Throw him out!" people yelled. In the lobby and on the street, hawkers sold America First buttons and copies of *The American Pacifist.*⁴⁹

Roosevelt's Lend-Lease proposal prompted countless other grassroots isolationist groups to form; antiwar "Mothers" groups sprouted around the country and were among the most visible and persistent protesters in the capital. In February, after the bill passed the House, the "Mothers' Crusade to Defeat Bill 1776" descended on Washington. Hundreds of mostly upper-middle-class and college-educated women from Chicago and New York paraded down Pennsylvania Avenue, carrying American flags, coffins, and signs that read "Kill Bill 1776, Not Our Boys," and chanting, "Our boys' bodies shall not rot in foreign graves, Down with King Franklin's

:d by Elizabeth Dilling, the crusade's founder, and financed
; Thomsen, the German chargé d'affaires in Washington,
nen stalked the halls of the Capitol, besieging intervention-
....bers of Congress. After much mayhem, Dilling was ar-
rested for disorderly conduct. Later, she would be indicted for
sedition and conspiracy.[50]

While the crusading mothers picketed the White House and
confronted members of Congress, another well-known American
mother spoke in favor of all possible aid to Britain. In a talk at
Hunter College in New York, Eleanor Roosevelt told the audience
that freedom was worth dying for. "I have four boys," she said, "and
I don't want to see them go to war any more than any other
mother would. Two of them happen to be in the Navy, which
would be the first in the war. But perhaps there are some things
you would rather die to prevent than see happen."[51]

In the last week of January, Senator Walter George of Georgia,
chairman of the Senate Foreign Relations Committee, opened
hearings on the Lend-Lease bill in the Senate's huge caucus chamber. The lead advocates, Hull, Morgenthau, Stimson, and Knox,
hewed closely to their previous testimony. Knox, however, added
an impassioned statement. The question, he said, was "would we
rather see Europe dominated by a democratic system or would we
rather see Europe dominated by a Hitler system? . . . If the Hitler
system is victorious, can any of us imagine that we can return
freely to the ways of the peace which we have known in the past?"
Asked by Gerald Nye to what lengths the administration would go
to save Britain, Knox replied that "if vital interests of the United
States are at stake, we have to fight. . . . And if the time comes
when we will not do that, we will cease to have a country."[52]

Another prominent defender was New York's mayor Fiorello
La Guardia, who acknowledged "selfish" reasons for supporting
the bill: it was in the interest not only of America but of New York
City in particular. "It so happens," he said, "that I am the chief executive of a town on the Atlantic coast and I want to be realistic
and take absolutely no chances."[53]

Once again, Charles Lindbergh testified for the opposition.
Internationalist senators Barkley, Connally, and Claude Pepper

prodded him to repeat his views in the starkest terms. Their aim, in the words of historian Warren Kimball, was to "isolate Lindbergh from the majority of the general public" and cut him off from the more moderate isolationists who agreed that some aid to Britain was in the American interest. "Gentlemen," Lindbergh announced to the committee, "I am opposed to this bill because I believe it endorses a policy that will lead to failure in war and to conditions in our own country as bad or worse than those we now desire to overthrow in Nazi Germany." But couldn't Britain beat Germany? one senator asked. No, replied the aviator: the combined productive capacities of the United States and Great Britain could not equal the air strength of Germany, much less surpass it. The danger to America, he added, did not lie in an invasion from abroad but "here at home in our own midst, and . . . it is exemplified by the terms of this bill." Moreover, there was no reason to believe that Hitler had designs on the Western Hemisphere. "They have more respect for the difficulty of invading this hemisphere than we ourselves seem to have," he observed. Senator Connally dryly congratulated him on his courage in "having such opinions and daring to express them."[54]

The isolationist faction in the Senate also invited testimony from AFC chairman Robert Wood, publisher Robert McCormick, historian Charles Beard, and others. Alf Landon, the former Kansas governor who had run against FDR in the 1936 election, testified against the bill, but began by repudiating noninterventionism; it was impossible for the United States, he said, to cut itself off from the affairs of the world. Still, when asked by Republican and isolationist senator Hiram Johnson of California if he could conceive of any danger to American democracy greater than the Lend-Lease bill, Landon replied, "No sir." His own modest proposal was that Congress simply appropriate a gift of several billion dollars for Britain instead of promising unlimited aid.[55]

Also testifying was the editor of the pacifist periodical *Christian Century*, Charles Clayton Morrison, who accused FDR of spinning "the weirdest fantasies" of an imminent invasion and of "deliberately" brainwashing Americans with the myth of British-American solidarity. "The state of mind of the American people," Morrison suggested, "is that of a vast psychopathic hospital." Then came a

Yale University senior, Kingman Brewster. Called upon by isolationists to represent the youth of America, Brewster, a future president of Yale and ambassador to the Court of St. James's under Jimmy Carter, expressed respect for the "courage and straightforwardness of Colonel Lindbergh" and then followed his hero's lead by attacking the warmonger in the White House.[56]

But the star of the Senate hearings was not La Guardia or Lindbergh or Landon—it was Wendell Willkie, FDR's rival for the White House in the 1940 election and still titular head of the Republican Party. Just days after that election, Willkie had told newspaper columnist Mark Sullivan that if the Republican Party let itself be recaptured by the "old-guard reactionaries" with their isolationist notions, the result would be "tragic." On January 12, he issued a statement to the press urging passage of Lend-Lease. Hammering the "appeasers, isolationists, and lip-service friends of Britain," he urged his fellow Republicans to put patriotism above partisanship and support the legislation. Otherwise, he warned, the GOP "will never again gain control of the American government."[57]

On February 11, the Senate caucus room was packed with more than a thousand people, eager to witness the dramatic spectacle of a defeated presidential candidate coming to the assistance of his one-time opponent. Willkie had just returned from England, where he had served as FDR's emissary, and was tired from his journey. But as photographers scrambled around looking for good angles, he appeared relaxed, lounging in his seat and puffing on a cigarette. He informed committee members that "the people of Britain are united almost beyond belief." They "are a free people," he said. "Millions of them will die before they give up that island. When the going gets tough they'll force that bunch of robbers to give up." Lend-Lease, he acknowledged, gave the president new powers. "Now I'm as much opposed as any man in America to undue concentration of power in the chief executive. And may I say," he added disarmingly, "that I did my best to remove that power from the present executive." Nevertheless, he hoped that the bill would be adopted with a "non-partisan and almost a unanimous vote."[58]

Isolationists in both parties grilled Willkie, and he answered their questions with wit, candor, and good humor. When asked about his biting criticism of FDR during the campaign, he breezily dismissed those remarks as "campaign oratory," adding that FDR "is my President now." When Democrat Robert Reynolds of North Carolina voiced doubt that the United States had any reason to intervene in the war, Willkie replied crisply: "Two madmen are at large and we cannot say where they will strike. If Britain collapsed tomorrow, we'd be in the war one month later."[59]

Republican anti-interventionists on the committee felt betrayed. For over an hour, Missouri's Bennett Clark pelted Willkie with hostile questions, reproaching him for acting as "the champion" of Roosevelt's foreign policy. When Clark slipped and addressed him as "Mr. President," the crowd in the galleries burst into applause. "You merely speak of what should have been," Willkie said with an impish smile.[60]

Willkie's dynamic testimony accelerated the trend among the press and the public to support the Lend-Lease bill. By now, Roosevelt was confident it would pass. His military aide Pa Watson assured him that of the twenty-eight Republicans in the Senate, ten could be counted on to vote for the bill; and of the sixty-six Democrats, no more than a dozen might vote against it. "This is a much better situation than there has been on any recent controversial bill in the Senate," South Carolina's Democratic senator Jimmy Byrnes told Watson.[61]

The real question was how quickly it would be approved by the Senate, where the arts and techniques of obstruction and delay were far more advanced than in the House. Hans Thomsen, the German chargé d'affaires, hoped for a dragged-out fight. He didn't doubt that Lend-Lease would ultimately pass, but as he wrote to his handlers in Berlin, isolationist propaganda could "contribute to lengthening the congressional debate, greatly strengthening the opposition to the law and . . . thereby demonstrate before the world that the interventionist policy is disapproved by certain portions of the people."[62]

At the end of Willkie's day in the Senate committee room, Roosevelt invited him to dinner in his White House study; it was an "old cronies dinner," recalled FDR's secretary, Grace Tully. "From the sounds of laughter in the Study where dinner was served, it was clear to me that the two men enjoyed being together."[63]

The next day, Willkie spoke at a Lincoln Day dinner in New York, a black-tie Republican affair at the Waldorf-Astoria. He implored his party to lead the fight to aid Britain and not commit political suicide by refusing to recognize the obvious threat from the gangsters of the Axis powers. "Have you got it in you?" he asked the crowd. "Have we the vision?" Willkie's rival for the 1940 GOP nomination, New York district attorney and gangbuster Thomas Dewey, agreed with him and endorsed Lend-Lease at another Lincoln Day dinner in Washington. "Our party stands almost unanimously for all-out aid to the heroic people of Great Britain," Dewey exclaimed. Although Ohio's Robert Taft stated that same evening that Willkie "does not and cannot speak for the Republican Party," in fact a Gallup poll showed that Willkie's support had helped persuade a plurality of Republicans to support Lend-Lease.[64]

Right after Willkie's testimony, Senator Wheeler, in an odd but inventive move, decided to launch an attack not against the Roosevelt administration or against Willkie, but against Hollywood. The studio heads, he charged in a radio address, were conspiring to push the country into war. He sought to put Americans on notice that "the war mongers and interventionists control most of our avenues of publicity, including the motion picture industry." The American film industry, with its anti-Nazi movies and newsreels, was "carrying on a violent propaganda campaign" in order to spur the American people to clamor for war. Threatening legislative action to censor Hollywood movies, he demanded that the film industry remain "impartial" between fascism and democracy and give equal consideration and coverage to "both sides."[65]

One example of the kind of film Wheeler wanted to muzzle had opened in theaters that past June. Director Frank Borzage's *The Mortal Storm* dramatized the brutality of the Third Reich with the story of the doomed effort of a young couple, played by Jimmy Stewart and Margaret Sullavan, to flee from Nazi Germany. In his review, *New York Times* movie critic Bosley Crowther noted that the film "falls definitely into the category of blistering anti-Nazi propaganda" and made for "grim and depressing" entertainment. But such movies were precisely what Crowther wanted Hollywood to make. Incensed by Wheeler's threat to gag the film industry, he wrote, "Freedom of the screen is as basic to our democratic system as freedom of the press." He demanded even more civic courage from the studios, more substantive reverence for Western values of democracy and freedom—and more films that put Nazi brutality on screen.[66]

On February 27, on a radio hookup from the White House, President Roosevelt paid tribute to the movie industry at the annual awards dinner of the Academy of Motion Picture Arts in Hollywood. In his remarks, he congratulated the motion-picture industry for reflecting and protecting, at home and abroad, the values of the Western humanist tradition. Hollywood's fine and intrepid films, he said, brought to the rest of the world "the aims and aspirations and ideals of free people and of freedom. That is the real reason that some governments do not want our American films exhibited in their countries."[67]

That same month, production got under way on another anti-Nazi movie—this one set during the First World War. Starring Gary Cooper and directed by Howard Hawks, *Sergeant York* would tell the story of a real-life Tennessee mountaineer with deep religious beliefs against killing who goes to war and discovers that sometimes violence is the only way to defend democracy, freedom, and the security of mankind.

In early January, the fifty-three-year-old Alvin York had listened to FDR's Four Freedoms speech on the radio. It was "one of the greatest speeches I've ever heard," he said. "I like especially his promise to the democracies that America will give them the arms they need. That's something we've got to do."[68]

CHAPTER EIGHT

Joint Talks

O N JANUARY 9, 1941, Prime Minister Churchill and the members of his Cabinet gathered in London for a farewell luncheon. The aloof, aristocratic, strikingly tall fifty-nine-year old Lord Halifax was about to leave Britain to take up his new post as ambassador to the United States. It was, Churchill said, a mission "as momentous as any that the monarchy has entrusted to an Englishman in the lifetime of the oldest of us here." Optimistic about the final outcome, he added, "We do not doubt the achievement of our purpose is within the power of the English-speaking peoples."[1]

Four days later, Churchill and Harry Hopkins, FDR's special envoy to Britain that winter, traveled to the Orkney Islands, at Scotland's northern tip, to bid a safe voyage to Halifax and his wife. They were sailing on a new British battleship, the *King George V,* accompanied by American and British officers, with an escort of destroyers.

Halifax had not asked for this mission, nor had he been Churchill's first choice. After Lord Lothian's death in mid-December, the prime minister wanted to appoint David Lloyd George, the World War I prime minister. He had even gotten President Roosevelt's approval, though American officials were privately dismayed that the energetic, effective Lothian would be replaced by a superannuated politician who had guided Britain through a devastatingly pyrrhic victory in 1918 and had until recently been an outspoken appeaser. Rumors of the White House's disappointment reached Churchill, and fortunately, Lloyd George withdrew, citing health reasons.[2]

Then Churchill turned to Edward Wood, Viscount Halifax. Halifax had also been a prominent appeaser in the 1930s, and a highly influential one after he became foreign secretary in 1938. But he had backed Churchill to succeed Neville Chamberlain in May 1940, and Churchill retained him as foreign secretary. Still, the prime minister never fully trusted him after Halifax pushed for a negotiated peace with Hitler shortly after Churchill took charge, when British forces were trapped at Dunkirk. Had Churchill not managed, narrowly, to turn the Cabinet away from Halifax's plan, he might have had to resign as prime minister.[3]

Now, however, the prime minister expressed complete confidence in his new ambassador. "I know that courage and fidelity are the essence of his being," Churchill said of Halifax at the sendoff luncheon. "He has vowed himself to prosecute this war against the Nazi tyranny at whatever cost until its last vestiges are destroyed." A few weeks earlier, Hopkins had met Halifax in London. "I liked him," he wrote. Though Halifax was too conservative for his taste, Hopkins felt that all that mattered was to "get on with our business of licking Hitler." For his part, Halifax was reluctant to move to a country he considered less cultivated than England, but as he wrote to Churchill the day after Christmas 1940, "In war one can but do what one is told!"[4]

At midafternoon on January 24, 1941, after a harrowing Atlantic crossing amid blizzards and prowling Nazi submarines, the *King George V* dropped anchor five miles from an Annapolis shore shrouded in fog and rain. A launch arrived to transport Lord and Lady Halifax from their ship to the *Potomac*, the presidential yacht where Franklin Roosevelt was waiting to receive them. This unprecedented break with protocol demonstrated the heightened significance of the Anglo-American alliance; the president of the United States had driven down from Washington and sailed out into foul weather to welcome Britain's new ambassador. After the formalities were completed—FDR assured Halifax "of our firm determination to continue on an ever-increasing scale our assistance to Great Britain"—ambassador and president had high tea and discussed the world situation.[5]

Speaking to reporters afterward on the presidential yacht, Halifax expressed gratitude to Roosevelt for the great honor of sailing out to meet him, and then he delivered Britain's plea: "The more quickly your generous help can be made effective, the sooner shall we be able to break this Nazi power that is trying to enslave Europe and the world." That evening, FDR accompanied his guests back to Washington and wished them a good night at the British embassy. It was, wrote the Associated Press, "one of the most dramatic scenes of international friendship in American history."[6]

Scarcely less dramatic were the remarkable scenes of Winston Churchill and Harry Hopkins barnstorming Scotland and England together on their return from the Orkney Islands. Everywhere they stopped, Churchill proudly introduced the ailing and unkempt Hopkins as "the personal representative of the President of the United States." At a formal dinner in Glasgow, Hopkins gave a brief talk that concluded with a quotation from the book of Ruth: "Whither thou goest, I will go . . ." He paused, then continued: "even to the end." Churchill wept, and the words soon spread all over Britain, boosting the morale of the battered people. Churchill's minister of aircraft production, Lord Beaverbrook, told Robert Sherwood that Hopkins's empathy for the British and his confidence in victory were "more tangible aid for Britain than all the destroyers and rifles and ammunition that had been sent previously."[7]

An official visit to Britain had been Hopkins's idea. He had been talking with the president late in 1940 about the many outstanding issues between the United States and Britain when FDR said, "You know—a lot of this could be settled if Churchill and I could just sit down together for a while." Hopkins replied, "What's stopping you?" Roosevelt reminded him that after Kennedy's resignation, there was no ambassador in London to arrange a meeting and no replacement yet for Lothian in Washington. "How about me going over, Mr. President?" FDR immediately shot the idea down; he couldn't spare Hopkins at one of the most critical moments of his presidency. But at a press conference on January 3, the president announced suddenly that Hopkins would go to London as his representative to maintain "personal relations between me and the British government." If Roosevelt couldn't meet face-to-face with Churchill, then his personal emissary would serve as the next best thing. This was a surprise to Hopkins, but three days later he was aboard a Pan-Am Clipper flight from New York to Lisbon and then on to London.[8]

When Churchill first heard of Hopkins's mission, he was puzzled. "Who?" he asked. But after he was briefed on his visitor's close relationship to Roosevelt, he arranged for special treatment, hosting FDR's friend and aide at 10 Downing Street and at Ditchley Park, making sure that he had access to ministers in the War Cabinet and military chiefs, and escorting him around the country. In his war memoir, the prime minister wrote that as soon as he met Hopkins, he realized that "here was an envoy from the President of supreme importance to our life." He was especially struck by Hopkins's "constrained passion" when the envoy assured him that "the President is determined that we shall win the war together" and that FDR would "carry you through, no matter what happens to him—there is nothing that he will not do so far as he has human power."[9]

Hopkins was also won over. He arrived bearing FDR's mistrust of Churchill and his own resentment at any suggestion that the prime minister could possibly be a better leader than his own boss. But twelve evenings with Churchill in the first two weeks after he arrived left him profoundly impressed. He assured the president that the prime minister had only positive feelings toward America and that he was leading Great Britain "magnificently in every respect." After meeting with British civilian and military officials at the highest levels, Hopkins concluded that "Churchill is the government in every sense of the word. ... He is the one and only person over here with whom you need to have a full meeting of minds."[10]

Hopkins's stay in England, originally scheduled for two weeks, was extended to nearly six, and by then this personal diplomacy had opened conduits of communication and information sharing between British and American officials, and especially between the prime minister and Roosevelt. Hopkins was, Churchill later wrote, "the most faithful and perfect channel of communication between the President and me."[11]

The press reported that Ambassador Halifax was accompanied on board the *King George V* by American officers Admiral Robert Ghormley and General Raymond Lee, who had been special observers in London acting as liaisons to British military officials. But the newspapers did not report that arriving along with them on January 24 were representatives of the British Chiefs of Staff. Disguised in civilian clothes, they presented themselves as "technical advisers" to the British Purchasing Commission. Their real assignment, however, was to participate in confidential discussions, scheduled to begin in less than a week, with their American counterparts to create a joint strategy for war.[12]

The two nations had first held such talks in January 1938, when naval planners met for what was little more than an exchange of information, with the United States insisting that the discussion was hypothetical and noncommittal. Even so, a furor erupted in Congress when news of the meeting leaked. In June 1939, a time of high tension in Europe when it was feared that war might break out at any moment, there was another round of joint staff talks. This time they were more substantive, dominated by the needs of the British, who were realizing how unready they were to fight Germany on land or sea. Once again, Roosevelt insisted that the talks involve no binding commitments, but the United States did agree that in the event of a European war, it would station its main fleet in Hawaii as a deterrent to Japan and would provide limited naval help in the western Atlantic.[13]

In the early fall of 1940, with the world situation radically changed, exploratory Anglo-American talks were held in London, headed on the American side by Admiral Ghormley. For the Americans, the talks were mainly an opportunity to gather information about Britain's prospects for survival and about Germany's strength and intentions. But in late November, Britain's worsening situation made another and more serious round of staff talks imperative.

The goal of Admiral Stark's Plan Dog was the defense of Britain and the defeat of Germany. But how would the Americans and British coordinate their military and naval actions? Stark saw his memorandum as the policy basis for joint Anglo-American strategic planning, and it was his proposal for secret British and American staff talks that mobilized American officials. "If we didn't have some talks with the British," General Marshall said later, "we would start with no basis at all if war developed later on, and at the time this conference was first established we needed to have some at least vague idea of what we could expect from the British—what sort of help they would want from us."[14]

At a White House Cabinet meeting on November 29, Navy Secretary Knox asked the president to invite the Churchill government to send over "some of its outstanding naval men" to work out strategic war plans with American experts. He and Stark were both worried, the admiral wrote that same day to General Marshall, that the British might not have "any long-range plan for themselves" or "realistic ideas" as to precisely what help they needed from the United States. Roosevelt had no objections to joint talks, and hours later Lord Lothian flashed the news to London: the talks would start in late January.[15]

Both Marshall and Stark had serious doubts about the British military chiefs' skills. In his Plan Dog memo, Stark had proposed the joint discussions in part because he distrusted the competence of British military leaders. Scoffing at their often amateurish "guess work," he feared that unless there was rigorous and accountable coordination between the senior staffs of both countries, the American military effort would be sabotaged by British ineptitude. The task for the American representatives at the talks, as Stark viewed it, was to focus on the interests of the United States and not on those of the British Empire. Any American intervention in the war, he counseled, should be based on a strategy that "will immediately promote *our own national interest.*" American officers must "insist upon *full equality* in the political and military direction of the war" and not entrust U.S. security to British military leaders. Echoing Stark's advice, two members of the Joint Planning Committee, Admiral Richmond Kelly Turner and Colonel Joseph McNarney, warned in their own memorandum that Washington "cannot afford, nor do we need to entrust, our national future to British direction. . . . Never absent from British minds are their post-war interests, commercial and military. We should likewise safeguard our own eventual interests."[16]

Roosevelt had demanded that the talks be absolutely secret, a stipulation that Lothian echoed in his message to Churchill, underscoring that "no knowledge of this should be allowed to obtain any kind of publicity." To head off any suspicions, the British officers would wear suits and ties while going to and from the meetings. From the president's point of view, secrecy was more important than ever. As the administration embarked on controversial new initiatives to align the United States more closely with the British, Roosevelt wanted no public discussion about collaborative war plans and strategy. If the Germans and Japanese had learned of the talks, "no great damage would have been done," commented Robert Sherwood, but if Congress had found out, "American preparation for war might well have been nigh wrecked and ruined."[17]

FDR also emphasized that any plans or decisions reached at the conference would not be binding on him, though that did not imply that the talks would be meaningless. On the contrary, General Marshall later wrote that one of the talks' successes was that American military leaders learned "what we needed to know without in any way involving [the president and the government] in any commitments of any kind." When the British-American discussions were over, in March 1941, Roosevelt's decision to express neither approval nor disapproval of the results left Marshall free to conclude, as he had with Plan Dog, that the army had FDR's tacit acquiescence in making the arrangements agreed on in the talks, and that for all practical purposes, decisions about the implementation of the overall strategy would be left to the military.[18]

On January 16, Roosevelt met with Hull, Stimson, Knox, Marshall, and Stark. "It was a very grave situation that the President put before us," Stimson wrote in his diary later that day. There was a one in five chance, FDR said, that Germany would invade Britain immediately, in which case Britain might survive for six months at best. With the joint staff talks set to begin in less than two weeks, the president emphasized the importance of keeping the British supplied with all they needed, even in the event of an Axis attack on the United States. The United States, he said, would simply have to be "ready to act with what we had available." Painfully aware of the unpredictable nature of the world crisis, he had remarked to Knox in late 1940, "This is a period of flux. I want no authorization for what may happen beyond July 1, 1941. All of us may be dead when that time comes!" That openness to change reflected FDR's leadership style. As the political historian James MacGregor Burns commented, Roosevelt liked to "keep open alternative lines of action, to shift from one line to another as conditions demanded."[19]

At the January 16 meeting, the president concluded with a general directive, transcribed by General Marshall. For the first time, he tacitly indicated his approval of Plan Dog: the Europe-first strategy that he wanted his staff to adopt at the joint talks would be based on Stark's memo. "That we would stand on the defensive in the Pacific with the fleet based on Hawaii ... that there would be no naval reinforcement of the Philippines; ... that the Navy should be prepared to convoy shipping in the Atlantic to England ... that the Army should not be committed to any aggressive action until it was fully prepared to undertake it; that our military course must be very conservative until our strength had developed; ... that we should make every effort to go on the basis of continuing the supply of materiel to Great Britain." The U.S. representatives at the Anglo-American talks had their marching orders.[20]

On January 29, five days after the arrival of the *King George V,* those secret talks got under way at the Navy Department. They would become known as the American-British-Canadian conversations—or ABC. Chairing the American delegation was General Stanley Embick, head of the army team, who had served on the Allied War Council in World War I. Leading the Navy team was Admiral Robert Ghormley, who had been working with the British since August. Also representing the Navy was Admiral Richmond Kelly Turner.

Embick proved a hard-nosed chairman. During the conference, one army officer remarked that he was "worth his weight in gold to the United States, for he thinks and acts American in his dealings with the British." In the 1930s, believing that American entry into World War I had been a mistake and stressing that "our vital interests lie in the continental United States," Embick advocated policies that, he wrote, were geared "to the maintenance of peace and the avoidance of any entanglements which would lead us into war." Admiral Turner—known to colleagues as "Terrible Turner"—was no less vigilant in defending the American position. Admiral Ghormley, on the other hand, was the group's conciliator, urging a genuine two-way discussion; he trusted that the British would engage, as he put it, with a "spirit of full cooperation and willingness to recognize [the] special interests of the United States."[21]

Among the British representatives were the four who had crossed the Atlantic incognito with Halifax: Rear Admiral Victor Hilary Danckwerts, former head of planning at the Admiralty; Rear Admiral R. M. Bellairs, considered one of the most brilliant men in the Royal Navy; Major General Edwin L. Morris, former planning director in the War Department; and Lieutenant Colonel A. T. Cornwall-Jones, War Cabinet Office secretary. In Washington, they were joined by Air Commodore J. C. Slessor of the British Purchasing Commission. The British team, more than the Americans, acted as a unit. As historian James Leutze pointed out, they worked as equals, each free to give his opinion regardless of rank, but when they entered the conference room, they presented a united front.[22]

The American opening statement, approved by FDR, was a spare, aggressive document; it explained the purpose of the talks while also setting the agenda and implicitly dictating the outcome. "The American people as a whole desire now to remain out of war, and to provide only material and economic aid to Great Britain," it asserted. But "should the United States be *compelled* to resort to war"—FDR had changed the wording from the more discretionary "*decide* to resort to war"—the Americans were committed to material assistance to Britain (though the United States would retain war materiel for its own future security), to the defeat of Germany ("most effectively attained" by America "exerting its principal military effort in the Atlantic"), and to the containment of Japan. If Japan should also enter the war, U.S. operations in the Pacific "would be conducted in such a manner as to facilitate the exertion of its principal military effort in the Atlantic or navally in the Mediterranean." All roads led to an Atlantic-first strategy: Plan Dog in a nutshell.[23]

Roosevelt recognized, however, that given the breadth of its empire, Britain's own defense plan had to be global. Acknowledging that Britain's defense of its home islands depended upon the various assets of its colonial system, FDR explained in late December 1940 that the British people existed in safety "not only because they have prepared strong local defenses but also because, as the heart and the nerve center of the British Empire, they have been able to draw upon vast resources for their sustenance and to bring into operation against their enemies economic, military and naval pressures on a world-wide scale." Roosevelt was willing to trim his anti-colonialist beliefs and work with a prime minister deeply committed to the perpetuation of the empire.[24]

But at the staff talks, the British representatives wanted more than this understanding. They were convinced that the defense of their vital interests in the Far East—from India and Burma to Australia and New Zealand—hinged on their naval base in Singapore. The problem was that any ships Britain sent to the Far East to check the Japanese would weaken its defenses in Europe. The only answer was an American fleet in the Pacific.

Under Plan Dog, part of the Pacific fleet at Pearl Harbor was to be redirected to the Atlantic in case of American involvement in warfare, but the British asked the Americans to agree to send a fleet to Singapore, whose loss, Admiral Bellairs wrote in a paper presented to the Americans, would be a "disaster of the first magnitude second only to the loss of the British Isles." Singapore's safety, he concluded, "must be assured." British obstinacy on this point only confirmed some Americans' view that the British wanted to drag the United States into the dirty work of salvaging their empire.[25]

The U.S. representatives met on February 13 to review Bellairs's strongly worded case for American defense of Singapore. They were angry, since Stark and Turner had warned the British in December that their views on Singapore were "quite unacceptable as the basis for staff discussions" and that British intransigence on this subject would doom the conference to failure. As one of the

American team members wrote to General Marshall, any concession to British demands on Singapore would be "a strategic error of incalculable magnitude."[26]

Terrible Turner was assigned the task of drafting the reply to Bellairs. The United States would not abandon its Atlantic-first strategy, he wrote, or overextend its forces in the Pacific. He acknowledged Singapore's strategic importance for Britain; holding on to it was "very desirable," but not if it required a diversion of American forces from the Atlantic that "might jeopardize the success of the main effort." The conclusion: it was Britain's responsibility to defend Singapore—and the British Empire—as best it could.[27]

The clash over Singapore became even more contentious when, in mid-February, British representatives at the talks informed Lord Halifax of the stalemate, and Halifax brought up the matter with Secretary Hull. For the Americans, this was an improper attempt to turn a military question into a political one, and the talks were temporarily suspended.

Enter Prime Minister Churchill. When he received a detailed account of the British position on Singapore, he exploded in rage. It was not the first time he had come into conflict with the British Chiefs of Staff. Even though the prime minister had recently created for himself the new post of minister of defence, putting him completely in charge of the prosecution of the war, he did not have the same authority over his Chiefs of Staff that Roosevelt did. In the United States, FDR was constitutionally the commander in chief of the armed forces, but in Britain this post was formally held by the king.[28]

Even before the joint staff talks began, Churchill had urged his staff to defer to American perspectives on the U.S. role in the Pacific. "It would be most unwise," he wrote in December, "to try to force our views on naval strategy in that [Pacific] theatre upon the U.S. Naval authorities." Recognizing that his country was in no position to make demands, Churchill wanted the British delegation to say only that Singapore was at the Americans' disposal. But the Admiralty saw the entire Pacific theater through the lens of Singapore and was determined to force its views on the United States.[29]

On February 17, 1941, the prime minister sent a furious message to the first sea lord, Sir Dudley Pound, criticizing Bellairs for
"making such heavy weather over all this." Churchill was more
concerned about the fate of Lend-Lease in Congress, and still
more about American entry into the war as a combatant as soon as
possible, than he was about U.S. ships anchoring in Singapore.

Contrary to what the prime minister had said in his radio address on February 9, what he really needed from the United States
was its "gallant armies," not merely the tools of war. "What has
been the use of all this battling?" Churchill demanded. "Anyone
could have seen that the United States would not base a battle-fleet
on Singapore and divide their naval forces." He tartly reminded
Pound that "our sole object is to get the Americans into the war,
and the proper strategic dispositions will soon emerge when they
are up against reality, and not trying to enter into hypothetical paper accords beforehand." In another memo to his military chiefs,
Churchill repeated how counterproductive it was to put before the
Americans "a naval policy which they will not accept, and which
will only offend them and make it more difficult to bring them into
the war. If they prefer Hawaii to Singapore there is no more to
be said."[30]

Bellairs sent a conciliatory message to the Americans. Apology
accepted; the matter was dropped and discussions resumed.[31]

For all of the conflict and for all the concessions made by
the British—"every paragraph had to be fought," Bellairs commented—the ABC talks, codified as ABC-1, brought substantial
agreements. Britain was assured of American help in the Atlantic,
and the two sides agreed on the exigent priority of defeating Nazi
Germany. The American presence in the Pacific would remain
defensive, its fleet stationed in Hawaii as a deterrent to Japanese
aggression. Still, the Americans agreed to take responsibility for
the central Pacific, the area that extended as far west as Guam
north of the equator but only as far west as the Fiji Islands south of
the equator. The British would be in charge of the rest of the
Pacific, including Singapore, and they would defend their empire
in the Mediterranean and the Far East as they saw fit.[32]

ABC-1, with its roots in Plan Dog, was a clear win for the
United States. The British had conceded American control of the

agenda and the outcome. Moreover, as Sherwood wrote, ABC-1 "provided the highest degree of strategic preparedness that the United States or probably any other nonaggressor nation has ever had before entry into war." The Americans regarded it, a British staff member informed Churchill, as "the Bible of our joint collaboration," and Rear Admiral Danckwerts cautioned his Admiralty colleagues against angering the Americans by departing from its provisions.[33]

But the real success of ABC-1 was that it was a win for the British as well. At a moment when Roosevelt was redefining U.S.-British relations and bringing the American people along with him, Churchill had succeeded in tying the United States ever more securely to his beleaguered country. He had involved the U.S. military in comprehensive planning for an armed intervention that, until recently, most Americans had regarded as a greater threat than Adolf Hitler. He had not yet "brought them into the war," but he had pulled them a large step closer.

As for Plan Dog, it also reflected London's priorities. Unless Germany were defeated, the prospects for Britain and its empire were bleak, and Plan Dog turned their preservation into a shared goal. Even after the Japanese attack on Pearl Harbor, when many Americans understandably demanded a Japan-first strategy, British and American leaders agreed that they would not abandon their plan to make Germany their primary target. Throughout the harsh and unpredictable course of the war, the priorities of Plan Dog remained intact.[34]

Disputes between Britain and the United States over strategic policy would continue; the two countries would calculate their decisions according to their own national and imperial interests; and the prime minister would not always be as yielding as when Lend-Lease and American entry into the war hung in the balance. But the ABC conference nevertheless set a precedent for cooperation that would withstand the bitterest disagreements. Neither Britain nor the United States would embark on war plans without consulting the other. They had created a partnership that would evolve into permanent joint staff missions in London and Washington, with personnel in the hundreds, though the number of actual negotiators remained small.[35]

For his part, Prime Minister Churchill was elated that a new era was dawning. "We were conscious," he would write after the war, "of the tremendous changes taking place in American opinion, and of the growing belief, not only in Washington, but throughout the Union, that their fate was bound up with ours." The ABC talks did much to cement that bond. Nine months before the United States entered the war, the Anglo-American alliance was now indestructibly anchored on both sides of the Atlantic.[36]

CHAPTER NINE

The Flames of World
Conflagration Lick Everywhere

I N MID-FEBRUARY 1941, AS the Senate Foreign Relations Committee was considering whether to approve the Lend-Lease Act and send it to the Senate floor, a lengthy article entitled "The American Century" appeared in *Life* magazine. Its author was Henry Luce, the anti-fascist and interventionist publisher of *Time*, *Life*, and *Fortune*. "Consider the 20th Century," Luce wrote. "It is America's first century as a dominant power in the world."[1]

Luce wanted to give history a push at this critical moment and wrench the United States from "the moral and practical bankruptcy of any and all forms of isolationism." Since the end of the First World War, he wrote, Americans had "failed to play their part as a world power—a failure which has had disastrous consequences for themselves and for all mankind." Now, however, they had the opportunity to exercise world leadership. "Like most great creative opportunities," Luce wrote, "it is an opportunity enveloped in stupendous difficulties and dangers. If we don't want it, if we refuse to take it, the responsibility of refusal is also ours, and ours alone." Scorning the idea of aid to Britain *short of war*, which he considered "typical of halfway hopes and halfway measures," he called on his

Republican Party to cleanse itself of the "virus of isolationist steril-
ity" and called on his fellow citizens to acknowledge and act on
their moral obligation to the rest of the world, and thereby recon-
ceive their nation's global role and destiny.

Lend-Lease, awaiting action in the Senate, would be the first
test of that new vision.

On February 13, two days after Wendell Willkie's testimony, the
Senate Foreign Relations Committee approved the Lend-Lease
Act by a vote of 15–8, mostly along party lines. Four days later, debate began on the Senate floor. The galleries were jammed with
unruly visitors, who were repeatedly scolded for their cheers as
well as their catcalls.[2]

One of the first senators to address his colleagues was
Democrat Claude Pepper of Florida. "Lay it down as a premise,"
he said as the galleries fell into a hush: "America will not let
England fall to Hitler." The time had come for a decision. "One or
the other shall live, totalitarianism or democracy, tyranny or freedom. One or the other must be crushed. There can't be peace and
there won't be peace until Hitler is crushed into an earth which ab-
sorbs and assimilates him until he is remembered only as a nightmare." The Democratic majority leader, Alben Barkley of
Kentucky, declared that what Hitler called a "revolution of young
nations" was in reality "an inhuman and bestial revolution against
every freedom for which men have striven through centuries of
hardship." If the Axis won, "the result is economic bondage. It is
religious bondage. It is political bondage. And it is intellectual
bondage. You cannot have intellectual freedom where the soul of
man is enslaved." Republican senator Warren Barbour of New
Jersey declared it "inescapable" that Britain's survival "is essential
at this critical hour to the defense of the United States."[3]

Interventionists like Pepper and Barkley welcomed to their
cause converts like Democrat Josiah Bailey of North Carolina. In
1939, Bailey had refused to reconsider American neutrality, con-
tending that if the United States entered the European war, "I
should think we were the greatest pack of fools history has ever recorded." But now he confessed that he had "utterly changed my
mind. . . . I am advocating intervention with all its implications."[4]

Isolationists were quick to insist that Lend-Lease was Roosevelt's backdoor to American military involvement in the conflict. "What is worse than war?" asked Washington State's Homer Bone, one of the handful of Democrats opposed to the bill. Warren Austin of Vermont, the bill's most energetic Republican supporter, had a strong and emotional rebuttal ready. "O, there are much worse things than war," Austin exclaimed, as he stood alone in the center aisle of the Senate. "A world enslaved by Hitler is much worse than war, it is worse than death. And a country whose boys will not go out and fight to save Christianity and the principles of freedom from ruthless destruction by a fiend—well, you won't find such boys in America. . . . If ever it becomes necessary for us to fight, we will fight!" Applause from the galleries drowned out a smattering of boos.[5]

But opponents of Lend-Lease, even with little new to say, dominated the floor debate, speaking three times more than the bill's supporters. Day after day, the business of the Senate was paralyzed by the unlimited debate permitted under Senate rules. Major bills lay in limbo. Sinking in public opinion and in the canvass of senators, the isolationists adopted a strategy of talking the bill to death or dragging out the proceedings with anesthetic repetition in hopes that, by some miracle, Americans would turn against it. Democrat William Bulow, an isolationist from South Dakota, maintained on February 20 that it made eminent sense for Congress to "debate this until Europe settles its own affairs." Hitler's way of settling affairs was to issue fresh threats. In March and April, he thundered, "a naval warfare will start such as the enemy has never expected. Wherever Britain touches the Continent we shall face her. Wherever British ships cruise, our U-boats will be sent against her until the hour of decision arrives."[6]

Isolationists fiddled on, scraping out well-worn themes such as branding Lend-Lease a Trojan horse that would lead to a Roosevelt dictatorship or insisting, as did Republican Henry Cabot Lodge Jr. of Massachusetts, that Britain's defeat would "not be fatal to our national existence." Ohio's Robert Taft drew laughter from the crowded galleries when he observed that "lending war equipment is a good deal like lending chewing gum—you certainly don't want the gum back."[7]

Anglophobes like Democrats Worth Clark of Idaho and Robert Reynolds of North Carolina had their day. England was fighting for nothing more than its own "commercial supremacy," Clark declared on February 24; "She has a right to kill her sons to preserve her empire if she wishes, but that is her affair and not ours." He saw little difference between British imperialism and Hitler's Nazism. As for Reynolds, a few days earlier he had launched into a long diatribe, insisting that the British wanted only to exploit American money and lives to protect their empire and demanding that rich Britons "strip themselves of their hunting lodges and castles, their hounds and their falcons, their horses and their dogs, their jewels, their cash, and their securities." Reynolds then pivoted to the oldest isolationist argument of all, claiming that the United States was well protected by two immense oceans and that Hitler was no more a menace to the United States than Napoleon had been in 1808. The North Carolinian came to a stop after two hours, though he had announced that he would speak for a minimum of four—silenced, Alben Barkley taunted, by "an attack of brevity."[8]

Attacks of brevity were rare. As February edged into March, senators orated before an almost empty chamber. The excitement filling the galleries had long since faded. Syndicated columnists Joseph Alsop and Robert Kintner described the scene on the Senate floor as a "haphazard collection of rather ordinary, rather elderly American men, paying their usual very intermittent attention to the proceedings." The two journalists lamented the pointless, rambling talk "in one of the supreme deliberative bodies of a great nation ... while the flames of world conflagration lick everywhere."[9]

The isolationist press was no more successful in breathing new life into frozen, discredited arguments. The *Chicago Daily Tribune*, which had warned of Roosevelt's dictatorial ambitions since the early days of the New Deal, editorialized that the "dictator bill" would lead to the downfall of democracy in America. But most of the nation's press gave solid backing to Lend-Lease, as did most of the public. A Gallup poll taken in mid-February showed that a majority of Americans supported it—from a high of 78 percent in the South to a low of 46 percent in the Midwest.[10]

The administration, meanwhile, was already preparing for Lend-Lease's rapid implementation. This was no secret. On February 17, White House press secretary Steve Early announced that the president had already spoken with legislative leaders and top Cabinet members about the program's launch. So sure was FDR that the bill would pass that in mid-February he appointed Averell Harriman to serve as a special defense liaison officer in London. Harriman, the former chairman of the Union Pacific Railroad and now the chief of the industrial materials division of the OPM, would be responsible for overseeing and expediting the flow of war materiel to Britain under Lend-Lease.[11]

"When the bill passes," a confident Steve Early told reporters, "many of the administrative requirements will be set and ready to be put into operation." One requirement was to decide on the size of the appropriations that would meet British needs. A sum of $8 billion, several billion down from the original British estimate, was agreed to, and the president reported that the congressional leaders with whom he discussed this figure "took it well." But to make the appropriations request easier for Congress to swallow, Treasury Secretary Morgenthau increased pressure on Britain to cash in more of its investments in the United States. He found a sacrificial lamb in a textile manufacturer, American Viscose, the largest British-owned company in the United States, and insisted that it be sold within seventy-two hours. In that high-profile forced sale, Morgan Stanley bought the company for $54 million, less than half its actual value, and quickly resold it for $62 million. Churchill found this a steep price, in both money and dignity, for American help. He drafted a bitter cable to Roosevelt, protesting that the administration's demands "wear the aspect of a sheriff collecting the last assets of a helpless debtor," but never sent it. Recognizing the impotence of his rage, he said to a Cabinet minister, "As far as I can make out, we are not only to be skinned but flayed to the bone."[12]

While Morgenthau handled the financial side of Lend-Lease, Henry Stimson and his War Department designed its administrative framework. Their plan called for an advisory committee made up of the secretaries of state, treasury, war, and navy—a committee the *New York Times* described as "in effect, a 'Ministry of Defense.'" Though FDR made clear that Lend-Lease would be under his overall control, the actual operations would be managed by an executive director replacing Morgenthau, who had taken the lead on Lend-Lease since the bill's origin in December. For the new job, FDR turned in April to his trusted friend Harry Hopkins. In the beginning, amid public doubts about Hopkins's health and his ability to manage such a heavy and complex task, Roosevelt minimized his role, suggesting that he was little more than a glorified accountant. But as the program expanded tremendously, Hopkins would become, according to Robert Sherwood, "the *de facto* Deputy President." Instead of dealing with breadlines and hurricanes, Sherwood continued, Hopkins would now have to confront "the greatest disaster that had ever befallen the human race." His mission was nothing less than "promoting in the American people an entirely new conception of their responsibilities and their capabilities."[13]

Having made diligent preparations to put Lend-Lease into operation, the administration had to wait for the congressional green light, which seemed to be dimming in a fog of rhetoric. As the debate wore on and as isolationists realized that they were making no headway in defeating the bill, they turned to another tactic. If the bill could not be killed outright, it might be crippled by amendments, a ploy that had already failed in the House.

The most dangerous of these amendments attacked the president's authority under the bill. Louisiana senator Allen Ellender proposed an amendment asserting that nothing in the bill gave the president "any additional powers" to deploy the American military outside the Western Hemisphere. Though Congress could not abridge the president's constitutional authority as commander in chief, the administration feared that such an amendment could be interpreted as blocking the president from sending American troops abroad. Stimson and Hull feared it might be an open invitation to Japanese aggression, including an attack on Singapore.[14]

The president broke his self-imposed silence at a press conference on February 25 to emphasize his opposition to any amendment that would hamper the government in extending all possible aid to Great Britain, a remark that was interpreted as criticism of the Ellender proposal. Still, Roosevelt had to proceed cautiously; if the administration fought back too hard against the amendment, isolationists would seize on that as proof of FDR's determination to send American troops into war.[15]

Also threatening the bill's integrity were amendments designed to strip the president of discretion in allocating armaments for Britain and other Lend-Lease recipients. South Carolina's James Byrnes, who was playing a major role in shepherding the bill through the Senate, and Virginia's Harry Byrd sought to defuse the opposition by offering compromise amendments that would preserve congressional control of the funds without tying the president's hands too tightly. Byrnes's proposal would require the president to seek congressional authorization not only for the appropriation of funds but for the transfer of war materiel paid for by those funds. Byrd proposed that money for Lend-Lease supplies be separate from the military budget, which would also give Congress greater control over the program. Taft, on the other hand, recommended that almost every transfer of armaments require congressional approval, a requirement that would have made Lend-Lease practically unworkable.

The administration reacted tardily to these challenges, and with Roosevelt bedridden with flu in early March, Stimson, Hopkins, Morgenthau, Knox, Marshall, and others fanned out to push back. Stimson in particular warned senators that such amendments "would utterly destroy the unity and flexibility which were intended by the President." Britain could even lose the war, he noted in his diary, if there were "a long debate every time we tried to give away to the British or to sell to them or to lend to them weapons."[16]

On Sunday, March 2, the secretary of war confided to the president how depressed he was over the bill's delay and the Senate leaders' inability to control "the little group of isolationists" who were making "a great deal of trouble." In January, Stimson had testified to the House Foreign Affairs Committee that it was of vital importance for the people's representatives to debate freely the grave issues that affected the nation's future but, he had underscored, it was equally important for those representatives to *act*.[17]

On March 3, Senator George, gentlemanly as always in his old-fashioned southern way, proposed that speeches be limited to one hour, but foes of Lend-Lease, led by Wheeler and Bennett

Clark, refused to give unanimous consent to his request. "I intend to fight it in any way I can," Wheeler howled on the Senate floor, threatening to filibuster the bill. Despite its "sugar-coated title"— "To Promote the Defense of the United States"—he maintained that Lend-Lease was in fact "designed for the defense of Singapore and foreign countries, and when the people can be brought to understand this, there will be such a public uprising as has never been seen here before."[18]

But by the next day, amid their colleagues' rising impatience, the bill's opponents withdrew their filibuster threat and agreed to end the debate so that the Senate could move on to consider proposed amendments. But this was no surrender. The intractable senators, refusing to acknowledge their waning support and expectantly awaiting Wheeler's "public uprising," professed their certainty that, as Wheeler said, "the overwhelming majority of the people" opposed Lend-Lease.[19]

Meanwhile, opponents would force the Senate to work through countless amendments to the bill. Some were significant, including a failed proposal to strike the bill's provision that assistance could be given to "any country whose defense the president deems vital to the defense of the United States" and instead limit aid recipients to Britain, Greece, and China. Some amendments were minor, including several clarifying ones that were adopted. Others were irrelevant, such as one offered by Senator Reynolds that would ban Communists from the federal bureaucracy.[20]

Roosevelt and Senate leaders met to discuss the Ellender amendment, which would prohibit the president from deploying troops outside of the Western Hemisphere, and agreed to a substitute that simply said that nothing in the Lend-Lease bill "shall be construed to change existing law relating to the use of the land and naval forces of the United States." That compromise, backed by Ellender himself, was approved by the Senate on March 7. As for the Byrnes and Byrd proposals, the Senate adopted a modified amendment that retained their heart but gave the president authority, in an emergency, to supply Britain or another nation with materiel directly from army or navy stocks. Even this less stringent amendment, Stimson judged, put an unwelcome limit on the president's discretionary power.[21]

The administration overcame its final hurdle on March 7, when the Senate emphatically rejected nine amendments. From sheer exhaustion and perhaps embarrassment, the Senate staggered toward a final vote.[22]

On Saturday, March 8, 1941, Americans were going about their lives—heading to the movies, playing bridge, listening to the radio or, in the Northeast, struggling through the thickest blizzard in six years. Across the Atlantic in London, the Luftwaffe launched its most brutal night attack in weeks; bombs crashed through the roof of a London nightclub crowded with dancers, decimated a public shelter, and killed pedestrians on a roadway. The Air and Home Security Ministries released updated figures on British casualties from June 1940 to the end of February 1941: 24,371 killed and 35,373 injured. Life in Britain, wrote Ernie Pyle, "has indeed become pretty bleak."[23]

In Washington, as senators prepared to cast their votes on Lend-Lease, a heavy police detail monitored the Senate galleries, which were packed to capacity with Cabinet members, senators' wives, and sightseers from all parts of the country. At one point, a woman in the front row of the galleries unfurled a banner reading "H.R. 1776 MEANS WAR. VOTE NO!" and was promptly evicted from the chamber.

Unwilling to surrender the limelight, Senator Nye, who had already spoken for twelve hours on the Senate floor, made a last-ditch attack on President Roosevelt, but he was interrupted by a determined chorus of "Vote! Vote!" The majority quickly rejected another gaggle of restrictive amendments, such as one excluding the Soviet Union from Lend-Lease aid.[24]

Finally, in a roll call just six minutes long, amid hushed silence, the senators individually called out their "ayes" or "nays." The tally was sixty in favor and thirty-one opposed. Fourteen Democrats voted no, while ten Republicans supported the bill, including, surprisingly, Senator Lodge. He divulged that he had asked the advice of General Marshall, who responded, not surprisingly, "In my opinion, the prompt enactment of this bill into law is a matter of great importance ... for national security." Also voting yes, though he had backed many opposition amendments, was Minority Leader

Charles McNary of Oregon, whose isolationism had been tempered by the fall of France and by his stint as Wendell Willkie's running mate in 1940.[25]

After the Senate vote on Lend-Lease, there was a "last-day-of school atmosphere," one reporter remarked. The two rival camps comfortably mingled; Bennett Clark and Jimmy Byrnes were seen walking down a Capitol corridor arm in arm.[26]

The long process was not quite over: the bill had to go back to the House for a final vote. After debating the Senate's amendments for less than two hours on March 11, the House approved the bill by an overwhelming vote of 317 to 71, an improvement on the initial House ballot in early February, when the tally was 260 to 165. Now some of the bill's opponents—isolationists like Hamilton Fish, Karl Mundt, and Minority Leader Joseph Martin—cast their votes in favor of Lend-Lease. Though Martin still feared that the bill would bring the country nearer to war, he thought it was improved by the amendments. "We accept the verdict of the majority," he said in a thoughtful call for national unity. "We may differ among ourselves but there is no division in our loyalty to our country or our determination to protect the security of our people. We are one people." Finally one. The word *congress* comes from the Latin—to come or walk together.[27]

Vice President Henry Wallace, as president of the Senate, and Speaker of the House Sam Rayburn signed the historic measure, and it was rushed over to the White House. The president read it quickly and wrote his name on it, making use of six pens that were later distributed as souvenirs to the congressional leaders who had played the greatest roles in bringing the bill across the finish line—Democrats Barkley, George, Byrnes, Rayburn, and McCormack, and Republican Austin. Fourteen minutes after the Lend-Lease bill arrived at the White House, on Tuesday, March 11, 1941, it became law.[28]

While FDR was signing the Lend-Lease legislation, Secretary Stimson was giving a speech in Washington to a conference of army public relations officers whose job it was to convey positive images of the army camps where draftees would be trained. "The success of any army depends upon its morale," he said, reminding his audience that a million men had been called "from their ordinary civilian lives . . . to train for their duties in national defense." The public relations officers' task was to inspire the new soldiers by helping them "to understand the purpose of their new life."[29]

That morning, the president had told Stimson that "we should be all ready to make a big jump forward as soon as the Bill is signed" and asked him to prepare a list of spare war materiel that could be sent to Britain at once. Greece, which had been reduced to near bankruptcy fighting off the Italians and now had a German army on its border with Bulgaria, was also eligible for immediate help. At last, Roosevelt had the discretion to direct the output of the "arsenal of democracy." That evening, Stimson phoned General Marshall with instructions, and before the night was over, Marshall had gotten in touch with the British Purchasing Commission and the Greek ambassador. Marshall "started the thing going," Stimson wrote in his diary. "That was the first action under the Lease and Lend Law."[30]

A week later, at a meeting with all the supply officers of the War Department, Stimson spoke about the "essential meaning" of Lend-Lease. Although he would have much preferred full-throttle participation in combat, he called Lend-Lease "an act of magnificent realism" that protected American self-interest and "virtually made the warring democracies an expeditionary force of our country of which we were the base and the supply of munitions."[31]

The Nazis were quick to react. A Berlin spokesman scoffed at the Lend-Lease bill, calculating the value of American intervention as "precisely nil." The official Nazi press assured its readers that the act would be no barrier to the construction of a "new European order."[32]

As for the Führer himself, his public response came days later in a speech at the Army Museum in Berlin. "No power and no support coming from any part of the world," he declared, "can change the outcome of this battle in any respect. England will fall." An American journalist present at the event expressed surprise that the Führer did not spew out his usual hate-filled wisecracks. Instead he spoke in a "calm, almost monotonous voice, utterly different from his usual fervent manner." Perhaps, the reporter surmised, Hitler was disappointed that the Tripartite Pact had not persuaded the

United States to abandon the idea of assisting England. He seemed less concerned about the fate of Britain than about American intentions. Or perhaps his attention was consumed by his army's imminent invasion—the largest in history, with 3 million soldiers—of his supposed ally, the Soviet Union.[33]

But for the English-speaking democracies, Lend-Lease was an unalloyed good, a pledge that together they would be victorious. In the United Kingdom, passage of the bill went a long way to boost morale. In the House of Commons on March 12, the day after Lend-Lease became law, Prime Minister Churchill expressed Britain's deep gratitude to the world's "most powerful democracy" for devoting its "overwhelming industrial and financial strength to insuring the defeat of Nazism in order that nations, great and small, may live in security, tolerance and freedom." Lend-Lease was not only a "monument of generous and far-seeing statesmanship," it was also "a new Magna Carta" that set forth "the rights and laws upon which a healthy and advancing civilization can alone be erected" as well as "the duty of free men and free nations" to enforce them.[34]

A week later, at a luncheon of the Pilgrim Society in London, Churchill declared that "the words and acts of the President and people of the United States come to us like a draught of life and they tell us by an ocean-borne trumpet call that we are no longer alone." Eight months later, on November 11, 1941, when the Lend-Lease program was still struggling to meet its production and delivery targets, Churchill spoke one of his most memorable lines of praise: "The lend-lease bill must be regarded without question as the most unsordid act in the whole of recorded history." Also deeply grateful were ordinary English men and women. In the shattered streets of London they joyously flew American flags— and many listened on the radio to a new hit song, "Thanks, Mr. Roosevelt."[35]

The American-British alliance was becoming an irresistible force that easily transcended diplomatic protocol. Just as President Roosevelt had broken precedent when he sailed out on Chesapeake Bay to meet Lord Halifax, King George returned that symbolic gesture. On March 1, 1941, wearing the uniform of a five-star field marshal, the highest rank in the British army, the king and his entourage were driven to the Windsor railroad station to greet John Winant, the new American ambassador. "I am glad to welcome you here," His Majesty said warmly to Winant, New Hampshire's Republican governor who had recently served as director of the International Labor Office, where he developed a friendship with Churchill's mobilization czar, Ernest Bevin. The new ambassador's sincerity, *Time* magazine noted, contrasted with "the smooth smiles of his predecessor Joseph Kennedy, who would rather be almost anywhere than in England." The king and his party escorted Winant to Windsor Castle for refreshments and discussion. It was a "striking tribute," commented the semi-official British Press Association, "to the strength of the Anglo-American friendship."[36]

Another distinguished American, James Conant, the president of Harvard University, also traveled to England that winter. President Roosevelt had asked him to set up a London office of the National Defense Research Committee, a group of American scientists, led by MIT's Vannevar Bush, who were developing complex weapons of war. Now the United States would strive to rescue civilization by furnishing Britain with secret weapons information as well as war supplies.[37]

On the day after he signed Lend-Lease, Roosevelt joined Robert Sherwood, Harry Hopkins, and Missy LeHand for a simple dinner on a card table in his study. The president, Sherwood reported, was enormously cheerful and "as usual, the talk was wildly irrelevant." Then they got to work on the speech FDR would give that weekend at the annual White House Correspondents' Association dinner.[38]

As Roosevelt brought to mind the isolationists' slurs about Lend-Lease and their attempts to frighten the American people, his mood darkened. "I'm going to get really tough in this one," he muttered. "I couldn't answer all these lies while the bill was still being debated, but now I'm really going to hand it to them." Pulling inflammatory quotations from newspaper clippings he had collected for the purpose, Roosevelt started to dictate his talk. "It was one of the most scathing, most vindictive speeches I have ever heard," Sherwood later wrote. Wasn't it disappointing, he reflected, that in his hour of triumph the president didn't show more magnanimity?[39]

But Harry Hopkins understood Roosevelt better and knew when he was just blowing off steam. The angry draft FDR dictated that evening was never seen again, and the final version of the speech, a relieved Sherwood wrote, contained "no evidence of petty vindictiveness." Instead, it was a verbal work of art, the words of a magnanimous, idealistic leader.[40]

On Saturday, March 15, while rescue workers in towns and cities all over Britain tried to clear away the rubble from Friday night's bombing raids, far away in Washington's Willard Hotel on Pennsylvania Avenue, reporters and editors mingled with hundreds of the capital's notables for the correspondents' dinner. Among the tuxedoed guests were Vice President Henry Wallace, House Speaker Sam Rayburn, Cabinet secretaries, senators, New York mayor La Guardia, Wendell Willkie, and Lord Halifax.

After songs by entertainers like Dinah Shore and comic skits by the reporters, the president spoke for more than half an hour. His words—and the loud applause that broke out again and again during the speech—were carried across the country on the radio and around the world on short-wave broadcasts, translated into fourteen languages.[41]

Roosevelt began his talk with a quip about the press conferences he held at least twice a week, telling the reporters that "you cannot ask me any questions tonight; and everything I have to say is word for word '*on* the record.' " Then, to his global audience, he pointed out that at his press conferences as well as at this dinner, reporters from many lands were present and "to most of them it is a matter of constant amazement that press conferences such as ours can exist in any Nation in the world."[42]

Over the past hundred days, Roosevelt had led the nation to a hard-won and historic achievement that broke with the past and set a confident course for the future. And Americans welcomed his leadership. A new Gallup poll showed that in Roosevelt's ninth year in office, 72 percent of the voting public supported him, compared with 55 percent four months earlier, when he ran against Wendell Willkie for the presidency. It was a "spectacular vote of confidence," commented the *New York Times*. Not since February 1934, when 69 percent of Americans backed him, had Roosevelt's approval reached such heights.[43]

But rather than strike a note of triumph, Roosevelt continued his speech with the confession that in 1939 he had not adequately grasped the mortal threat to freedom and democracy posed by fascism. "Before the present war broke out on September 1, 1939," he admitted, "I was more worried about the future than many people—indeed, than most people. The record shows that I was not worried enough. That, however, is water over the dam. Do not let us waste time in reviewing the past, or fixing or dodging the blame for it. History cannot be rewritten by wishful thinking." With the Lend-Lease Act, "we, the American people, are writing new history today. The big news story of this week is this: The world has been told that we, as a united Nation, realize the danger that confronts us—and that to meet that danger our democracy has gone into action." The passage of Lend-Lease marked "the end of any attempts at appeasement in our land; the end of urging us to get along with dictators; the end of compromise with tyranny and the forces of oppression."

Despite his anger at the delaying tactics of congressional anti-interventionists, he portrayed their opposition to Lend-Lease as proof of the vitality of American democracy. "America is not a country which can be confounded by the appeasers, the defeatists, the backstairs manufacturers of panic. It is a country that talks out its problems in the open, where any man can hear them. ... Yes, the decisions of our democracy may be slowly arrived at," he acknowledged. "But when that decision is made, it is proclaimed not with the voice of any one man but with the voice of one hundred and thirty million. It is binding on us all. And the world is no longer left in doubt."

The "great task of this day" was to put American industrial production into full swing. "Today, at last—today at long last—ours is not a partial effort," he announced. "It is a total effort and that is the only way to guarantee ultimate safety." The new watchword was "Speed, and speed now"—which, he hoped, would "find its way into every house in the Nation."

Reaching out simply and plainly to his fellow Americans, he painted an honest picture of the road ahead. "Whether you are in the armed services; whether you are a steel worker or a stevedore; a machinist or a housewife; a farmer or a banker; a storekeeper or a manufacturer—to all of you it will mean sacrifice in behalf of your country and your liberties. . . . The light of democracy must be kept burning." The Four Freedoms he had described in January, he said, constituted "the ultimate stake." Civilization itself tottered on the edge of an abyss. "If we fail—if democracy is superseded by slavery—then those four freedoms, or even the mention of them, will become forbidden things. Centuries will pass before they can be revived."

The response to this peril was an unstoppable determination to help Britain defeat the Nazi regime, a determination that Roosevelt expressed with a powerful and fervent crescendo of repetition emphasizing the short, ordinary verb *get*:

> The British people and their Grecian allies need ships. From America, they will *get* ships. They need planes. From America, they will *get* planes. From America they need food. From America, they will *get* food. They need tanks and guns and ammunition and supplies of all kinds. From America, they will *get* tanks and guns and ammunition and supplies of all kinds. . . .
>
> And so our country is going to be what our people have proclaimed it must be—the arsenal of democracy.

And then came his transformational pledge that the United States "must continue to play its great part in the period of world reconstruction for the good of humanity."

"Never, in all our history," he concluded, "have Americans faced a job so well worth while. May it be said of us in the days to come that our children and our children's children rise up and call us blessed."

It was a remarkable performance; it encompassed past, present, and future, the practical and the visionary, urgency as well as respect for democratic deliberation and tolerance for dissent—a fitting capstone to three extraordinary months of ferment, conflict, and decisive action. Roosevelt's delivery was unusually emotional, his voice revealing his deep feelings. "He was stirring," Robert Sherwood observed, "because he himself seemed deeply stirred."[44]

This address at the White House Correspondents' Dinner signaled the end not only of the president's own public ambivalence but also the end of an era—the era of American retreat from world affairs that had begun in 1919. Woodrow Wilson had championed the League of Nations at the Paris peace talks as a forum for global cooperation that would prevent future wars. But the Senate rejected the Treaty of Versailles, and the League with it. The leader of the opposition, Senator Henry Cabot Lodge Sr., had attacked it as a "deformed experiment" that would undermine American security.[45]

Wilson himself was a late convert to internationalism. At the outbreak of the war in August 1914, he had felt only outrage and disgust, writing that the combatants deserved "utter condemnation" and insisting that the United States would remain "neutral in fact as well as in name, impartial in thought as well as in action." Soon he developed a loftier and more idealistic rationale for his policy of isolation, declaring in 1915 that "the example of America must be a special example"—that of peace. "Peace is the healing and elevating influence of the world and strife is not. There is such a thing as a man being too proud to fight. There is such a thing as a nation being so right that it does not need to convince others by force that it is right."[46]

When Wilson finally led the country into World War I in 1917, it was on such idealistic and exalted terms—the United States would no longer be simply peace's exemplar but would deliver that peace to all humanity based on the highest American values of justice, self-determination, and freedom—that the real world could only disappoint him. His intervention in the European conflict ironically led his country to a fresh rejection of the endless strife in the bad Old World and a deepening of the isolationist strain that he himself had embraced in 1914. No one could have expressed the isolationists' attitude toward international affairs more concisely than George Harvey, an opponent of the League of Nations whom Warren Harding appointed ambassador to Britain. Upon leaving his post in 1923, Harvey declared that "the national American foreign policy is to have no foreign policy."[47]

As Wilson's self-righteous refusal to compromise with Republican opponents of the Versailles Treaty and the League showed, he lacked Franklin Roosevelt's political skills and realism. FDR had an idealistic streak in common with Wilson, who had been his boss when he was assistant secretary of the navy, but Roosevelt was an idealist without illusions. He possessed a tough-minded understanding of how the world—and Congress—worked, and he had learned from Wilson's failures. During the Senate's debate over the League in August 1919, Wilson supporter John Williams presciently asked how another war could be averted "if we are to be actuated by a mean, selfish spirit of nationalism." By 1941, Roosevelt had succeeded in devitalizing that mean, selfish nationalism.[48]

"Our effort to find security in isolation has failed," the *New York Times* editorialized in March 1941. "We proclaim our decision that in collective security and only in collective security can the democratic nations survive." After the war, Henry Stimson blamed isolationism for America's failure to stop Nazi Germany before it could set the world afire with the most destructive war in human history. "Our refusal to catch up with reality during those years," he wrote, "was the major source of our considerable share of the responsibility for the catastrophe of World War II. . . . We had in 1941 let it become too late to save ourselves by peaceful methods." This was the past that, as Roosevelt said, could not be rewritten; perhaps the future could be swayed by his Four Freedoms and his vision of a postwar world where all nations would unite to protect those freedoms.[49]

The president had a "mighty fine time" at the correspondents' dinner that evening, Sam Rosenman recalled. FDR knew most of the journalists by first name and greeted them buoyantly when they came to his table to congratulate him on the Lend-Lease fight. After the dinner, Rosenman wrote, a small group returned to the White House. "We all had a fine hour of post-mortems over a glass of beer, discussing the speech and how well it had gone over."[50]

CHAPTER TEN

The Third Hundred Days

F RANKLIN ROOSEVELT'S THIRD HUNDRED DAYS were one of the most fertile periods of his long presidency: three months during which his administration rejected isolationism, made a commitment to victory, and put in motion the means necessary to achieve it. Those hundred days also marked a decisive, irreversible shift in national consciousness.[1]

During those months, the president for the first time used speeches and press conferences to turn American foreign policy in a frankly internationalist direction. He educated Americans about the challenges the nation faced; laid out his intentions and policies and the causes and values behind them; and underscored the sacrifices he would ask his fellow citizens to make in order to achieve the goal of defeating Germany. All of these had previously been only half spoken. The passage of Lend-Lease powerfully demonstrated his success in shaping public opinion.[2]

The Lend-Lease Act announced to the world that American neutrality, though still on the statute books, had effectively vanished. Sam Rosenman commented that the act represented "the end of deviousness and evasion in sending help to the Allies. It was the beginning of forthright action." Henry Stimson called it a "new departure." During a March 1941 meeting with War Department supply officers, he praised Lend-Lease for ending the "old folly of remaining shackled by rules which the potential enemies of the country would not recognize." In a world in which international law had ceased to exist, Stimson emphasized, "the only law that was left was the law of self-defense."[3]

Still, there was no disguising Roosevelt's ambivalence about unrestricted American involvement in the war. His belief that the country needed more time to rearm, and especially his insistence that he required some major provocation from the Axis powers to "push" him into armed conflict, boxed him into his policy of "aid short of war." As a result, the United States in March 1941 was neither fully at peace nor fully at war. And yet during his third Hundred Days, Roosevelt approved crucial preparations for war. Plan Dog, the ABC talks, the prodigious acceleration of industrial defense production, the creation of the Office of Production Management, and the jewel in the crown, Lend-Lease, were all irrevocably under way. If they were not quite a public announcement of intent, taken together they amounted to a covert declaration of war.[4]

But during his third Hundred Days, Roosevelt accomplished even more than that. His administration began to envision and plan for the postwar world, after the destruction of Nazism. He pictured an era of American ascendancy across military, political, economic, and moral realms. In those winter months, the United States took its first strides toward becoming the world's superpower, with all the benefits and costs that status entailed.

On August 9, 1941, a conference began aboard the American cruiser *Augusta* in Placentia Bay, Newfoundland, offshore from one of the U.S. Navy's largest bases. Franklin Roosevelt and a small entourage, including Harry Hopkins, General Marshall, and Admiral Stark, held secret meetings about general strategy with Winston Churchill and his advisors. FDR, in a summer business suit, and Churchill, in nautical garb, face-to-face at last, greeted each other warmly, then quickly went to work. The prime minister was desperately hoping for a commitment from Roosevelt to enter the war. Earlier, when his bodyguard had suggested that the meeting would make history, Churchill replied, "Yes, and more so if I get what I want from him."[5]

He would not bow to Hitlerism, but the president was still waiting to be pushed into war—though as Churchill reported upon returning to London, he promised the prime minister that "he would wage war, but not declare it," that he "would become more and more provocative," and that the Germans, if they "did not like it, could attack American forces!" Fortunately, these comments were not leaked to the press. Roosevelt had told Churchill that he "was skating on pretty thin ice in his relations with Congress."[6]

Meanwhile, Churchill had to be satisfied with military and diplomatic commitments that tied the two nations in an ever tighter partnership. Roosevelt also promised massive amounts of aid, including almost unlimited access to American weapons. The United States would immediately send Britain bombers and tanks and more than a hundred thousand rifles. The president also said he would soon ask Congress for another $5 billion in Lend-Lease aid, in addition to the $7 billion already allocated. That news came as a major boost to the prime minister, another reassurance that the American president was fully committed to the Allied cause, even if he hesitated at the threshold of war. Churchill's entourage noticed that he returned from conferences with FDR in a higher mood and more animated.[7]

What the president wanted from the prime minister was less tangible than rifles and tanks: a joint statement of war aims. Though the Newfoundland meeting took place four months before Pearl Harbor and America's entry into the war, FDR had been telling the American people about his goals, the Four Freedoms, and the world he glimpsed on the far side of the war. Now he wanted the two allies to declare to the world where they stood and what they stood for. The president sought, as Undersecretary of State Sumner Welles put it, a way of "keeping alive . . . some principles of moral and human decency." Shortly before leaving for Newfoundland, FDR expressed his desire for a joint Anglo-American statement that would "hold out hope to the enslaved peoples of the world."[8]

That declaration would become known as the Atlantic Charter. It was drafted by the Americans and assented to, after some negotiations, by Churchill. The United States and Great Britain, the charter began, "deem it right to make known certain common principles ... on which they base their hopes for a better future for the world." The two nations pledged to renounce territorial aggrandizement; to permit territorial changes only when the people concerned approved them; to respect the right of people to choose their form of government; and "to see sovereign rights and self-government restored to those who have been forcibly deprived of them." FDR wanted that clause to apply not just to the victims of the Axis powers but to all people living under European colonialism, although to the disappointment of Americans and British moderates, Churchill interpreted it as referring to the nations under the Nazi yoke and not to the "regions and peoples which owe allegiance to the British Crown."[9]

The charter explicitly referred to two of FDR's Four Freedoms—freedom from want and freedom from fear. The United States and Britain expressed their desire to advance prosperity by supporting free trade among nations, though with "due respect" for the United Kingdom's "existing obligations" to British Commonwealth countries; by improving labor standards and assuring social security; and they pledged to encourage disarmament and "the abandonment of the use of force" in order to create "a peace which will afford to all Nations the means of dwelling in safety within their own boundaries, and which will afford assurance that all men in all the lands may live out their lives in freedom from fear and want."[10]

The charter was not a formal agreement between the two nations. For FDR, however, it was far more than a gesture; it was a statement of his vision for the postwar world. He wanted to build forward from the Four Freedoms and his defense of democratic principles; he believed in those ideals and principles, and he wanted people around the world to believe in them too. At the end of a war that would leave behind unimaginable devastation and grief, the Four Freedoms would bring hope and life and light. As Roosevelt's friend Felix Frankfurter wrote to him, the Atlantic Charter "was all grandly conceived and finely executed. ... The deed and the spirit and the invigoration of a common human fraternity in the hearts of men will endure—and steel our will and kindle our actions toward the goal of ridding the world of this horror."[11]

Aboard the *Augusta* on August 12, Churchill and Roosevelt shook hands. It was "a very moving scene," FDR wrote to a friend, as Churchill and his officers "received full honors going over the side." The two men had formed a bond born of circumstance. Tragedy had brought them together at a crossroads, and now they shared the road forward. A *New York Times* reporter wrote that Churchill and Roosevelt had been "cast up by a happy fate or a wise Providence into places of supreme power and responsibility."[12]

On August 14, the White House released the text of the charter, and a week later, Roosevelt presented it to Congress. It reconfirmed the bond between Britain and the United States, largely on American terms, but it also expressed the goals of an expanding alliance of free nations. In July 1944, at the Bretton Woods conference in New Hampshire, which designed a financial system for the postwar world, delegates from the forty-four Allied nations approved an agreement to end economic nationalism, lower barriers to trade, and encourage open markets and the movement of capital. After the war, the Atlantic Charter's principles and FDR's Four Freedoms were incorporated into one of the founding statements of the United Nations, the Universal Declaration of Human Rights. In its preamble, drafted in part by Eleanor Roosevelt in 1948, the declaration announced that the "advent of a world in which human beings shall enjoy freedom of speech and belief and freedom from fear and want has been proclaimed as the highest aspiration of the common people."[13]

In his essay "The American Century," Henry Luce had exhorted the United States, as "the most powerful and the most vital nation in the world," to realize its destiny by repudiating "ignorant and foolish" isolationism and by accepting "wholeheartedly our duty and our opportunity" to play the leading political, military, and moral role in global affairs. In a fireside chat two days after the attack on Pearl Harbor, which forever canceled the image of America as an impregnable fortress, President Roosevelt echoed Luce, stating that it was finally time for the United States to abandon "once and for all the illusion that we can ever again isolate ourselves from the rest of humanity."[14]

Six years later, on his eightieth birthday, Henry Stimson wrote his own essay, entitled "The Challenge to Americans." In a sense, it was a postwar coda to Luce's article. Dismissing the idea that "America can again be an island to herself," he urged the nation to accept its obligation to think and act with a sense of global responsibility. "No private program and no public policy, in any sector of our national life," Stimson wrote, "can now escape from the compelling fact that if it is not framed with reference to the world, it is framed with perfect futility." He described his long career in public service—which dated back to 1911, when Taft named him secretary of war—as "devoted to issues arising from the fact that the United States is not alone in the world."[15]

Lend-Lease was the star example of America's global responsibility; Stimson pronounced it "one of the most important legislative achievements of the entire war." In 1945, theologian Reinhold Niebuhr called Lend-Lease "one of the greatest political achievements" of Franklin Roosevelt. Perhaps even George Washington would have been pleased by FDR's leadership. In his Farewell Address in 1796, the nation's first president spoke of his hope that the United States, as "a free, enlightened, and at no great distant period, a great nation," would "give to mankind the magnanimous and too novel example of a people always guided by an exalted justice and benevolence."[16]

American resolve to act, as Stimson put it, "with reference to the world" would continue after the war, when Lend-Lease would be transmuted in 1947 into the Marshall Plan, designed to heal the war wounds of a devastated Europe. "The Marshall Plan is really lend-lease," wrote Clark Eichelberger, who had helped draft the original charter for the United Nations. Whereas the purpose of Lend-Lease was to win the war, the Marshall Plan, he said, was "lend-lease to win the peace."[17]

From Lend-Lease to the Marshall Plan, from the Four Freedoms to the United Nations, the essential global leadership role of the United States emerged during Franklin Roosevelt's third Hundred Days. And the transformation began on December 9, when a naval plane dropped a letter from Winston Churchill onto the deck of the *Tuscaloosa* and on December 17 when, at a press conference, the president spoke about a neighbor's house on fire and a garden hose.

Four months later, at a press conference in mid-April 1941, a light-hearted Roosevelt told reporters that he didn't have anything for them "except a little human interest thing" and "a rather nice little coincidence." He had just looked over the first Lend-Lease list submitted by Britain for nonmilitary equipment—"and it suddenly brought back something to me. I remember, once upon a time, I was talking about what people would do if their neighbor's house caught fire—if they happened to have some garden hose in the cellar they would take it out and lend it to their neighbor to put his fire out. . . . Well, the last three items on that list were for 900,000 feet of garden hose!" The reporters laughed wholeheartedly as Roosevelt clarified: "Not garden hose but fire hose—actually fire hose."[18]

Notes

Chapter One. The God of No Foreign War

1. Franklin D. Roosevelt, Press Conference, March 4, 1941, in *Public Papers and Addresses of Franklin D. Roosevelt* (hereafter *PPA*), 13 vols., ed. Samuel I. Rosenman (New York: Macmillan, 1941), 9:42.

2. *New York Times*, March 5, 1941, "Crisis Greater Today Than in 1933"; *Washington Post*, March 5, 1941, "U.S. Faces Crisis More Serious Than 1933's."

3. James MacGregor Burns, *The Crosswinds of Freedom* (New York: Knopf, 1989), 166.

4. Robert Dallek, *Franklin D. Roosevelt and American Foreign Policy, 1932–1945* (New York: Oxford University Press, 1979), 10.

5. In April 1935, FDR wrote to Edward House that he hoped France, Italy, and England would lead other European countries in a complete blockade of Germany and that, if it succeeded, "recognition by us would obviously follow." But the Stresa Conference at which a blockade was discussed produced only platitudes. FDR to House, April 10, 1935, in *F.D.R.: His Personal Letters*, ed. Elliott Roosevelt (New York: Duell, Sloan, and Pearce, 1950), 1:472–74.

6. *New York Times*, August 16, 1936, "President Roosevelt's Chautauqua Address." See also Alonzo Hamby, *Man of Destiny: FDR and the Making of the American Century* (New York: Basic Books, 2015), 77–78.

7. *New York Times*, August 16, 1936, "President Roosevelt's Chautauqua Address."

8. *Los Angeles Times*, October 6, 1937, "Text of World Peace Speech."

9. *Washington Post*, October 6, 1937, "League's Bid for Positive Action"; *Atlanta Constitution*, October 6, 1937, "The President and Peace"; *Saint Louis Globe Democrat* and *Cincinnati Inquirer*, quoted in *New York Times*, October 6, 1937, "Nation-wide Press Comment on President Roosevelt's

Address"; *New York Times*, October 10, 1937, "Policy in the Making"; *Atlanta Constitution*, October 14, 1937, "Tinkham Talks Removal of F.D.R."; *Atlanta Constitution*, October 17, 1937, "Fish Asserts F.D.R. Should Be Ousted"; *Hartford Courant*, October 6, 1937, editorial. The *New York Herald Tribune* also warned that the speech "was an appeal for a popular emotional mandate to the president to take whatever course in our international relations that seemed to him best," quoted in *Los Angeles Times*, October 6, 1937, "Editorial Comment Varies on President's Address." See also Dorothy Borg, "Notes on Roosevelt's 'Quarantine' Speech," *Political Science Quarterly*, 72, 3, September 1957, 405.

10. *Los Angeles Times*, October 10, 1937, "Neutrality Favored as Best Hope of Peace"; Harvey Cantril and Mildred Strunk, eds., *Public Opinion, 1935–1941* (Princeton: Princeton University Press, 1951), 966–67. See also Burns, *The Crosswinds of Freedom*, 153.

11. Robert Herzstein, *Roosevelt and Hitler: Prelude to War* (New York: Paragon House, 1989), 94–95; *New York Times*, October 6, 1937, "President Hits Out"; *New York Times*, October 8, 1937, "Two Foreign Policies." See also Dallek, *Franklin D. Roosevelt and American Foreign Policy*, 148.

12. James MacGregor Burns, *Roosevelt: The Lion and the Fox* (New York: Harcourt Brace Jovanovich, 1956), 355; *Los Angeles Times*, April 29, 1939, "Text of Hitler's Answers." See also William Shirer, *The Nightmare Years: 1930–1940* (Boston: Little, Brown, 1984), 2:402.

13. FDR, Fireside Chat on the European War, September 3, 1939, Miller Center, http://millercenter.org/president/fdroosevelt/speeches/speech-3315.

14. *Hartford Courant*, September 22, 1939, "Roosevelt Message Text."

15. *New York Times*, October 22, 1939, "Basic Fear of War Found in Surveys"; *New York Times*, May 9, 1939, "Senators Revive Ludlow War Vote"; *Atlanta Constitution*, March 8, 1939, "War Referendum Plan Continues"; Burns, *The Crosswinds of Freedom*, 159.

16. Roosevelt to Francis Sayre, December 13, 1939, and FDR to William Allen White, December 14, 1939, in Roosevelt, *F.D.R.: His Personal Letters*, 2:965, 967–68. See also Dallek, *Franklin D. Roosevelt and American Foreign Policy*, 214–15; Franklin D. Roosevelt, Annual Message to the Congress, January 3, 1940, in *PPA*, 9:2–4.

17. FDR to Neville Chamberlain, February 14, 1940, and FDR to Edouard Daladier, February 14, 1940, in Roosevelt, *F.D.R.: His Personal Letters*, 2:1001–2; William L. Langer and S. Everett Gleason, *The Challenge to Isolation: The World Crisis of 1937–1940 and American Foreign Policy*, 2 vols. (New York: Harper Torchbooks, 1952), 1:365, 374. See also Irwin F. Gellman, *Secret Affairs: Franklin Roosevelt, Cordell Hull, and Sumner Welles* (Baltimore: Johns Hopkins University Press, 1995), 193; Dallek, *Franklin D. Roosevelt and American Foreign Policy*, 218; Robert E. Sherwood, *Roosevelt and Hopkins: An Intimate History* (New York: Harper and Brothers, 1948), 137.

18. See David Reynolds's important article, "1940: Fulcrum of the Twentieth Century?" *International Affairs*, 66, 2, 1990, 325–50; Churchill to Franklin Roosevelt, May 15, 1940, in Warren F. Kimball, ed., *Churchill and Roosevelt: The Complete Correspondence* (Princeton: Princeton University Press, 1984), 1:37–38; *Hartford Courant*, June 5, 1940, "Mr. Churchill Sums It Up."

19. Mark A. Stoler, *George C. Marshall: Soldier-Statesman of the American Century* (New York: Twayne, 1989), 71.

20. Franklin D. Roosevelt, "The President Again Asks for Additional Appropriations for National Defense," in *PPA*, 9:289, 291; FDR, Fireside Chat, May 26, 1940, *PPA*, 230, 237; *New York Times*, May 29, 1940, "President Sets Up a Defense Council to Hasten Arming"; John M. Schuessler, "The Deception Dividend: FDR's Undeclared War," *International Security*, 34, 4, Spring 2010, 133–65.

21. *Los Angeles Times*, October 31, 1940, "Order Pushed by President"; Sherwood, *Roosevelt and Hopkins*, 191; John Morton Blum, *From the Morgenthau Diaries*, vol. 2, *Years of Urgency, 1938–1941* (Boston: Houghton Mifflin, 1965), 196; Thomas Paterson, J. Garry Clifford, et al., *American Foreign Relations* (Boston: Cengage Learning, 2014), 2:195; *Daily Boston Globe*, July 18, 1940, "Democratic Party Platform: Promises Not to Send U.S. Troops Abroad Except in Case of Attack."

22. Franklin Roosevelt, Campaign Address in Madison Square Garden, October 28, 1940, in *PPA*, 508; Sherwood, *Roosevelt and Hopkins*, 189, 201.

23. James MacGregor Burns, *Roosevelt: The Soldier of Freedom* (New York: Harcourt Brace Jovanovich, 1970), 42.

24. Anne Morrow Lindbergh, *The Wave of the Future: A Confession of Faith* (New York: Harper, Brace, 1940), 11–12, 18–21, 24, 34. "Are we afraid," she wrote, "not only of German bombers but also of change, or responsibility, of growing up?" Susan Dunn, *1940: FDR, Willkie, Lindbergh, Hitler—The Election amid the Storm* (New Haven: Yale University Press, 2013), 242–44. In the text of his August 4, 1940, speech, Charles Lindbergh also referred to "democracy" and the "so-called democratic nations." *New York Times*, August 5, 1940, "Text of Col. Lindbergh Speech." See also *New York Times*, January 6, 1941, "Hits Fear in Book by Mrs. Lindbergh." Mrs. Lindbergh was convinced that she was making, as she improbably told her mother, "the *moral* argument for isolationism— which I think no one has yet presented." Anne Morrow Lindbergh, *War Within and Without: Diaries and Letters of Anne Morrow Lindbergh, 1939– 1944* (New York: Harcourt Brace Jovanovich, 1980), AML to Elizabeth Morrow, September 4, 1940, 143, emphasis added. Mrs. Lindbergh borrowed her metaphor from Lawrence Dennis, the theoretician of fascism who had similarly written that the misdeeds of the Nazis were merely the "foam" on that unstoppable fascist wave. Lawrence Dennis, *The Dynamics of War and Revolution* (New York: *Weekly Foreign Newsletter*, 1940), xxiv. Willkie's foreign policy advisor, Raymond Buell, who was also an editor

at *Fortune*, met with Dennis. After his meeting, he wrote that Dennis and Lindbergh were close friends and that both believed that "the war is a product of the Wall Street plutocracy, Jews, etc. and Dennis figures that if a small number of intellectuals have been 'right' on this war issue and have a clear-cut fascist alternative, they will be able to seize power." Raymond Buell, Memorandum on Foreign Affairs for Henry Luce, January 8, 1941, p. 34, Raymond Leslie Buell Papers, Manuscript Division, Library of Congress, courtesy of J. Garry Clifford.

25. *New York Times, Sunday Times Magazine*, December 29, 1940, "Is It 'The Wave of the Past'?" by Allan Nevins; *New York Times*, May 20, 1940, "Two Views of America's Past," by Allan Nevins. Thomas W. Lamont, a partner of J. P. Morgan & Co., gave a speech on November 15, 1939, in which he said: "What we have been witnessing in Germany since 1933 . . . has been a violent social revolution. A German friend described it to me in terms of a great tidal wave. It came rolling in . . . overwhelming the country, bore out to sea and oblivion the stable elements of the community, leaving cast upon the shore all the strange creatures of the undersea world of society." Thomas W. Lamont, "Economic Peace," *Vital Speeches of the Day* (a semi-monthly magazine), 6:108–10.

In her "My Day" newspaper column of April 18, 1949, Eleanor Roosevelt mentioned a book by Reuben Markham entitled *The Wave of the Past*, published in 1941 by the University of North Carolina Press. Markham's book, Roosevelt wrote, "is apparently inspired by Anne Lindbergh's book, *The Wave of the Future*. Mr. R. H. Markham writes that 'the past has its mark and the future has its mark. The one is slavery and the other is freedom.' I think you will find both of these books of interest."

26. Eleanor Roosevelt, *The Moral Basis of Democracy* (New York: Howell, Soskin, 1940), 48, 43, 57.

27. Ibid., 68, 52–53, 68–69, 77, 74.

28. FDR reportedly said this to Douglas Fairbanks Jr. on November 26, 1940. See David Reynolds, "Lord Lothian and Anglo-American Relations, 1939–1940," *Transactions of the American Philosophical Society*, n.s., 73, 2, 1983, 42.

29. Churchill to Franklin Roosevelt, November 6, 1940, in Kimball, *Churchill and Roosevelt*, 1:81; Winston Churchill, *The Second World War*, vol. 2, *Their Finest Hour* (Boston: Houghton, Mifflin, 1949), 553–54.

30. *Time*, November 11, 1940, "Post-election: To the Lighthouse."

31. *Life*, February 17, 1941, "The American Century," by Henry Luce.

Chapter Two. Lousy November

1. *New York Times*, November 6, 1940, "Roosevelt Looks to 'Difficult Days' "; James MacGregor Burns, *Roosevelt: The Soldier of Freedom*

(New York: Harcourt Brace Jovanovich, 1970), 3; Kenneth S. Davis, *FDR: Into the Storm* (New York: Random House, 1993), 625; *Washington Post*, October 2, 1940, "On the Record"; James Roosevelt, *My Parents: A Differing View* (Chicago: Playboy, 1976), 164.

2. *New York Times*, November 8, 1940, "Washington Hails Roosevelt Return"; Leila Stiles, November 7, 1940, Leila Stiles File, Franklin D. Roosevelt Library (hereafter FDRL), Hyde Park, NY, courtesy of J. Garry Clifford. *Time*, November 18, 1940, "The Presidency: Full Desk." The country as well as the president seemed to be in a post-election "slump," bemoaned *New York Herald Tribune* columnist Dorothy Thompson, who had heard rumors that the president was in a "down" mood. Washington was sinking into a "swamp," *Time* magazine remarked.

3. *New York Times*, November 8, 1940, "London Raid Heavy"; *New York Times*, November 8, 1940, "De Valera Warns Britain on Ports"; *New York Times*, November 3, 1940, "Nazis Report Wide Raids"; *Time*, November 18, 1940, "World War: Formidable Dangers."

4. John Gunther, *Roosevelt* (New York: Harper, 1950), 22–23.

5. Roosevelt, Press Conference of November 8, 1940, in *Complete Presidential Press Conferences of Franklin D. Roosevelt*, 25 vols., ed. Jonathan Daniels (New York: Da Capo, 1972), 16:305.

6. William Langer and S. Everett Gleason, *The Undeclared War, 1940–1941* (Gloucester, MA: P. Smith, 1968), 236; Forrest C. Pogue, *George C. Marshall: Ordeal and Hope, 1939–1942*, 2 vols. (New York: Viking, 1965), 2:64–65, 67; The Henry Lewis Stimson Diaries, September 9, 1940, Yale University Library; Daniel Todman, *Britain's War: Into Battle, 1937–1941* (Oxford: Oxford University Press, 2016), 468.

7. Henry Lewis Stimson and McGeorge Bundy, *On Active Service* (New York: Harper, 1948), 355.

8. Roosevelt, Press Conference, November 8, 1940, in Daniels, *Complete Presidential Press Conferences of Franklin D. Roosevelt*, 16:298–99.

9. *New York Times*, November 9, 1940, "Hitler Forswears 'Any Compromise.'" This article mentions that the *Deutsche Allgemeine Zeitung* wrote that Hitler "knows he is sent by Providence to lead Germany to victory, and the German nation knows it also." See also Burns, *Roosevelt: The Soldier of Freedom*, 14ff.; *New York Times*, November 11, 1940, "Jews' Fate Linked to Britain's Peril."

10. *New York Times*, November 10, 1940, "R.A.F. Fired Cellar After Hitler Left"; *Chicago Daily Tribune*, November 10, 1940, "British Call Hit on Hitler's Beer Cellar Mistake"; *Los Angeles Times*, November 10, 1940, "Bombs Peril Adolf Hitler."

11. *New York Times*, September 29, 1938, "Text of Prime Minister Chamberlain's Address"; *New York Times*, October 1, 1938, " 'Peace with Honor,' Says Chamberlain."

In June 1939, before receiving an honorary degree at his alma mater Hamilton College, the pro-fascist poet Ezra Pound announced that "the British Government, except for Chamberlain, is rotten." *Daily Boston Globe*, June 10, 1939, "Britishers Begin to Fight Charges of Encirclement."

12. *New York Times*, March 16, 1939, "Excerpts from Commons Speeches."

13. *New York Times*, November 17, 1940, "War Winter II"; *New York Times*, November 11, 1940, "Chamberlain Goal Was World Peace."

14. *New York Times*, November 15, 1940, "Chamberlain's Ashes Laid to Rest"; *New York Times*, November 17, 1940, "War Winter II"; *New York Times*, November 11, 1940, "Chamberlain Goal Was World Peace."

15. *New York Times*, November 12, 1940, "Raid Alarm in London"; *New York Times*, November 12, 1940, "Grim Nations Observe 1918 Peace."

16. Eleanor Roosevelt, "My Day," November 12, 1940, https://www.gwu.edu/~erpapers/myday/displaydoc.cfm?_y=1940&_f=md055733; *New York Times*, November 12, 1940, "West, South Swept by Raging Storms"; *Time*, November 25, 1940, "Weather: Hunter's Storm"; *Los Angeles Times*, November 13, 1940, "Icy Storm Fatal for 98."

17. Address on Armistice Day, November 1, 1940, in *Public Papers and Addresses of Franklin D. Roosevelt* (hereafter *PPA*), 13 vols., ed. Samuel I. Rosenman (New York: Macmillan, 1941), 9:571.

18. A 1935 book by newspaper reporter Walter Millis, *The Road to War*, captured public attention. Millis held war profiteers responsible for America's involvement in the First World War. Ironically, Millis published a short book in 1941 called *The Faith of an American* that supported American entry into the Second World War.

19. Steven Casey, *Cautious Crusade: Franklin D. Roosevelt, American Public Opinion, and the War against Nazi Germany* (New York: Oxford University Press, 2001), 77.

20. *Washington Post*, November 12, 1940, "President's Armistice Text."

21. *New York Times*, November 13, 1940, "Roosevelt Omits Press Conference." FDR just wanted "a chance to sleep," noted Secretary of the Interior Harold Ickes. *The Secret Diary of Harold L. Ickes*, vol. 3, *The Lowering Clouds* (New York: Simon and Schuster 1954), November 17, 1940, 370.

22. Stimson Diaries, November 13 and 14, 1940, 122. *Time*, November 25, 1940, "The Presidency, the Congress, Foreign Relations: F.D.R. Goes Fishing"; Frank Costigliola, *Roosevelt's Lost Alliances: How Personal Politics Helped Start the Cold War* (Princeton: Princeton University Press, 2012), 119.

23. *New York Times*, November 14, 1940, "Roosevelt Calls for Unity in U.S."

24. Costigliola, *Roosevelt's Lost Alliances*, 78, 80.

25. Samuel Rosenman, 1959, Columbia University Center for Oral History, 108; Frank Costigliola, "Broken Circle: The Isolation of Franklin D.

Roosevelt in World War II," *Diplomatic History*, 32, 5, November 2008, 677–718. Rosenman said that Missy was "the one indispensable person around the Executive Mansion and later around the White House." Joseph Lash, ed., *From the Diaries of Felix Frankfurter* (New York: Norton, 1975), 162; Joseph Lash Interview with Anna Roosevelt Halsted, 1966–1967, box 44, Lash Papers, FDRL.

26. Justus Doenecke, introduction to *Debating Franklin D. Roosevelt's Foreign Policies*, ed. Justus Doenecke and Mark Stoler (Lanham, MD: Rowman and Littlefield, 2005), 6; Robert H. Jackson, *That Man: An Insider's Portrait of Franklin D. Roosevelt* (New York: Oxford University Press, 2003), 137. Jackson, who accompanied the president on that cruise as well as on several such trips, wrote that the usual routine during a presidential cruise was "much reading, much sleep, much discussion, much work, and much play."

27. Frederick Taylor, *Coventry: November 14, 1940* (New York: Bloomsbury, 2015), 58, 217ff.; *Time*, November 25, 1940, "The Presidency, the Congress, Foreign Relations: F.D.R. Goes Fishing."

28. *New York Times*, November 15, 1940, "Revenge by Nazis"; Heather Wiebe, *Britten's Unquiet Pasts: Sounds and Memory in Postwar Reconstruction* (Cambridge: Cambridge University Press, 2012), 192.

29. Allan Nevins, *This Is England Today* (New York: Scribner's, 1941), 32–34; *New York Times*, November 15, 1941, "Revenge by Nazis"; *Daily Boston Globe*, March 9, 1941, "Ernie Pyle in Coventry"; *New York Times*, November 17, 1940, "War Winter II."

30. Nevins, *This Is England Today*, 38; *New York Times*, November 17, 1941, "Hamburg Pounded in 'Reply' by R.A.F."

31. *New York Times*, November 21, 1940, "Coventry Dead Laid in One Grave," by Raymond Daniell.

32. *New York Times*, August 15, 1939, "Roosevelt to Move Thanksgiving"; *New York Times*, August 20, 1939, "All New England Says 'No!' "; Eleanor Roosevelt, "My Day," November 25, 1940, https://www.gwu.edu/~erpapers/myday/displaydoc.cfm?_y=1940&_f—d055744.

33. *New York Times*, November 21, 1940, "Feasts, Devotions"; *New York Times*, November 22, 1940, "Feasts and Prayer"; *New York Times*, November 22, 1940, "27th's Troops Hail Thanksgiving Day."

34. *New York Times*, November 22, 1940, "Thanks Services Sound Grave Note"; *Los Angeles Times*, November 22, 1940, "American Liberty Stressed in Thanksgiving Services."

35. *New York Times*, November 22, 1940, "Feasts and Prayer"; *Daily Boston Globe*, November 22, 1940, "Thanksgiving: President Notes Day"; Roosevelt Press Conference Number 695, November 19, 1940, in Daniels, *Complete Presidential Press Conferences of Franklin D. Roosevelt*, 16:309.

36. *Daily Boston Globe*, November 22, 1940, "King Says U.S. Supplies Ever Increasing"; *New York Times*, November 22, 1940, "Parliament Opens on

Confident Note"; Churchill to Roosevelt, May 15, 1940, in Warren F. Kimball, ed., *Churchill and Roosevelt: The Complete Correspondence*, 3 vols. (Princeton: Princeton University Press, 1984), 1:37.

37. Memo of May 25, 1940, in David Reynolds, "1940: Fulcrum of the Twentieth Century?" *International Affairs*, 66, 2, 1990, 332.

38. *Washington Post*, November 23, 1940, "All Aid Given, Says President."

39. *New York Times*, November 24, 1940, "Envoy Flies Here." It is often repeated that Lothian remarked, "Well, boys, Britain's broke. It's your money we want." But David Reynolds finds no evidence that Lothian said this, nor do I. See David Reynolds, "Lord Lothian and Anglo-American Relations, 1939–1940," *Transactions of the American Philosophical Society*, n.s., 73, 2, 1983, 48–49. The headline in the *Chicago Daily Tribune*, however, was "Envoy Lothian Claims Britain Going Broke," November 24, 1940.

40. David P. Billington Jr., *Lothian: Philip Kerr and the Quest for World Order* (Westport, CT: Praeger Security International, 2006), 114, 127–29. See also William Dodd, *Ambassador Dodd's Diary, 1933–1938* (New York: Harcourt, Brace, 1941), May 6, 1937, 407.

41. Billington, *Lothian*, 135–36; Winston Churchill, *The Second World War*, vol. 2, *Their Finest Hour* (Boston: Houghton, Mifflin, 1949), 555, 399. George Sylvester Viereck, the naturalized American citizen who was a Nazi agent (and later convicted), wrote a pamphlet entitled "Lord Lothian vs. Lord Lothian," in which he quoted some of the new ambassador's pro-appeasement statements from the 1930s alongside his more recent attacks on Nazi Germany. Billington, *Lothian*, 144.

42. Reynolds, "Lord Lothian," 48 and see note; Warren Kimball, *The Most Unsordid Act: Lend-Lease, 1939–1941* (Baltimore: Johns Hopkins University Press, 1969), 101, 148; John Morton Blum, *From the Morgenthau Diaries*, 3 vols., vol. 2, *Years of Urgency, 1938–1941* (Boston: Houghton Mifflin, 1965), 199–200, 223–24. On December 2, 1941, Morgenthau spoke with Lothian: "I told him that I was very sorry that he had made the remark which he did on landing about the British finances as that would date the matter in the minds of the public. I explained further what I mean by saying that if Senator Nye or any other senator called me on the Hill they would say, 'Well, on such and such a date Ambassador Lothian said the English were running short of money. By what authority did you let them place additional orders in this country?' This seemed to be a new idea to him [Lothian]. He said that he had made the remark on his own authority." Nye introduced a resolution for congressional investigation of all property, real and otherwise, in the United States owned by Great Britain. He wanted to prove that Britain did not need financial aid. His proposed resolution was buried in the Senate Foreign Relations Committee. *New York Times*, November 27, 1940, "Aid Now Unlikely."

43. FDR, Press Conference, November 26, 1941, No. 697, in Daniels, *Complete Presidential Press Conferences of Franklin D. Roosevelt*, 16:324. Nor did Roosevelt have anything to say about the troubling front-page stories in the *New York Times* that day: Slovakia, following the example of Hungary and Rumania, had just joined the Axis powers; members of the Norwegian resistance were wrecking railroad lines and roads and triggering landslides in an attempt to disrupt communication and transportation in their Nazi-occupied land; the Luftwaffe was bombing the British port of Bristol; an explosion capsized the British ship *Patria* in the port of Haifa, with eighteen hundred Jewish refugees on board, after British authorities denied it permission to dock in Palestine; and California senator Hiram Johnson vowed to "fight to the last ditch" to prevent any modification of the 1934 Johnson Act that prohibited loans to countries—including Britain—behind on repayment or in default of their debt from the First World War. The only country not in default was Finland. *New York Times*, November 26, 1940, "International Situation"; *New York Times*, November 26, 1940, "Refugee Ship off Palestine Is Sunk by Blast."

44. Ickes, *Secret Diary*, November 9, 1940, 3:367. See also Kimball, *The Most Unsordid Act*, 92; Lord Lothian to Halifax, November 26, 1940, reel 12, 4909, telegram 2802, marked "Important," British Foreign Office Records, FO 371 series, Public Record Office; Robert E. Sherwood, *Roosevelt and Hopkins: An Intimate History* (New York: Harper and Brothers, 1948), 222.

45. Frankfurter to FDR, November 29, 1940, in *Roosevelt and Frankfurter: Their Correspondence*, ed. Max Freedman (Boston: Little, Brown, 1967), 564.

46. Robert Dallek, *Franklin D. Roosevelt and American Foreign Policy, 1932–1945* (New York: Oxford University Press, 1979), 243–44; James MacGregor Burns, *Roosevelt: The Lion and the Fox* (New York: Harcourt Brace, 1956), 438; FDR to Knox, July 22, 1940, in *F.D.R.: His Personal Letters*, ed. Elliott Roosevelt (New York: Duell, Sloan and Pearce, 1950), 2:1049; Ickes, *Secret Diary*, 3:283.

47. Dallek, *Franklin D. Roosevelt and American Foreign Policy*, 246–47; *The Papers of George Catlett Marshall*, 6 vols., ed. Larry I. Bland et al. (Baltimore: Johns Hopkins University Press, 1986), 2:246–47, 295, note 2. See also *New York Times*, September 4, 1940, "The Quid Pro Quo That Was Always Indicated," by Arthur Krock.

48. *Chicago Daily Tribune*, September 9, 1940, "Col. M'Cormick Hails Isle Bases as Defense Aid"; *Atlanta Constitution*, September 4, 1940, "Destroyers-Bases"; *Christian Science Monitor*, September 4, 1940, "A Stroke for Defense." The *St. Louis Post-Dispatch* was virtually alone in denouncing the deal, editorializing that FDR "committed an act of war." Reprinted in the *New York Times*, September 4, 1940, "Display Ad 55."

49. Robert Shogan, *Hard Bargain: How FDR Twisted Churchill's Arm* (New York: Scribner, 1995), 222.

50. Churchill to British Embassy, December 28, 1940, C-53x, not sent, in Kimball, *Churchill and Roosevelt*, 1:119; *New York Times*, August 21, 1940, "Text of Prime Minister Churchill's Speech"; Churchill, *Their Finest Hour*, 404.

51. Stimson Diaries, September 27, 1940, 201; Pogue, *George C. Marshall: Ordeal and Hope*, 2:66–67.

52. Pogue, *George C. Marshall: Ordeal and Hope*, 2:64; Stimson Diaries, November 12, 1940, 129.

53. Pogue, *George C. Marshall: Ordeal and Hope*, 65–66; Memorandum for the President, November 13, 1940, and Memorandum for General Watson, November 20, 1940, in Bland et al., *The Papers of George Catlett Marshall*, 2:348–49, 352–53. See also George C. Marshall: Interviews and Reminiscences for Forrest Pogue, tape 9, 288–89, http://marshallfoundation. org/library/collection/george-c-marshall-interviews-reminiscences/#!/collection=341.

    Marshall would later recall the lessons this episode taught him about the complex process of wartime decision making. First, he learned that instead of trying to evade constitutional restrictions, it was more prudent to get them revoked; and second, it illustrated how easy it was for the British and the Americans to misunderstand one another—"their confusion about us, and our confusion about ourselves and about them. The matter of the Flying Fortresses was very illuminating to me, that we could be so far off-center on the matter and not realize it at all. . . . We just didn't understand them and they certainly didn't understand us. And they had information as to the battle efficiency of things that we just refused to accept." Bland et al., *Papers of George Catlett Marshall*, 2:353; George C. Marshall: Interviews and Reminiscences for Forrest Pogue, tape 9, 289.

54. *New York Times*, August 15, 1939, "Roosevelt to Move Thanksgiving." *Christian Science Monitor*, November 27, 1940, "Boston Slips into Galoshes"; *Christian Science Monitor*, November 29, 1940, "Plymouth Cheers Its Namesake"; *Daily Boston Globe*, November 29, 1940, "Home of First Thanksgiving Has Brilliant Pageant."

55. *New York Times*, November 29, 1940, "Raid on Port Heavy; Bombed Town Carries On"; *New York Times*, November 29, 1940, "Plymouth, in U.S., Hails Bombed City." After the attack on Plymouth, the Ministry of Home Security that monitored British morale reported: "Though raids were the principal topic of conversation, an unusual proportion of the raid talk was cheerful or humorous. There was relatively much whistling and laughing, relatively little grumbling. . . . There is no doubt, however, that there is considerable depression and much pessimism about the future underlying a determination to carry on." Todman, *Britain's War*, 516–17.

56. *New York Times*, November 29, 1940, "Liverpool Afire"; *New York Times*, November 17, 1940, "War Winter II"; *Washington Post*, November 29, 1940, "Nazis Claim Havoc in Plymouth Raid"; *New York Times*, November 29, 1940, "Raid on Port Heavy."

57. *New York Times*, December 16, 1940, "Roosevelt Hints of Crisis in Saying 'If World Survives' "; *Time*, December 16, 1940, "State of Business: Down the Stretch."

Chapter Three. Plan Dog

1. James O. Richardson, *On the Treadmill to Pearl Harbor* (Washington, DC: Naval History Division, 1973), 387; James R. Leutze, *Bargaining for Supremacy: Anglo-American Naval Collaboration, 1937–1941* (Chapel Hill: University of North Carolina Press, 1977), 180–81; Walter R. Borneman, *The Admirals* (New York: Little, Brown, 2012), 190.

2. James MacGregor Burns, *Roosevelt: The Soldier of Freedom* (New York: Harcourt Brace Jovanovich, 1970), 20.

3. William L. Langer and S. Everett Gleason, *The Undeclared War, 1940–1941* (New York: Harper and Brothers, 1953), 30.

4. Richardson, *On the Treadmill to Pearl Harbor*, 432.

5. Langer and Gleason, *The Undeclared War*, 41.

6. Richardson, *On the Treadmill to Pearl Harbor*, 432; Skipper Steely, *Pearl Harbor Countdown: Admiral James O. Richardson* (Gretna, LA: Pelican, 2008), 230.

7. Mark M. Lowenthal, *Leadership and Indecision: American War Planning and Policy Process, 1937–1942*, 2 vols. (New York: Garland, 1988), 1:399; The Henry Lewis Stimson Diaries, October 14, 1940, 52, Yale University Library.

8. Forrest C. Pogue, *George C. Marshall: Ordeal and Hope, 1939–1942*, 4 vols. (New York: Viking, 1965), 2:23.

9. Stimson to FDR, October 12, 1940, in Stimson Diaries, September 9, 1940, 46ff.

10. Stimson Diaries, November 7, 1940, 112, and December 18, 1940, 41. See also Henry Lewis Stimson and McGeorge Bundy, *On Active Service* (New York: Harper, 1948), 367.

11. *New York Times*, March 16, 1939, "14 Navy Officers Take High Command"; Leutze, *Bargaining for Supremacy*, 184; B. Mitchell Simpson III, *Admiral Harold R. Stark, Architect of Victory, 1939–1945* (University of South Carolina Press, 1989), 1–2; FDR to Stark, March 22, 1939, in *F.D.R.: His Personal Letters*, ed. Elliott Roosevelt (New York: Duell, Sloan and Pearce, 1950), 2:864.

12. *George C. Marshall: Interviews and Reminiscences for Forrest C. Pogue: Transcripts and Notes, 1956–1957* (Lexington, VA: Marshall Research Foundation, 1986), March 6, 1957, 86–87; Mark A. Stoler, *George C.*

Marshall: Soldier-Statesman of the American Century (New York: Twayne, 1989), 65–66; Joseph Persico, *Roosevelt's Centurions* (New York: Random House, 2013), 20–21.

13. Persico, *Roosevelt's Centurions*, 25.

14. Stimson and Bundy, *On Active Service*, 87; David Schmitz, *Henry L. Stimson* (Wilmington, DE: SR Books, 2001), 38; *New York Times*, October 17, 1919, "Stimson Opposes Big Regular Army"; *New York Times*, March 27, 1917, "Send Army Abroad, Stimson Demands"; *New York Times*, January 31, 1916, "Points to Lesson of 1812."

15. Stimson and Bundy, *On Active Service*, 268–69; Schmitz, *Henry L. Stimson*, 87–89; Stimson Diaries, November 18, 1931. Earlier in his career, Stimson had served as U.S. attorney for the Southern District of New York. He was "the nearest thing to a New England conscience on legs I have ever known," said a lawyer who once opposed him on a case.

16. Stimson Diaries, April 17, 1932; Schmitz, *Henry L. Stimson*, 91; Stimson and Bundy, *On Active Service*, 281, 305, 307, 312, 316. Stimson quotes from his own "outburst" on November 30, 1932. A resolute and determined leader in the United States in the 1930s, he later wrote, might have been able to "squirt Hitler and his gang out of their posts in the way you squeeze the pus out of an ulcer." *New York Times*, August 1, 1932, "Right Parties Fail to Carry Germany"; *Time*, July 18, 1932, "Foreign News: Lausanne Peace on Earth"; *Time*, June 29, 1931, "The Presidency: Moratorium"; Henry L. Stimson, "The Challenge to Americans," *Foreign Affairs*, 26, 1, October 1947, 7; *New York Times*, October 7, 1937, "Text of Former Secretary Henry L. Stimson Letter"; *New York Times*, October 7, 1937, "Stimson Favors Action on Japan."

17. Schmitz, *Henry L. Stimson*, 114; Stimson and Bundy, *On Active Service*, 292–93; Stimson Diaries, June 25, 1940, 56.

18. *New York Times*, June 19, 1940, "Stimson Demands Military Training."

19. *New York Times*, October 3, 1936, "Denies Roosevelt Averted a Revolt"; *New York Times*, September 3, 1936, "Knox Sees 'Aliens' Ruling Democrats"; *New York Times*, October 8, 1936, "Knox Warns Labor against New Deal." On the campaign trail, Knox oscillated between charging that the president's "squandering" of public money was the "recourse of a dictator" (*New York Times*, October 8, 1936, "Knox Warns Labor against New Deal") and allowing that the New Deal "is not planning a dictatorship; it just has delusions of grandeur" (*New York Times*, September 8, 1936, "Knox Warns Labor to Shun 'Iron Hand' ").

20. Susan Dunn, *1940: FDR, Willkie, Lindbergh, Hitler—The Election amid the Storm* (New Haven: Yale University Press, 2013), 92–94; *New York Times*, October 3, 1936, "Denies Roosevelt Averted a Revolt"; *New York Times*, September 3, 1936, "Knox Sees 'Aliens' Ruling Democrats"; *New York Times*, October 8, 1936, "Knox Warns Labor against New Deal"; *Hartford Courant*, May 14, 1940, "Time for America to Face Facts";

Steven M. Mark, "An American Interventionist: Frank Knox and United States Foreign Relations" (PhD diss., University of Maryland, 1977), 192, 211; *New York Times*, May 12, 1940, "Knox Demands Defense Arming"; *New York Times*, May 18, 1940, "Col. Knox to Form Air 'Plattsburghs' "; *New York Times*, February 1, 1941, "Secretary Knox's Statement to Senate Group."

21. *New York Times*, November 12, 1940, "Knox Urges Defense of Entire Hemisphere"; *New York Times*, November 12, 1940, "Navy Chiefs Warn We Must Be Ready"; *Daily Boston Globe*, November 12, 1940, "Text of Armistice Day Speech by President."

22. Stimson Diaries, December 3, 1940, 11.

23. *The Churchill War Papers*, 3 vols., ed. Martin Gilbert (New York: Norton, 2000), 3:1283; Frederick W. Marks, *Wind over Sand: The Diplomacy of Franklin Roosevelt* (Athens: University of Georgia Press, 1988), 165. King George VI, in a private letter to President Roosevelt, wrote, "I have been so struck by the way you have led public opinion by allowing it to get ahead of you" (Conrad Black, *Franklin Delano Roosevelt* [New York: Public Affairs, 2003], 634, 492). Stimson and Bundy, *On Active Service*, 367; Samuel I. Rosenman, *Working with Roosevelt* (New York: Da Capo, 1967), 167; FDR to Helen Rogers Reid, June 6, 1940, Reid Family Manuscripts, Library of Congress, quoted in J. Garry Clifford, "Both Ends of the Telescope," *Diplomatic History*, 13, 2, April 1989, 220.

24. FDR, Commonwealth Club Address, September 23, 1932, http://www.heritage.org/initiatives/first-principles/primary-sources/fdrs-commonwealth-club-address.

25. See Michael Desch, *When the Third World Matters* (Baltimore: Johns Hopkins University Press, 2003), ch. 3, on the perceived Nazi threat to the Western Hemisphere. *Los Angeles Times*, December 1, 1940, "Speakers Shy from Doctrine"; Lindbergh, speech, October 13, 1939, http://teachingamericanhistory.org/library/document/neutrality-and-war/.

   Strangely, Italy's fascist dictator Benito Mussolini came out with a modest proposal building on the idea of America's defense of its own hemisphere. In early October 1940, his official newspaper, *Il Popolo d'Italia*, announced that the Axis would recognize the "natural Lebensraum" of the United States in the Western Hemisphere in exchange for American recognition of the same right of territorial expansion of Germany and Italy in Europe and Japan in Asia. In brief, the United States was invited, fatuously, to join the Axis in "a new system of division of the world." *New York Times*, October 9, 1940, "Italians Bid U.S. Join Axis or Fight."

26. FDR, Press Conference, February 25, 1941, in *Complete Presidential Press Conferences of Franklin D. Roosevelt*, 25 vols., ed. Jonathan Daniels (New York: Da Capo, 1972), 17:152–53.

27. Robert Dallek, *Franklin D. Roosevelt and American Foreign Policy, 1932–1945* (New York: Oxford University Press, 1979), 246–47; *The Papers of George Catlett Marshall*, 6 vols., ed. Larry I. Bland et al. (Baltimore: Johns Hopkins University Press, 1986), 2:295, note 2; *New York Times*, September 14, 1940, "Text of the Selective Service Measure."

28. Roosevelt, Columbus Day Address, October 12, 1940, in *Public Papers and Addresses of Franklin D. Roosevelt* (hereafter *PPA*), 13 vols., ed. Samuel I. Rosenman (New York: Macmillan, 1941), 9:463; Warren Kimball, *The Most Unsordid Act: Lend-Lease, 1939–1941* (Baltimore: Johns Hopkins University Press, 1969), 168.

29. Warren Kimball, *Forged in War: Roosevelt, Churchill, and the Second World War* (New York: W. Morrow, 1997), 66–67; Address on Hemisphere Defense, October 12, 1940, in *PPA*, 9:460–67; *New York Times*, October 27, 1940, "Roosevelt Hails Navy for Defense."

30. *New York Times*, October 27, 1940, "Roosevelt Hails Navy for Defense."

31. Historian James MacGregor Burns aptly commented that FDR's strategy was often to "keep open alternative lines of action, to shift from one line to another as conditions demanded, to protect his route to the rear in case he wanted to make a sudden retreat, and, foxlike, to cross and snarl his trail in order to hide his real intentions." James MacGregor Burns, *Roosevelt: The Lion and the Fox* (New York: Harcourt Brace, 1956), 409.

32. Stimson's meeting with Marshall in Stimson Diaries, November 25, 1940, 156. See also Fred Greene, "The Military View of American National Policy, 1904–1940," *American Historical Review*, 66, 2, January 1961, 354–77; Ernest May, "The Development of Political-Military Consultation in the United States," *Political Science Quarterly*, 70, June 1955, 163ff.; Louis Morton, "National Policy and Military Strategy," *Virginia Quarterly Review*, 46, Winter 1960, 4–7.

33. In mid-December, the American ambassador to Japan Joseph Grew sent the following warning to Navy Secretary Knox: "Dear Frank, Sooner or later, unless we are prepared . . . to withdraw bag and baggage from the entire sphere of 'Greater East Asia including the South Seas' . . . we are bound eventually to come to a head-on clash with Japan." Grew called for a progressively grim policy on the part of the United States; although it entailed "inevitable risks," he wrote that "these risks are less in degree than the far-greater future dangers which we would face if we were to follow a policy of laissez faire." Grew ended his message by complimenting FDR on "playing a masterly hand in our foreign affairs," but historian James MacGregor Burns suggests that those remarks were both "pleasing and barbed," for FDR had yet to play realpolitik. Burns, *Roosevelt: The Soldier of Freedom*, 22.

34. Stetson Conn and Byron Fairchild, *The Framework of Hemisphere Defense* (Washington, DC: Office of the Chief of Military History, Department of the Army, 1960), 89; memorandum from Marshall to Stark, November

29, 1940, in Bland et al., *The Papers of George Catlett Marshall*, 2:361. Stark responds that Marshall's assumptions "preclude war in the Far East altogether" (2:362, note 2).

That fall, retired U.S. Navy rear admiral Yates Stirling Jr. pushed hard for an aggressive Atlantic-first strategy. Writing opinion pieces on the Navy for United Press, Stirling cast Germany as "America's enemy number one" and urged Americans to view the Atlantic Ocean as "our greatest responsibility." The bottom line was that if the Allies lost the Atlantic, "the defeat of America will be certain and absolute." *New York Times*, September 28, 1940, "Stirling, at Fair, Sees Reich Main Foe." Germany, Stirling warned, would try to trick the United States into keeping its fleet concentrated in the Pacific, but Americans needed to stay focused on the Atlantic and on Great Britain. "England is on the firing line and her navy and air force are our first line of defense," he wrote. Only by giving all possible aid to Great Britain and saving it from defeat would it be possible to eliminate "Hitlerism in Europe." *Atlanta Constitution*, September 30, 1940, "Forget Japan for Time, Eye Axis, U.S. Told"; *Atlanta Constitution*, October 11, 1940, "America Can't Appease Japan"; *Washington Post*, October 22, 1940, "The War at Sea," by Yates Stirling Jr.

35. Marshall to Stark, November 29, 1940, in Bland et al., *The Papers of George Catlett Marshall*, 2:361; Kimball, *The Most Unsordid Act*, 46.

36. Mark Skinner Watson, *Chief of Staff: Prewar Plans and Preparations* (Washington, DC: Historical Division, Department of the Army, 1950), 312; Stoler, *George C. Marshall*, 75; notes on conference in OCS, June 17, 1940, Misc. Conf, binder 3, p. 30, quoted in Louis Morton, "The Critical Summer of 1940," in *Command Decisions*, ed. Kent Roberts Greenfield (Washington, DC: Office of the Chief of Military History, Department of the Army, 1960), 29; Stimson Diaries, October 8, 1940, 23. The author of the quote is then major (but later lieutenant general and General Eisenhower's chief of staff) Walter Bedell Smith.

37. Conn and Fairchild, *The Framework of Hemisphere Defense*, 417.

38. Stimson Diaries, November 12, 1940, 132–33; *New York Times*, November 15, 1940, "Text of Address on National Defense by Secretary Knox," emphasis added. See also *Christian Science Monitor*, November 15, 1940, "Fleet Is Ready"; Lothian to British Foreign Office, November 19, 1940, reel 6, No. 2723, telegram 2632, British Foreign Office Records, FO 371 series, Public Record Office, courtesy of J. Garry Clifford.

39. *New York Times*, November 15, 1940, "Knox in Warning of Perilous Times Denounces Hitler." Lord Lothian agreed; he wired the Foreign Office in London that Knox was "refreshingly outspoken." Lothian to British Foreign Office, November 19, 1940, reel 6, no. 2723, telegram 2632, British Foreign Office Records, FO 371 series, Public Record Office, courtesy of J. Garry Clifford.

40. Stimson Diaries, November 25, 1940, 158; Stimson and Bundy, *On Active Service*, 374–75, 366. On January 5, Stimson had a telephone conversation with Grenville Clark during which Clark informed Stimson about his idea for the president to announce a change in policy from "short of war" to all-out war. He wanted the president to appoint a committee of notables to consider all-out war—with Justice Hughes, Justice Roberts, General Pershing, Hull, Knox, Stimson, some senators, and some distinguished citizens including Wendell Willkie and William Allen White. Stimson Diaries, January 5, 1941, 83.

41. *New York Times*, October 13, 1940, "17% of U.S. Voters Seen Favoring War." See J. Garry Clifford, "Both Ends of the Telescope: New Perspectives on FDR and American Entry into World War II," *Diplomatic History*, 13, 2, April 1989, 229; Robert E. Sherwood, *Roosevelt and Hopkins: An Intimate History* (New York: Harper and Brothers, 1948), 299. In *A World at Arms: A Global History of World War II* (Cambridge: Cambridge University Press, 1994), historian Gerhard Weinberg uncovered clear evidence of FDR's refusal to be provoked into war by anything less than an attack. "On August 22, 1940, when trying to get the support of the chairman of the Senate Naval Affairs Commission for the destroyers for bases deal, Roosevelt engaged the argument that such a step might lead to war with Germany because of retaliatory acts by the latter. He argued that if the Germans wanted to go to war with the United States, they would always find an excuse to do so, but that the United States would not fight unless attacked" (239). "When recordings of press conferences made in the White House in the fall of 1940 became available recently, and it turned out that a machine had been inadvertently left turned on, extraordinarily similar remarks by Roosevelt in private conversation came to light. On October 4 and on October 8, he explained to political and administrative associates that the United States would not enter the war unless the Germans or Japanese actually attacked; even their considering themselves at war with the United States would not suffice" (240).

42. Leutze, *Bargaining for Supremacy*, 191. For Plan Dog memorandum, see https://en.wikisource.org/wiki/Plan_dog_memo.

43. David Kaiser, *No End Save Victory: How FDR Led the Nation into War* (New York: Basic Books, 2014), 140.

44. George C. Marshall: Interviews and Reminiscences for Forrest Pogue, tape 9, 288, http://marshallfoundation.org/library/collection/george-c-marshall-interviews-reminiscences/#!/collection=341; Leutze, *Bargaining for Supremacy*, 200.

45. Admiral Harold Stark, Plan Dog Memo, November 12, 1940, https://en.wikisource.org/wiki/Plan_dog_memo.

46. At the end of his Plan Dog memorandum, Stark wrote: "I make the specific recommendation that, should we be forced into a war with Japan, we

should, because of the prospect of war in the Atlantic also, definitely plan to avoid operations in the Far East or the Mid-Pacific that will prevent the Navy from promptly moving to the Atlantic forces fully adequate to safeguard our interests and policies in the event of a British collapse. We ought not now willingly engage in any war against Japan unless we are certain of aid from Great Britain and the Netherlands East Indies."

47. Mark A. Stoler, *Allies and Adversaries: The Joint Chiefs of Staff, the Grand Alliance, and U.S. Strategy in World War II* (Chapel Hill: University of North Carolina Press, 2000), 32.

48. *Washington Post*, October 31, 1940, "Text of Roosevelt's Boston Speech."

49. Marshall, too, came to realize that victory would eventually call for boots on the ground. "I never had any idea that we could settle the question in Europe by purely air offensive," he later wrote. "You've got to get down and hold things. . . . You can destroy plants. You can destroy cities . . . but that doesn't win." George C. Marshall: Interviews and Reminiscences for Forrest Pogue, tape 9, 290–91, http://marshallfoundation.org/library/collection/george-c-marshall-interviews-reminiscences/#!/collection=341.

50. For descriptions of the five different RAINBOW plans, created by the Joint Planning Board in 1939, see Leutze, *Bargaining for Supremacy*, 40.

51. Pogue, *George C. Marshall: Ordeal and Hope*, 2:127. See also Mark Skinner Watson, *Chief of Staff: Prewar Plans and Preparations* (Washington, DC: Historical Division, U.S. Department of the Army, 1950), 119.

52. Stoler, *Allies and Adversaries*, 33–34; Bland et al., *Papers of George Catlett Marshall*, 2:360.

53. Lowenthal, *Leadership and Indecision*, 1:413.

54. Stoler, *Allies and Adversaries*, 36; Stark to General Marshall, November 22, 1940, WPD 4175–15, Secret (courtesy of Mark Stoler); Burns, *Roosevelt: The Soldier of Freedom*, 85; Lowenthal, *Leadership and Indecision*, 1:412, 424ff., 280, note 47, 352ff. Roosevelt's muted response seemed in keeping with his usual pattern of decision making; as historian Arthur Schlesinger Jr. noted, his favorite technique "was to keep grants of authority incomplete." Arthur Schlesinger Jr., *The Coming of the New Deal* (Boston: Houghton, Mifflin, 1958), 528. Were there other factors contributing to Roosevelt's reluctance to formally associate himself with a plan that took almost for granted that war would come, perhaps very soon? He may have been ambivalent about a straight and narrow Atlantic-first strategy. Several weeks later, he would write to Woodrow Wilson's son-in-law, Francis Sayre, asking whether, inasmuch as the hostilities in the Atlantic and Pacific were linked, the United States would "be rendering every assistance possible to Great Britain were we to give our attention wholly and exclusively to the problems of the immediate defense of the British Isles and of Britain's control of the Atlantic." He explained that the British Isles, "as the heart and the nerve center of the

British Empire," depended on the vast economic and strategic resources of its overseas colonies and that America's strategy "must envisage both sending of supplies to England and helping to prevent a closing of channels of communication to and from various parts of the world." And, he added, "we have no intention of being 'sucked into' a war with Germany." FDR to Sayre, December 31, 1940, in Roosevelt, *F.D.R.: His Personal Letters*, 2:1094–95. Historian Robin Prior, on the other hand, wrote that "Britain in 1940 and 1941 survived with no significant outside help except that freely given by the Dominions, especially Canada.... That Roosevelt refused to show any leadership in this matter is also beyond question. The defender of liberal democracy in 1940–1941 was not Britain along with the United States; it was Britain and the Dominions. They fought freedom's battle while the largest democracy on earth occasionally threw them some crumbs.... For Roosevelt the survival of Fortress America seemed to be sufficient." I disagree with that interpretation. Robin Prior, *When Britain Saved the West: The Story of 1940* (New Haven: Yale University Press, 2015), 280, 285.

55. Historian and security expert Lowenthal wrote that the "flaw" in the Stark memorandum lay not in the document but in what it said about the policy process itself. "The drafting of this document was a necessary usurpation of the President's fundamental policy function in the face of his own virtual abdication of this function." Lowenthal notes the time-consuming revisions and negotiations in the month following the drafting. But, he writes, "the ultimate failure of the Stark memorandum was President Roosevelt's unwillingness to either formally approve it or offer a preferred alternative." Still, he agrees that FDR's "quick acceptance" of ABC talks meant a tacit acceptance of the memorandum. Lowenthal, *Leadership and Indecision*, 425ff. See also Mark M. Lowenthal, "Roosevelt and the Coming of War," *Journal of Contemporary History*, 16, 1981, 426.

56. Louis Morton, *Strategy and Command: The First Two Years* (Washington, DC: Office of Military History, United States Department of the Army, 2000), 295; Mark Stoler, "George C. Marshall and Europe-First, 1939–1951," *Journal of Military History*, 79, 2, April 2015; Burns, *Roosevelt: The Soldier of Freedom*, 87; Stoler, *Allies and Adversaries*, 32. In July 1942, the United States would begin to launch, from England, air raids on Germany; and in late 1942 there would be a quarter of a million Allied troops in North Africa.

Chapter Four. Cruising in December

1. Robert E. Sherwood, *Roosevelt and Hopkins: An Intimate History* (New York: Harper and Brothers, 1948), 222; *The Secret Diary of Harold L. Ickes*, vol. 3, *The Lowering Clouds* (New York: Simon and Schuster 1954), December 21, 1940, 395.

2. *Complete Presidential Press Conferences of Franklin D. Roosevelt*, 25 vols., ed. Jonathan Daniels (New York: Da Capo, 1972), December 3, 1940, 16:337–38.

3. *New York Times*, September 14, 1941, "Two Men with One Idea."

4. *Time*, December 30, 1940, "The Presidency: Quiet Christmas"; Sherwood, *Roosevelt and Hopkins*, 222; *New York Times*, December 4, 1940, "Wind Brings Cold of 10."

5. David Kaiser, *No End Save Victory: How FDR Led the Nation into War* (New York: Basic Books, 2014), 138; Winston Churchill, *The Second World War*, vol. 2, *Their Finest Hour* (Boston: Houghton, Mifflin, 1949), 556.

6. *Christian Science Monitor*, December 20, 1940, "Mirror of World Opinion."

7. David Reynolds, "Lord Lothian and Anglo-American Relations, 1939–1940," *Transactions of the American Philosophical Society*, n.s., 73, 2, 1983, 51; Robert Dallek, *Franklin D. Roosevelt and American Foreign Policy, 1932–1945* (New York: Oxford University Press, 1979), 253; William L. Langer and S. Everett Gleason, *The Undeclared War, 1940–1941* (New York: Harper and Brothers, 1953), 228; *Time*, December 16, 1940, "National Affairs: Timetables"; Ickes, *Secret Diary*, November 9, 1940, 3:367. Churchill later complained about some of the "harsh and painful" actions taken by the American War Department. He wrote: "The President sent a warship to Capetown to carry away all the gold we had gathered there. The great British business of Courtaulds in America was sold by us at the request of the United States government at a comparatively low figure, and then resold through the markets at a much higher price from which we did not benefit. I had a feeling that these steps were taken to emphasize the hardship of our position and raise feelings against the opponents of Lend-Lease. Anyhow, in one way or another, we came through." Churchill, *Their Finest Hour*, 573.

8. Langer and Gleason, *The Undeclared War*, 229.

9. The Henry Lewis Stimson Diaries, December 3, 1940, 12, Yale University Library; Langer and Gleason, *The Undeclared War*, 229–230; Warren Kimball, *The Most Unsordid Act: Lend-Lease, 1939–1941* (Baltimore: Johns Hopkins University Press, 1969), 104.

10. FDR to Grace Roosevelt Clark and Ellen Roosevelt, December 3, 1940, in *F.D.R.: His Personal Letters*, ed. Elliott Roosevelt (New York: Duell, Sloan and Pearce, 1950), 2:1987; *Los Angeles Times*, December 5, 1940, "President's Ship Cruising off Cuba"; Sherwood, *Roosevelt and Hopkins*, 223.

11. *Chicago Daily Tribune*, December 8, 1940, "Roosevelt Finds Bad Fishing Weather"; *New York Times*, December 8, 1940, "Roosevelt Works for Hours at Mail"; *Christian Science Monitor*, December 10, 1940, "President Widens

Caribbean Cruise"; *Atlanta Constitution*, December 5, 1940, "Smooth Seas Greet F.D.R."; *New York Times*, December 6, 1940, "Roosevelt Views Jamaica Defense"; *New York Times*, December 5, 1940, "Roosevelt Inspects Base at Guantanamo"; *New York Times*, December 14, 1940, "Windsor Confers with Roosevelt on Island Bases." See also *Life*, July 16, 1956, "My Garden," by H.R.H. The Duke of Windsor, 41, 3, 62; Reynolds, "Lord Lothian and Anglo-American Relations" 45, note. Reynolds mentions that he believes that mail was delivered only twice to the ship during the whole cruise. Sherwood, *Roosevelt and Hopkins*, 222.

12. Since 1946 the French colony of Martinique has been a Department of France and an integral part of the nation. Langer and Gleason, *The Undeclared War*, 90.

13. *New York Times*, December 3, 1940, "International Situation"; *New York Times*, December 4, 1940, "Chief Nazi Attack Aimed at Midlands"; *New York Times*, December 7, 1940, "Nazis Strike Hard at South England"; *New York Times*, December 9, 1940, "Bombs Rain on City." The official German news agency boasted that the Luftwaffe dropped an average of eight hundred thousand pounds of explosives a night.

14. Churchill, *Their Finest Hour*, 2:558; Sherwood, *Roosevelt and Hopkins*, 223.

15. Churchill, *Their Finest Hour*, 2:558–67.

16. Memorandum by George Beckwith on a Conversation with Alexander Hamilton, October 1789, in Susan Dunn, ed., *Something That Will Surprise the World: The Essential Writings of the Founding Fathers* (New York: Basic Books, 2006), 149. In 1768, a young John Adams, after examining all systems of government, modern and ancient, concluded that "the liberty, the unalienable, indefeasible rights of man, the honor and dignity of human nature ... and the universal happiness of individuals, were never so skillfully and successfully consulted as in ... the common law of England." Adams, "On Private Revenge," 1768, in *The Revolutionary Writings of John Adams*, ed. C. Bradley Thompson (Indianapolis: Liberty Fund, 2000), 14. David Reynolds mentions that, in creating a close Anglo-American bond in 1940 and 1941, "the shared language, stripped of all extravagant myths, proved particularly potent. It facilitated more extensive and more intensive personal relationships than would otherwise have been possible." David Reynolds, *The Creation of the Anglo-American Alliance, 1937–1941* (Chapel Hill: University of North Carolina Press, 1982), 267. *New York Times*, February 1, 1941, "Secretary Knox's Statement."

17. Sherwood, *Roosevelt and Hopkins*, 270.

18. Churchill, *Their Finest Hour*, 2:560.

19. William Manchester, *The Last Lion: Winston Spencer Churchill*, 4 vols. (Boston: Little, Brown, 1983–2012), 3:219; Churchill, *Their Finest Hour*, 2:219.

20. Churchill, *Their Finest Hour*, 2:562.

21. Ibid., 2:559.

22. Ibid., 2:560.

23. Ibid., 2:566.

24. Warren F. Kimball, ed., *Churchill and Roosevelt: The Complete Correspondence*, 3 vols. (Princeton: Princeton University Press, 1984), 1:108; Kimball, *The Most Unsordid Act*, 112.

25. Reynolds, "Lord Lothian and Anglo-American Relations," 45; Churchill, *Their Finest Hour*, 2:554, 558; Kimball, *Churchill and Roosevelt: The Complete Correspondence*, 1:88, editor's note on Lend-Lease.

26. Kimball, *Churchill and Roosevelt: The Complete Correspondence*, 1:88, editor's note, 94–95, 101–9; Manchester, *The Last Lion*, 3:220.

27. Kimball, *Churchill and Roosevelt: The Complete Correspondence*, 1:93. There were also reminders of the "Nazi and Fascist tyranny" (109), "Nazi power," "mortal danger" and "slaughter" of civilians," and the "agony of civilization" (102–9).

28. Churchill to FDR, December 2, 1940, quoted in Dallek, *Franklin D. Roosevelt and American Foreign Policy*, 254; *New York Times*, November 24, 1940, "Envoy Flies Here"; Reynolds, "Lord Lothian," 45.

29. Lothian to British Foreign Office, December 5, 1940, reel 6, Weekly Political Summary no. 2927, British Foreign Office Records, FO 371 series, Public Record Office, courtesy of J. Garry Clifford.

30. Nicholas Cull, *Selling War: The British Propaganda Campaign against American Neutrality* (Oxford: Oxford University Press, 1995), 123.

31. *New York Times*, December 12, 1940, "Lothian Declares Victory or Defeat Rests on Our Help." The telegram from the British embassy in Washington to the Foreign Office reads as follows: "Lord Lothian seemed perfectly normal on Saturday when he played golf, and on Sunday morning when he had a long conversation with Mr. Hull. On Sunday afternoon he fainted and though he was still able to do business in his bedroom, he was in a very weak condition with internal pains. He requested Christian Science treatment from a Boston practitioner Mr. Cudworth whom he has known for many years. . . . On Sunday and Monday an apparent stoppage of the bladder action was causing distress, weakness and difficulty of breathing. His condition improved in the course of the day and voiding took place on Tuesday on which day his condition seemed generally better. On Wednesday night Lord Lothian had . . . some restful hours but between 1 and 1:30 a.m. suffered a sudden seizure of shortness of breath and from this he never recovered." Telegrams no. 3482 and no. 3056, Department (SECRET), A5071 301/45. The Foreign Office wrote that Lothian was "another victim for Christian Science." Cull, *Selling War*, 123; *Time*, December 23, 1940, "Foreign Relations: Death of Lothian." The British press regarded Lothian's death as nothing short of a calamity, for, wrote *New York Times* reporter Raymond Daniell, "it was believed that somehow he found the formula

for dealing with the United States." *New York Times*, December 29, 1940, "British Face Calmly a Crucial War Year."

32. *Washington Post*, December 17, 1940, "Fog Shrouds Rites for Lord Lothian"; *New York Times*, December 20, 1940, "Prime Minister Churchill's Speech in the House of Commons."

33. Kimball, *Churchill and Roosevelt: The Complete Correspondence*, 1:109.

34. *Wall Street Journal*, December 6, 1940, "Great Game of Politics."

35. *New York Times*, December 11, 1940, "Hitler Challenges World Democracy"; *New York Times*, December 11, 1940, "Excerpts from the Text of Hitler's Speech to Arms Workers"; *Daily Boston Globe*, December 13, 1940, "Dorothy Thompson: Hitler's Last Speech"; James MacGregor Burns, *Roosevelt: The Soldier of Freedom* (New York: Harcourt Brace Jovanovich, 1970), 18; *Washington Post*, December 11, 1940, "Roosevelt Extends Iron Exports Curb; Blow to Japan"; *New York Times*, December 11, 1940, "Metals Restricted." The week before, the *New York Times* had published the text of a speech given the previous spring by Germany's minister of agriculture, Richard-Walther Darré. A fervent believer in a new predatory breed of German supermen and a vast substratum of dehumanized, non-Aryan slaves, Darré enthusiastically depicted his notion of a "new aristocracy of German masters." The elite German nation "will have slaves assigned to it," he declared, "these slaves to be their property and to consist of landless, non-German nationals. Please do not interpret the word 'slaves' as a parable or as a rhetorical term; we actually have in mind a modern form of medieval slavery which we must and will introduce because we urgently need it in order to fulfill our great tasks. These slaves will by no means be denied the blessings of illiteracy. ... The United States also will be forced by Germany to complete and final capitulation." *New York Times*, December 6, 1940, "Nazis Envisage Chattel Slavery for People of Conquered Nations," 1. The *Times* explained that how the speech came into the possession of *Life* magazine could not be divulged but the *Times* had performed a "thorough investigation" and believed that the address was authentic.

36. *New York Times*, December 10, 1940, "Matsuoka Doubts Conflict with U.S."; *Washington Post*, December 11, 1940, "Roosevelt Extends Iron Exports Curb; Blow to Japan"; *New York Times*, December 11, 1940, "Metals Restricted"; Burns, *Roosevelt: The Soldier of Freedom*, 21.

37. *Wall Street Journal*, December 6, 1940, "Great Game of Politics," by Frank Kent. Arthur Krock of the *New York Times* was also concerned about the "spell of official languor" that gripped the nation's capital, but he held out high hopes for the second half of December. Though declining to reveal his sources, he suggested that the president would soon announce important news. "His impending return is confidently expected to inaugurate a period of greater activity in the armament effort than ever before," Krock reported. He believed that the president would

soon address crucial policy questions: how to speed up—and finance—defense production; how to provide more significant assistance to Great Britain; how to dispel the psychology that had persuaded many Americans that the United States faced no peril from the Axis powers. Krock felt certain that the president was ready to give all possible aid to Britain, "to the very limits of national security." *New York Times*, December 8, 1940, "Vital Decisions Near," by Arthur Krock.

38. *Time*, December 23, 1940, "The Presidency: What of the Night."

39. *Boston Globe*, November 10, 1940, "Kennedy Says Democracy All Done in Britain"; *New York Times*, December 6, 1940, "British Solidarity in War Affirmed," by Raymond Daniell.

40. *New York Times*, November 14, 1940, "Raid Taranto Base"; *New York Times*, December 12, 1940, "London Puts Crux of War Up to U.S."; *Christian Science Monitor*, December 10, 1940, "New British Aid Plan Waits President's Return."

41. Sherwood, *Roosevelt and Hopkins*, 224.

42. Ibid., 225.

43. *New York Times*, December 15, 1940, "President Implies Agency Bill Veto; Silent on Defense"; *New York Times*, December 16, 1940, "Roosevelt Hints of Crisis in Saying 'If World Survives,'" emphasis added; Sherwood, *Roosevelt and Hopkins*, 225.

44. Sherwood, *Roosevelt and Hopkins*, 225; *New York Times*, December 16, 1940, "Roosevelt Hints of Crisis in Saying 'If World Survives'"; *Atlanta Constitution*, December 17, 1940, "If World Survives."

45. *Time*, December 23, 1940, "The Presidency: What of the Night?"

46. Stimson Diaries, December 16, 1940, 32.

47. Morgenthau, Presidential Diaries, December 17, 1940, reel 1, book 3, Franklin D. Roosevelt Library (hereafter FDRL), Hyde Park, NY, courtesy of J. Garry Clifford.

48. John Morton Blum, *From the Morgenthau Diaries: Years of Urgency, 1938–1941*, 3 vols. (Boston: Houghton Mifflin, 1965), 2:208–9.

49. Ibid.; Kimball, *The Most Unsordid Act*, 124.

50. Morgenthau, Presidential Diaries, December 17, 1940.

51. Morgenthau, Presidential Diaries, December 31, 1940, reel 1, book 3, FDRL, courtesy of J. Garry Clifford.

52. *Time*, December 23, 1940, "The Presidency: What of the Night?"

53. Press Conference, December 17, 1940, in *Public Papers and Addresses of Franklin D. Roosevelt*, 13 vols., ed. Samuel I. Rosenman (New York: Macmillan, 1941), 9:604–15.

54. *New York Times*, May 13, 1917, "Asks Law to Seize Mosquito Craft"; James MacGregor Burns, *Roosevelt: The Lion and the Fox* (New York: Harcourt, 1956), 63; Ickes, *Secret Diary*, November 9, 1940, 3:367, 411; Morgenthau Diaries, November 8, 1940, quoted in Langer and Gleason, *The Undeclared War*, 217. See also Kimball, *The Most Unsordid Act*, 92.

55. Ickes to Roosevelt, August 2, 1940, quoted in Kimball, *The Most Unsordid Act*, 77, 121.

56. Press Conference, December 17, 1940.

57. James MacGregor Burns and Susan Dunn, *The Three Roosevelts: Patrician Leaders Who Transformed America* (New York: Atlantic Monthly, 2001), 435. Kimball remarks that there were other times during World War II when one ally was content to let another do the fighting: when the British left the French to face the Nazi onslaught in June 1940; when the Anglo-Americans delayed the second front and left it to the Russians to hold off the Nazi army. Warren Kimball, *Forged in War: Roosevelt, Churchill, and the Second World War* (New York: W. Morrow, 1997), 74.

58. *Washington Post*, December 19, 1940, "Today and Tomorrow," by Walter Lippmann; *New York Times*, December 19, 1940, "Greater Aid for Britain"; *Time*, December 30, 1940, "1940: The First Year of War Economy"; *Washington Post*, December 6, 1940, "On the Record: The Slump at Washington," by Dorothy Thompson; *Washington Post*, December 23, 1940, "Which New Order?" by Dorothy Thompson; *Atlanta Constitution*, December 22, 1940, "Thou Wilt Lament Hereafter—."

59. *Chicago Daily Tribune*, December 19, 1940, "Mr. Roosevelt's Crisis," emphasis added; *Chicago Daily Tribune*, December 18, 1940, "Britain's Vast Assets in U.S. Left Untapped"; *Chicago Daily Tribune*, December 19, 1940, "Roosevelt Plan Held Scheme to Put U.S. in War."

60. Kimball, *The Most Unsordid Act*, 126–27.

61. Langer and Gleason, *The Undeclared War*, 245; *Atlanta Constitution*, December 22, 1940, "Policy 'Impossible' America Warned"; *Atlanta Constitution*, December 22, 1940, "Washington Calm Despite Warning"; *Hartford Courant*, December 23, 1940, "The Warning from Germany."

62. Langer and Gleason, *The Undeclared War*, 245. See also Susan Dunn, *1940: FDR, Willkie, Lindbergh, Hitler—The Election amid the Storm* (New York: Yale University Press, 2013), 106, 236.

63. Mr. Butler to British Foreign Office, December 18, 1940, reel 6, telegram 3107, British Foreign Office Records, FO 371 series, Public Record Office, courtesy of J. Garry Clifford.

64. Churchill, telegram, December 31, 1940, C-50x, draft B, not sent. The final version was sent out on January 2, 1941. Kimball, *Churchill and Roosevelt: The Complete Correspondence*, 1:122.

Chapter Five. The Arsenal of Ideas

1. *New York Times*, December 26, 1940, "International Situation"; *New York Times*, December 26, 1940, "No Raids in Britain."

2. *New York Times*, December 26, 1940, "Britain on 'Path of Victory,' King Says," by Raymond Daniell; George Orwell, *The Lion and the Unicorn* (London: Secker and Warburg, 1941), 114.

3. *New York Times*, December 26, 1940, "Britain on 'Path of Victory,' King Says"; *New York Times*, December 22, 1940, "The Star Gleams through the Blackout."

4. *New York Times*, December 25, 1940, "President Says Christmas Signifies Bettering World in 'Voluntary Way' "; *Atlanta Constitution*, December 25, 1940, " 'If We Are All Here in 1941'—Roosevelt."

5. The President's Christmas Greeting to the Nation, December 24, 1940, in *Public Papers and Addresses of Franklin D. Roosevelt* (hereafter *PPA*), 13 vols., ed. Samuel I. Rosenman, (New York: Macmillan, 1941), 9:631–33.

6. *Time*, December 30, 1940, "Foreign News: Blitzmas."

7. *Washington Post*, December 26, 1940, "Bounteous Christmas Cheers D.C."; *Hartford Courant*, December 26, 1940, "Norwegian Royalty Are FDR Guests"; *Washington Post*, December 26, 1940, "President Hears Plea for Christian Unity"; *New York Times*, December 23, 1940, "Bishop Credits Joy in U.S. to Britain"; *Time*, February 24, 1941, "Religion: Churchmen & the War"; *New York Times*, December 22, 1940, "Mutual Good-Will Is Hailed by Rabbis"; *Los Angeles Times*, December 25, 1940, "Jews Begin Feast of Lights."

8. *New York Times*, December 25, 1940, "Spellman Pleads for World Peace"; *New York Times*, December 25, 1940, "Pope Voices Plea for 'a Just Peace' "; *Los Angeles Times*, December 25, 1940, "Battle-Scarred Europe Faces Dark Christmas"; *New York Times*, December 26, 1940, "Christmas Is Gay in a Few Nations in Blackout World."

9. *Washington Post*, December 26, 1940, "Bounteous Christmas Cheers D.C."; *Hartford Courant*, December 26, 1940, "Norwegian Royalty Are FDR Guests"; *Washington Post*, December 26, 1940, "President Hears Plea for Christian Unity"; *New York Times*, December 23, 1940, "Bishop Credits Joy in U.S. to Britain"; *Time*, February 24, 1941, "Religion: Churchmen & the War."

10. *Time*, February 3, 1941, "Religion: The Church & the War"; *Time*, February 17, 1941, "Religion: Practical Pacifists." See also Michael Thompson, "An Exception to Exceptionalism: A Reflection on Reinhold Niebuhr's Vision of 'Prophetic' Christianity and the Problem of Religion in U.S. Foreign Policy," *American Quarterly*, 59, 3, September 2007, 833–55; Ray Abrams, "The Churches and the Clergy in World War II," *Annals of the American Academy of Political and Social Science*, 256, March 1948, 112; *Time*, February 17, 1941, "The Congress: 260–165." Retired Yale English professor William Lyon Phelps wrote, in a letter to the *New York Times*, that although "isolation is suicide," he believed that members of the clergy should "stop talking about the war." Americans, he wrote, "need religious faith" and he noted "how sick and weary college students are of hearing the war dominate sermons. ... What every individual needs is the regeneration that comes through religion." *New York Times*, February 16, 1941, "Ministers Urged to Preach Religion Instead of War."

11. Reinhold Niebuhr, "Why the Christian Church Is Not Pacifist," in *The Essential Reinhold Niebuhr: Selected Essays and Addresses*, ed. Robert McAfee Brown (New Haven: Yale University Press, 1986), 110.

12. Ibid., 118; *Time*, February 3, 1941, "Religion: The Church & the War"; Reinhold Niebuhr, "World Crisis," in *A Reinhold Niebuhr Reader*, ed. Charles C. Brown (Philadelphia: Trinity Press International, 1992), 56–61. See also Thompson, "An Exception to Exceptionalism," 846; Niebuhr, "The War Situation," in *Christianity and Society*, 6, Winter 1940–41, 3–4; Niebuhr, "An End to Illusions," in *The Roosevelt Era*, ed. Milton Crane (New York: Boni and Gaer, 1947), 435–37; *Time*, February 3, 1941, "Religion: The Church & the War." Another group, the Interfaith Committee for Aid to the Democracies, underscored that the British people were almost alone in fighting for "the ideals of our civilization." But the great courage of the British people would not suffice. "They must be supplied with planes and ships, with munitions and food." *New York Times*, December 29, 1941, "3 Faiths' Leaders Plead for Britain."

13. *Time*, February 3, 1941, "Religion: The Church & the War."

14. *Time*, February 17, 1941, "The Congress: 260-to-165"; *Atlanta Constitution*, December 25, 1940, "Men Who Still Cling to Church in Germany Face Bleak Yule"; *Time*, December 23, 1940, "Religion: German Martyrs."

15. *Los Angeles Times*, December 29, "What I Liked Last Week"; *Atlanta Constitution*, December 25, 1940, "Men Who Still Cling to Church in Germany Face Bleak Yule"; *Time*, December 23, 1940, "Religion: German Martyrs." *New York Times*, December 22, 1940, "Christmas Article."

16. Leland V. Bell, *In Hitler's Shadow: The Anatomy of American Nazism* (Port Washington, NY: Kennikat, 1973), 104.

17. *New York Times*, June 14, 1940, "British Pin Their Hope on Blockade of Europe," by Raymond Daniell; *Los Angeles Times*, December 25, 1940, "Mrs. Anne Lindbergh Makes Appeal for Starving Europe."

18. Herbert Hoover Presidential Library, http://hoover.archives.gov/exhibits/Hooverstory/gallery07/.

19. *New York Times*, February 26, 1941, "35 Doctors Fight Hoover Food Plan"; *New York Times*, December 2, 1940, "Churchmen Assail Hoover Food Plan"; *New York Times*, December 2, 1940, "Hoover Food Plan Assailed at Rally"; *New York Times*, December 11, 1940, "Catholic Laymen Fight Hoover Plan."

20. Lord Lothian's official statement read: "His Majesty's Government has had in mind the noble services rendered by Mr. Hoover to the people of Belgium and other countries during and after the last war. After the most careful consideration, however, His Majesty's Government has been reluctantly forced to the conclusion that under present conditions any such scheme must be of material assistance to German's war effort and would

thereby postpone the day of liberation of these peoples from German subjugation. The Government [is] therefore not able to give permission for the passage of food through the blockade. . . . Moreover it must be remembered that the war against Great Britain is being actively and ruthlessly prosecuted from the countries under German occupation." *New York Times*, December 11, 1940, "Britain Bars Hoover Food Plan as Aiding German War Effort." FDR, Memorandum for Harry Hopkins, March 1, 1941, in *F.D.R.: His Personal Letters*, ed. Elliott Roosevelt (New York: Duell, Sloan and Pearce, 1950), 2:1129; Justus D. Doenecke, *Storm on the Horizon: The Challenge to American Intervention, 1939–1941* (Lanham, MD: Rowman and Littlefield, 2000), 94–99.

21. *Hartford Courant*, December 29, 1940, "FDR Makes Final Draft of Address."

22. *The Secret Diary of Harold L. Ickes*, vol. 3, *The Lowering Clouds* (New York: Simon and Schuster 1954), December 1, 1940, 376.

23. *Time*, December 30, 1940, "The Presidency: Quiet Christmas"; *New York Times*, December 24, 1940, "Prince Olaf Arrives in Clipper"; *Hartford Courant*, December 26, 1940, "Norwegian Royalty Are FDR Guests"; *Christian Science Monitor*, December 26, 1940, "President Backs Yule Plea by Dining Royal Refugees."

24. *Washington Post*, December 26, 1940, "Bounteous Christmas Cheers D.C."

25. Samuel I. Rosenman, *Working with Roosevelt* (New York: Da Capo, 1967), 227. Thereafter, as Rosenman recalled, they all moved into the White House and were thus able to work closely with FDR. "We all lived at the White House," and because of the holidays, "we were able to get long periods with the president" (258).

26. Robert E. Sherwood, *Roosevelt and Hopkins: An Intimate History* (New York: Harper and Brothers, 1948), 215.

27. The Henry Lewis Stimson Diaries, December 29, 1940, October 14, 1940, Yale University Library.

28. Sherwood, *Roosevelt and Hopkins*, 228; Rosenman, *Working with Roosevelt*, 261.

29. *Los Angeles Times*, December 30, 1940, "Roosevelt Redrafts Speech Seven Times Before Delivery"; *Time*, January 6, 1941, "The Presidency: The President Speaks"; *Atlanta Constitution*, December 30, 1940, "Gable, Lombard Are in Room."

30. *Washington Post*, December 30, 1940, "D.C. Man in the Street Agrees with Roosevelt on Dictators"; *New York Times*, December 29, 1940, "President Works All Day on 'Chat.'"

31. FDR, Fireside Chat, December 29, 1940, in *PPA*, 9:633–44.

32. Rosenman, *Working with Roosevelt*, 262; Sherwood, *Roosevelt and Hopkins*, 227.

33. *Time*, January 6, 1941, "The Presidency: The President Speaks."

34. Jean Edward Smith, *FDR* (New York: Random House, 2008), 486.

35. Sherwood, *Roosevelt and Hopkins*, 226; *New York Times*, May 12, 1940, "The Broadway Stage Has Its First War Play." The article is about Sherwood's play *There Shall Be No Night*. Rosenman, *Working with Roosevelt*, 261. In May 1940, the English novelist Phyllis Bottome visited the United States and told reporters that Britain did not desire an "expeditionary force" but rather needed the United States to act as an "arsenal." Bottome's passionately anti-Nazi novel *Mortal Storm* was made into a movie starring Jimmy Stewart and Robert Young that would be released in June 1940 *Hartford Courant*, May 6, 1940, "Says British Need U.S.A. as 'Arsenal.' "

36. Rosenman, *Working with Roosevelt*, 261.

37. Sherwood, *Roosevelt and Hopkins*, 228.

38. *Washington Post*, December 20, 1940, "Thousands Battle Inferno"; *New York Times*, December 30, 1940, "Flames Leap High," by Raymond Daniell. In fact the casualties were extraordinarily heavy. Raymond Daniell, *Civilians Must Fight* (Garden City, NY: Doubleday, Doran, 1941), 303.

39. Ernie Pyle, "London on Fire," December 29, 1940, in *Reporting World War II*, vol. 1, *American Journalism, 1938–1944*, ed. Samuel Hynes, Anne Matthews, et al. (New York: Library of America, 1995), 147–48; *Christian Science Monitor*, December 30, 1940, "Buildings Smashed." See also Sherwood, *Roosevelt and Hopkins*, 228.

40. *New York Times*, December 31, 1940, "Guildhall Housed Many Treasures"; *New York Times*, December 31, 1940, "Churchill Rebukes Question on Peace."

41. *New York Times*, December 31, 1940, "Churchill Rebukes Question on Peace"; Winston Churchill, *The Second World War*, vol. 2, *Their Finest Hour* (Boston: Houghton, Mifflin, 1949), 573–74.

42. Rosenman Papers, December 29, 1940, box 1, Franklin D. Roosevelt Library, Hyde Park, NY.

43. *Washington Post*, December 30, 1940, "D.C. Man in the Street Agrees with Roosevelt on Dictators."

44. *Chicago Daily Tribune*, January 12, 1941, "A Bill to Destroy the Republic"; *Chicago Daily Tribune*, January 3, 1941, "Roosevelt Talk Incendiary"; *Washington Post*, December 30, 1940, "U.S. Press, in General, Praises President's Fireside Address"; *New York Times*, December 31, 1940, "An American Doctrine."

45. *New York Times*, January 12, 1941, "Will We Stay Out?" by Arthur Krock; *Atlanta Constitution*, December 31, 1940, "Majority of U.S. Editors Praise Roosevelt's Stand on War"; *New York Times*, December 31, 1940, "An American Doctrine."

46. *New York Times*, December 30, 1940, "Capital Prepares for Early Action."

47. *New York Times*, December 31, 1940, "Wheeler Offers 'Quick' Peace Plan"; *New York Times*, December 31, 1940, "Text of Senator Wheeler's

Speech"; *Daily Boston Globe*, December 30, 1940, "Mingled Criticism"; *Atlanta Constitution*, March 4, 1941, "The Capital Parade," by Joseph Alsop and Robert Kintner; *Chicago Daily Tribune*, December 31, 1940, "Halt War Drive—Wheeler"; *Chicago Daily Tribune*, December 31, 1940, " 'America First' Drive Spreads across Nation." See also Wayne Cole, *America First: The Battle against Intervention* (Madison: University of Wisconsin Press, 1953), 43.

48. Steven Casey, *Cautious Crusade: Franklin D. Roosevelt, American Public Opinion, and the War against Nazi Germany* (New York: Oxford University Press, 2001), 23, 27, and table; *Atlanta Constitution*, December 29, 1940, "60 Per Cent in U.S. Favor Risking War to Assist England"; *Time*, January 6, 1941, "War and Peace: Exquisite Befuddlement."

49. *New York Times*, January 3, 1941, "U.S. Security Seen Linked to Britain"; *Atlanta Constitution*, January 2, 1941, "Gallup to Give U.S. Reaction to Roosevelt's Fireside Chat"; *Atlanta Constitution*, January 10, 1941, "South Leads U.S. in Sentiment for War." See also Susan Dunn, *Roosevelt's Purge: How FDR Fought to Change the Democratic Party* (Cambridge, MA: Harvard University Press, 2010).

50. Roosevelt Press Conference, #705, December 31, 1940, 4:10 p.m., in *Complete Presidential Press Conferences of Franklin D. Roosevelt*, 25 vols., ed. Jonathan Daniels (New York: Da Capo, 1972), 16:389, 595.

51. *New York Times*, January 1, 1941, "Hits Democracies."

52. Ibid. Hitler reminded German soldiers that he was "your supreme commander" to whom they had all sworn a "sacred oath." That oath was: "I swear by God this sacred oath that to the Leader of the German empire and people, Adolf Hitler, supreme commander of the armed forces, I shall render unconditional obedience and that as a brave soldier I shall at all times be prepared to give my life for this oath."

53. *New York Times*, January 1, 1941, "Hitler's Year."

54. *New York Times*, January 1, 1941, "New Year Revelry."

55. *Time*, January 13, 1941, "The Presidency: Aide to Britain"; Stimson Diaries, January 1, 1941, 72.

56. Eleanor Roosevelt, "My Day," January 2, 1941, http://www.gwu.edu/~erpapers/myday/.

57. Roosevelt, Annual Message to Congress, January 6, 1941, in *PPA*, 9:663–72.

58. *Time*, January 13, 1941, "National Affairs: For Four Human Freedoms."

59. Roosevelt, Annual Message to Congress, January 6, 1941.

60. Rosenman, *Working with Roosevelt*, 262–64.

61. In his annual message, FDR also said: "Just as our national policy in internal affairs has been based upon a decent respect for the rights and the dignity of all our fellow men within our gates, so our national policy in foreign affairs has been based on a decent respect for the rights and dignity of all nations, large and small. And the justice of morality must and

will win in the end." Elizabeth Borgwardt points out that Norman Rockwell's illustrations of the Four Freedoms portrayed them in an exclusively American context, whereas FDR had stressed that the Four Freedoms were an international vision. Elizabeth Borgwardt, "FDR's Four Freedoms as a Human Rights Instrument," *OAH Magazine of History*, 22, 2, April 2008, 8–13.

62. *Life*, February 17, 1941, "The American Century," by Henry Luce.

63. See Mark R. Shulman, "The Four Freedoms: Good Neighbors Make Good Law," *Fordham Law Review*, 77, 2, 2008; Frederick W. Marks, *Wind over Sand: The Diplomacy of Franklin Roosevelt* (Athens: University of Georgia Press, 1988), 166–68.

64. Sherwood, *Roosevelt and Hopkins*, 219.

65. *New York Times*, January 20, 1941, "4,000 Attend Gala"; *Washington Post*, January 21, 1941, "Goddess of Freedom and Sun Smile on Roosevelt."

66. *Washington Post*, January 20, 1941, "Inaugural Gala Delights Critic"; Herb Galewitz, *Music: A Book of Quotations* (n.p.: Dover, 2001), 4. Two weeks later, Berlin would introduce his latest song, "When That Man Is Dead and Gone." Sung in a jazz style called "swing," it was about Satan—"Satan with a small moustache"—stalking the earth, dressed as a man, and turning the world into hell. The refrain was: "When that man is dead and gone / When that man is dead and gone / We'll go dancing down the street / Kissing everyone we meet / When that man is dead and gone." *New York Times*, February 2, 1941, "Two New Berlin Songs Are Heard on Radio."

67. *Time*, January 27, 1941, "The Presidency: Third Term Begins."

68. *Washington Post*, January 19, 1941, "Last Twelve Years," by Ernest Lindley.

69. *New York Times*, January 21, 1941, "In the Nation," by Arthur Krock.

70. FDR, Third Inaugural Address, January 20, 1941, in *PPA*, 10:3–6.

71. *Atlanta Constitution*, January 21, 1941, "The Sacred Fire of Liberty"; *New York Times*, January 21, 1941, "Faith in Democracy"; *Washington Post*, January 21, 1941, "Today and Tomorrow"; Rosenman, *Working with Roosevelt*, 271, 269.

72. Stimson Diaries, January 20, 1941, 118.

73. *New York Times*, January 21, 1941, "Defense Program Is Parade Keynote."

74. *New York Times*, January 21, 1941, "Wider Nazi Help Expected in Rome," by Herbert Matthews.

75. *Life*, February 17, 1941, "The American Century," by Henry Luce.

Chapter Six. Make the Army Roll

1. Donald Nelson, "What Industry Did," in *While You Were Gone: A Report on Wartime Life in the United States*, ed. Jack Goodman (New York: Da Capo, 1974), 215; Leo Cherne, *Your Business Goes to War* (Boston:

Houghton Mifflin, 1942), 50–52; *New York Times*, February 2, 1941, "New Skills for Defense."

2. *Time*, December 16, 1940, "National Affairs: Timetables."

3. *Time*, February 17, 1941, "War Front: Defense Boom in Dixie." In the summer of 1940, Congress passed the five-year amortization plan that enabled industry to write off, for five years, new plants and improvements.

4. *New York Times*, February 2, 1941, "New Skills for Defense"; *Time*, February 3, 1941, "Building: Let Them Eat Summer Resorts"; Paul Gallico, "What We Talked About," in *While You Were Gone*, ed. Goodman, 30; Samuel Rosenman, 1960, 185, Oral History Research Office, Columbia University, https://clio.columbia.edu/?q=samuel+rosen man&datasource=quicksearch&search_field=all_fields&search=true. Eleanor Roosevelt was very critical of Charles Palmer's attitude. He said that "sociology was not part of his job." See Blanche Wiesen Cook, *Eleanor Roosevelt: The War Years and After* (New York: Viking, 2016), 414–15.

5. *New York Times*, January 16, 1941, "Defense Industry Revives a City."

6. Ibid.; *Atlanta Constitution*, October 14, 1933, "Boycott of German Goods Voted by American Labor."

7. *The Industrial Mobilization for War: History of the War Production Board and Predecessor Agencies, 1940–1945* (Washington, DC: United States Civilian Production Administration, 1947), 1:14; Henry Lewis Stimson and McGeorge Bundy, *On Active Service* (New York: Harper, 1948), 356.

8. *Washington Post*, September 27, 1939, "War Resources Board to Die as It Reports."

9. *New York Times*, May 29, 1940, "President Sets Up a Defense Council"; *New York Times*, June 2, 1940, "Advisers on Defense Face a Gigantic Task"; *New York Times*, June 9, 1940, "Defense Applied to Cost of Living."

10. *Boston Globe*, November 30, 1940, "A Director of Aircraft Production"; *Time*, December 23, 1940, "Defense Week: Big Bill's Answer."

11. Frances Perkins, *The Roosevelt I Knew* (New York: Viking, 1946), 357–59.

12. *New York Times*, September 19, 1982, "David Dubinsky—A Reporter's Memoir"; *New York Times*, November 21, 1940, "A.F.L. Men in Row," by A. H. Raskin; *New York Times*, November 22, 1940, "Dubinsky to Press Racketeering Test."

13. *Time*, December 2, 1940, "Labor: Wars to Lose, Peace to Win"; *New York Times*, September 18, 1982, "David Dubinsky, 90, Dies"; *Daily Boston Globe*, November 20, 1940, "Lewis Blasts Labor Peace Move." See also Philip Taft, *The A. F. of L. in the Time of Gompers* (New York: Harper, 1957), 425–26.

14. *New York Times*, November 20, 1940, "Lewis Shuts Door to Unity of Labor."

15. Wartime Record of Strikes and Lock-outs, 1940–1945, Senate, 79th Congress, 2nd Session, Document No. 136.

16. *Washington Post*, October 12, 1939, "Roosevelt Asks C.I.O."; *Daily Boston Globe*, October 4, 1939, "F.D.R. Bids Labor Heal Rift."

17. *New York Times*, November 20, 1940, "Roosevelt Urges A.F.L. to Seek Peace"; *New York Times*, November 20, 1940, "Text of President's Message Urging Federation to Seek Peace."

18. *Washington Post*, November 23, 1940, "C.I.O. Hails Murray."

19. Maurice Winger, "Restrictive Wartime Labor Measures in Congress," *Law and Contemporary Problems*, 9, 3, Summer 1942, 502–21.

20. *Los Angeles Times*, November 18, 1940, "Washington Intervenes in Vultee Strike"; *New York Times*, November 27, 1940, "Agreement Ends the Vultee Strike"; *Time*, November 25, 1940, "National Defense: Vultee Struck"; Wartime Record of Strikes and Lock-Outs, 1940–1945, Senate, 79th Congress, 2nd Session, Document No. 136, 17; Eleanor Roosevelt, "My Day," December 10, 1940; *Time*, April 7, 1941, "Labor: Stormy Weather"; *New York Times*, July 1, 1940, "Film Folk Rule High Salary List."

21. *Washington Post*, December 2, 1940, "Perspective on a Strike," by Ernest Lindley; *Washington Post*, November 25, 1940, "The Strike Weapon"; *Atlanta Constitution*, November 23, 1940, "Is This Significant?"

22. *Time*, November 25, 1940, "National Defense: Vultee Struck"; *Atlanta Constitution*, November 30, 1940, "The Capital Parade," by Joseph Alsop and Robert Kintner. See also Maurice Winger, "Restrictive Wartime Labor Measures in Congress," *Law and Contemporary Problems*, 9, 3, Summer 1942, 503; The Henry Lewis Stimson Diaries, November 26, 1940, 159, Yale University Library; *Chicago Daily Tribune*, November 27, 1940, "Vultee Strike Settled"; *Time*, December 9, 1940, "Under a New Leader"; *Hartford Courant*, November 24, 1940, "Vultee Strike Blamed on Communists"; *New York Times*, November 30, 1940, "20,000 Auto Workers Made Idle"; *New York Times*, November 29, 1940, "Aluminum Strike Ended"; *New York Times*, November 20, 1940, "Syracuse Strike Hits Arms"; *New York Times*, November 13, 1940, "Strike Shuts Steel Mill"; *New York Times*, November 8, 1940, "Strike Threatens Aircraft Supplies"; *New York Times*, December 1, 1940, "Enforcing Labor Peace in Defense Industries," by Arthur Krock.

The issue of the Vultee strike was inflamed by charges that it was the work of Communist subversives. The day after the president's November 26 press conference, Texas's Martin Dies, the chairman of the House Committee on Un-American Activities, released a lengthy White Paper purporting to show that Communists had gained significant power in the American labor movement. Attorney General Robert Jackson, though expressing some criticism of Dies's fiery report, nevertheless confirmed that the FBI had identified Vultee strike leaders as Communists or Communist sympathizers.

Ironically, American Communists at the time shared the anti-interventionism of fanatically anti-Communist isolationists like Charles Lindbergh. The Communists' stance was dictated by the August 1939 nonaggression pact between Hitler and Stalin. Thus, in some cases, American Communists used their footholds in unions to encourage strikes and derail American efforts to aid Britain, because they believed that aid to Britain would lead to American intervention in the war. Business leaders had long exploited such charges of Communist influence in unions. Panic over subversion provided them with an opportune lever to insist that labor rights be rolled back and to deflect attention from their own failure to speed up defense production.

There was, however, scant evidence that in 1940 Communists were to any measurable extent impeding the military buildup. Nor did the Vultee strike reveal anything more subversive than American workers trying to improve their lives. "Some persons think any man who wants more than $20 a week is a Communist," said Wyndham Mortimer, a UAW founder who oversaw the Vultee strike. "We deny Attorney General Jackson's charges and we say the strike was caused by wages and not by communism or any other ism."

23. Susan Dunn, *1940: FDR, Willkie, Lindbergh, Hitler—The Election amid the Storm* (New Haven: Yale University Press, 2013), 60; *Washington Post*, November 20, 1998, "Ford and GM Scrutinized for Alleged Nazi Collaboration." See also *Nation*, January 24, 2000, "Ford and the Führer," by Ken Silverstein.

24. *Daily Boston Globe*, November 7, 1940, "Ford Awarded Contract for 4000 Warplane Engines"; *Wall Street Journal*, November 7, 1940, "Ford Receives $122,323 Army Defense Contract."

25. *Time*, March 17, 1941, "Labor: Model T Tycoon"; *Daily Boston Globe*, December 14, 1940, "Hillman Protests Defense Contract to Ford Company."

26. Kenneth Davis, *FDR: The War President* (New York: Random House, 2000), 50–51.

27. *New York Times*, December 28, 1940, "Army Overrules Hillman Protest on Ford Contract"; *Daily Boston Globe*, December 14, 1940, "Hillman Protests Defense Contract to Ford Company."

28. *New York Times*, March 5, 1933, "Text of the Inaugural Address."

29. *New York Times*, December 20, 1940, "The International Situation."

30. *Los Angeles Times*, December 11, 1940, "Defense Czar for Aviation Production Reported Needed"; *Hartford Courant*, December 11, 1940, "Idea Broached for 'Czar' over Aviation Industry."

31. Stimson Diaries, November 22, 1940, 153.

32. *Atlanta Constitution*, November 27, 1940, "Factories Delay Defense Plans, Stimson Says"; *Washington Post*, November 27, 1940, "Roosevelt Tells Airlines Not to Expand"; *Wall Street Journal*, October 4, 1940,

"Douglas Aircraft Gets $141,320,610 Contract for Army Planes";
Stimson Diaries, November 27, 1940, 162; FDR, Press Conference,
November 26, 1940, in *Public Papers and Addresses of Franklin D. Roosevelt*
(hereafter *PPA*), 13 vols., ed. Samuel I. Rosenman (New York: Macmillan,
1941), 9:581.

33. Geoffrey Perret, *Days of Sadness, Years of Triumph* (New York: Coward
McCann, 1973), 73. In October 1941, Roosevelt ordered the War
Department to take over the operations of the Air Associates plant in
Bendix, New Jersey, when the owners refused to let workers who had
gone on strike return to their jobs. In his executive order, the com-
mander in chief wrote: "Due to the failure on the part of the Air
Associates Company, ... the complete cessation of production is now im-
minent at said plant. ... I, Franklin D. Roosevelt, pursuant to the powers
vested in me by the Constitution ... hereby authorize and direct the
Secretary of War immediately ... to take possession of and operate the
Bendix, N.J. plants of Air Associates, Incorporated. ... Our country is in
serious danger. The products of this plant play an indispensable part in
its defense. I call upon all workers in this plant to cooperate with the War
Department in insuring an immediate resumption of maximum produc-
tion." *Christian Science Monitor,* October 31, 1941, "Text of President's
Order"; *Hartford Courant,* October 31, 1941, "President Says Bendix
Firm 'Failed Its Part.' "

34. *New York Times,* December 19, 1940, "Britons Foresee More U.S. Effort,"
by Raymond Daniell.

35. *Washington Post,* February 23, 1941, "Three Principles for Defense," by
Joseph Alsop and Robert Kintner; *New York Times,* January 12, 1941,
"Labor Gains New Stature"; Daniel Todman, *Britain's War: Into Battle,
1937–1941* (Oxford: Oxford University Press, 2016), 618; George
Orwell, *The Lion and the Unicorn* (London: Secker and Warburg, 1941),
67; *Washington Post,* April 2, 1940, "Privilege Hitherto Known Must
Disappear"; Bevin, quoted in Allan Nevins, *This Is England Today* (New
York: Scribner's Sons, 1941), 67; *Time,* February 3, 1941, "Foreign News:
Labor Conscripted"; *New York Times,* January 22, 1941, "Britain to Draft
All Needed Labor," by Raymond Daniell; *Washington Post,* February 17,
1941, "Emotional Troubles"; *New York Times,* March 17, 1941, "British
Girls, Men Drafted for Work."

36. *New York Times,* December 1, 1940, "When Democracy Must Trim Its
Sails," by Allan Nevins; Nevins, *This Is England Today,* 4, 19; *Daily Boston
Globe,* April 5, 1941, "Globe Exclusives! Strikes Will End if Public
Realizes Danger," by Walter Lippmann. As for sacrifice, when the Gallup
poll asked respondents if, in order to speed up defense production, facto-
ries should be operating twenty-four hours a day, 90 percent of
Americans said yes. *New York Times,* January 5, 1941, "U.S. Public Ready
for Defense Fight."

37. *New York Times*, December 11, 1940, "Roosevelt Calls Business and U.S. Partners in Crisis."

38. *Daily Boston Globe*, December 14, 1940, "Knudsen Warns Plane Output Lags"; *Atlanta Constitution*, December 18, 1940, "Mr. Knudsen's Appeal," by Dorothy Thompson; *New York Times*, September 4, 1940, "Knudsen Resigns All GMC Offices." Also speaking at the National Association of Manufacturers meeting was General Robert E. Wood, the chairman of Sears Roebuck and the head of the isolationist America First Committee. Misguided Americans along with British propagandists, he charged, were conspiring to prepare the United States for a "plunge into war." Though he hoped for a British victory, he explained that the safest course for the United States was simply to remain neutral.

39. Keith Eiler, *Mobilizing America: Robert P. Patterson and the War Effort* (Ithaca: Cornell University Press, 1997), 80; Stimson Diaries, December 17, 1940.

40. Executive Order no. 8629, January 7, 1941, in *PPA*, 9:689–92.

41. One columnist noted that none of the four heads of the new OPM was a Democrat: Stimson and Knox were Republicans, Hillman was a member of the American Labor Party, and Knudsen had no known political affiliation. *New York Times*, December 18, 1940, "C.I.O. Chief Blames Industry for Lag in Defense Output." Buying "wisely" meant studying the production capacity of industries and marshaling the production facilities not only of a handful of corporate goliaths but also of thousands of small, independent companies that so far had remained idle.

42. *New York Times*, December 21, 1940, "President Names a Four-Man Board for Defense Drive"; *New York Times*, January 19, 1941, "Plane Production Rose in December"; *New York Times*, January 8, 1941, "President's Orders Revamping Defense Set-up"; *New York Times*, January 12, 1941, "Labor Gains New Stature"; *Christian Science Monitor*, January 8, 1941, "Knudsen and Hillman Get Unlimited Power"; *Washington Post*, January 9, 1941, "Double Headship," by Mark Sullivan.

43. *New York Times*, January 12, 1941, "Labor Gains New Stature"; *Time*, January 20, 1941, "Defense Week: Two Heads for One."

44. Stimson Diaries, December 17, 1940, 2.

45. Roosevelt, Press Conference, December 20, 1940, in *PPA*, 9:623, 630.

46. Stimson and Bundy, *On Active Service*, 355; Stimson Diaries, December 17, 1940, 2; Donald Nelson, *Arsenal of Democracy: The Story of American War Production* (New York: Harcourt, Brace, 1946), 114–15. See also *New York Times*, February 6, 1941, "President Decides Dispute in OPM." Nelson was made head of the War Production Board in 1942. See Perkins, *The Roosevelt I Knew*, 364.

47. *New York Times*, January 12, 1941, "Labor Gains New Stature"; Stimson Diaries, December 20, 1940, 49 and December 21, 1940, 51–53.

48. Eiler, *Mobilizing America*, 82. For duties and functions of the new OPM, see http://ibiblio.org/hyperwar/ATO/Admin/OPM/OPM-Duties/index. html.

49. FDR to Wayne Johnson, March 3, 1941, in *F.D.R.: His Personal Letters*, ed. Elliott Roosevelt (New York: Duell, Sloan and Pearce, 1950), 2:1131; Donald Nelson, "What Industry Did," 215.

50. Robert E. Sherwood, *Roosevelt and Hopkins: An Intimate History* (New York: Harper and Brothers, 1948), 288; FDR to Wayne Johnson, March 3, 1941, 2:1131. Knudsen told FDR that April that he had "searched the whole country over. There's no Democrat rich enough to take a job at a dollar a year" (Roosevelt, *F.D.R.: His Personal Letters*, 2:1131). Nelson, "What Industry Did," 215; John Morton Blum, *V Was for Victory*, quoted in Bruce Miroff, *Icons of Democracy* (Lawrence: University Press of Kansas, 1993), 269; Bruce Catton, *The War Lords of Washington* (New York: Harcourt Brace, 1949), 310.

51. *Washington Post*, May 22, 1941, " 'Bone-Headedness' at Army Camp Charged by Truman"; *Hartford Courant*, November 29, 1941, "Truman Charges Army Promoted Men 'for Waste' "; *Christian Science Monitor*, April 24, 1941, "War Department Is Accused of Dodging the Camps Issue"; *Christian Science Monitor*, December 12, 1942, "Key Workers at Jack & Heintz Plants Receive Paid Vacations"; *Hartford Courant*, March 30, 1942, "Jack and Heintz to Give Workers War Bonds"; *Hartford Courant*, March 25, 1942, "Jack & Heintz"; *Chicago Daily Tribune*, October 17, 1943, "Truman Committee Watchdog"; Nelson, "What Industry Did," 222, 225.

52. *New York Times*, March 28, 1941, "Allis Strike Hits Thirty Companies"; *New York Times*, March 15, 1941, "Strike Mediation"; *New York Times*, March 16, 1941, "Progress in Handling Defense Labor Trouble"; *New York Times*, May 18, 1941, "Labor Mediation Board Swamped by Calls on It." In June 1941, President Roosevelt commanded the War Department to take over the North American Aviation Corporation plant in Inglewood, California, that had been shut down by a rogue union. *New York Times*, June 10, 1941, "Roosevelt Explains Seizure." In October 1942, the CIO refused to deal with the NDAC; and in January 1941, the National Defense Mediation Board was replaced by the War Labor Board. In November 1941, the *New York Times* complained that the mediation board had become a "board of award," siding with labor and recommending a steady stream of wage increases. *New York Times*, November 13, 1941, "Biography of a Board." *New York Times*, October 28, 1941, "Terminated 39 Strikes"; *New York Times*, July 27, 1941, "21 Strikes Averted in June."

53. *New York Times*, June 21, 1941, "Henry Ford Signs C.I.O. Contract."

54. You can hear the rest of the lyrics to the labor song on YouTube: https:// www.youtube.com/watch?v=sEEWUQtqNCY. R. J. Thomas, "What Labor Did," in Goodman, *While You Were Gone*, 198–99.

Chapter Seven. Have We the Vision?

1. Warren F. Kimball, *The Most Unsordid Act: Lend-Lease, 1939–1941* (Baltimore: Johns Hopkins University Press, 1969), 144, 153, note 5, 177; Thomas G. Paterson, J. Garry Clifford, and Kenneth J. Hagan, *American Foreign Relations: A History*, 2 vols. (Lexington, MA: Heath, 1995), 2:184. The point of the bill's simple title, suggested by Justice Felix Frankfurter, was that aid for Britain was indispensable to American security but would not require American manpower.

2. Paterson, Clifford, and Hagan, *American Foreign Relations*, 2:184. See also Kimball, *The Most Unsordid Act*, 153, note 5.

3. Kimball, *The Most Unsordid Act*, 131. Langer and Gleason note that the original British estimate of 1941–42 requirements "totaled upwards" of $10 billion and that the Americans reduced the figure to $8 billion. William L. Langer and S. Everett Gleason, *The Undeclared War, 1940–1941* (New York: Harper and Brothers, 1953), 420. *Christian Science Monitor*, January 4, 1940, "President Roosevelt Transmits Annual Budget Message to Congress."

4. Kimball, *The Most Unsordid Act*, 134; Langer and Gleason, *The Undeclared War*, 256.

5. Kimball, *The Most Unsordid Act*, 145, 132.

6. Churchill to FDR, January 2, 1941, Corres C-50X, in Warren F. Kimball, ed., *Churchill and Roosevelt: The Complete Correspondence*, 3 vols. (Princeton: Princeton University Press, 1984), 1:124.

7. FDR, Press Conference, January 10, 1941, in *Complete Presidential Press Conferences of Franklin D. Roosevelt*, 25 vols., ed. Jonathan Daniels (New York: Da Capo, 1972), 17:68–69; Roosevelt to King George VI, November 22, 1940, in *F.D.R.: His Personal Letters*, ed. Elliott Roosevelt (New York: Duell, Sloan and Pearce, 1950), 2:1084; Kimball, *The Most Unsordid Act*, 132.

8. Kimball, *The Most Unsordid Act*, 218.

9. Ibid., 192, 195, 197, 199; *New York Times*, January 15, 1941, " 'Rotten,' 'Dastardly,' Roosevelt Says."

10. Robert Sherwood, *Roosevelt and Hopkins* (New York: Harper and Brothers, 1948), 242–43.

11. *New York Times*, January 13, 1941, "House Plans Speed"; Kimball, *The Most Unsordid Act*, 161.

12. *Washington Post*, January 16, 1941, "Lack of Dollars Cutting British Orders"; *Time*, January 27, 1941, "The Congress: Matter of Faith"; *Christian Science Monitor*, January 15, 1941, "Hull Charges Aggressors Violate All Neutral Rights"; *New York Times*, January 16, 1941, "Secretary of State Hull's Statement to House Committee"; *New York Times*, January 16, 1941, "Peril in Quibbling"; Kimball, *The Most Unsordid Act*, 166, 158, 169. Kimball notes that FDR wrote "at least part of Hull's opening statement." When Hull testified before the Senate committee, Texas senator

Tom Connally pitched the secretary of state a softball question: "Is there any possibility of our mollifying Mr. Hitler by pussy-footing a little more than we are or by avoiding a policy of violation of neutrality?" The answer was obvious: No.

13. Langer and Gleason, *The Undeclared War*, 260, 264; *Washington Post*, January 16, 1941, "Lack of Dollars Cutting British Orders to Trickle."

14. *New York Times*, January 17, 1941, " 'Crisis Exceeds '17.' "

15. *Chicago Daily Tribune*, January 11, 1941, "Senators to Fight F.D.R. Bill"; The Henry Lewis Stimson Diaries, February 17, 1941, 112, Yale University Library.

16. Stimson and Bundy, *On Active Service*, 365; *New York Times*, January 17, 1941, " 'Crisis Exceeds '17' "; Stimson Diaries, February 17, 1941, 112.

17. *New York Times*, January 30, 1941, "Four Amendments," emphasis added; Stimson and Bundy, *On Active Service*, 365; Stimson Diaries, January 29 1941, 135; James F. Byrnes, *Speaking Frankly* (New York: Harper and Brothers, 1947), 12.

18. *New York Times*, January 13, 1941, "Wheeler Sees 'Open War.' "

19. Stimson Diaries, December 29, 1940, 63; Document 28, Stimson memorandum relative to Bill 1776, January 22, 1941, in *Documentary History of the Franklin D. Roosevelt Presidency*, 40 vols., ed. George T. McJimsey (Bethesda, MD: University Publications of America, 2001–8), 2:147; Langer and Gleason, *The Undeclared War*, 266.

20. *New York Times*, January 18, 1941, "Knox's Statement of the Perils Facing Britain and America."

21. *Daily Boston Globe*, June 21, 1940, "Views of Our New Secretary of Navy"; *New York Times*, January 18, 1941, "British Fleet Key"; *Daily Boston Globe*, February 9, 1941, "Amendment to Balk Lease of Original Colonies Voted Out."

22. *New York Times*, January 18, 1941, "Knox's Statement of the Perils Facing Britain and America."

23. *New York Times*, January 19, 1941, "OPM Head for Bill."

24. Kimball, *The Most Unsordid Act*, 163; *New York Times*, January 17, 1941, " 'Crisis Exceeds '17.' "

25. Will Swift, *The Kennedy Family amidst the Gathering Storm* (Washington, DC: Smithsonian Books, 2008), 220. When Harry Hopkins was in England in January 1941 as FDR's representative, he met with Churchill, Anthony Eden, and other military leaders and Cabinet ministers. Lady Astor invited Hopkins for a weekend at Cliveden and told him that he had been making great mistakes in meeting with the wrong people. Sherwood, *Roosevelt and Hopkins*, 260; James MacGregor Burns, *Leadership* (New York: Harper and Row, 1978), 34; *New York Times*, October 20, 1938, "Kennedy for Amity with Fascist Bloc." See also Amanda Smith, ed., *Hostage to Fortune: The Letters of Joseph P. Kennedy* (New York: Viking, 2001), editor's notes, 228; Knox to Hull, October 25,

1938, in Wayne S. Cole, *Roosevelt and the Isolationists* (Lincoln: University of Nebraska Press, 1983), 290.

26. John Morton Blum, *From the Morgenthau Diaries: Years of Urgency, 1938–1941*, 3 vols. (Boston: Houghton Mifflin, 1965), 2:102; Cole, *Roosevelt and the Isolationists*, 290. In February 1939 Father Charles Coughlin named Joseph Kennedy "The Man of the Week" in his Jew-baiting weekly, *Social Justice*. See Isaac Kramnick and Barry Sherman, *Harold Laski: A Life on the Left* (New York: Allen Lane/Penguin, 1993), 429–30; *Boston Globe*, November 10, 1940, "Kennedy Says Democracy All Done in Britain"; *New York Times*, August 9, 1940, "Farley Withdraws from the Cabinet"; *Atlanta Constitution*, December 6, 1940, "The Capital Parade," by Joseph Alsop and Robert Kintner; Swift, *The Kennedy Family amidst the Gathering Storm*, 293; *New York Times*, November 12, 1940, "Kennedy Disavows Interview on War"; *Atlanta Constitution*, November 14, 1940, "Capital Parade." "I think he must be planning on resigning his post," commented Charles Lindbergh after reading the Kennedy interview. Charles A. Lindbergh, *The Wartime Journals of Charles A. Lindbergh* (New York: Harcourt Brace Jovanovich, 1970), November 11, 1940, 415. Anne Morrow Lindbergh wrote in her diary that Kennedy was "evidently very irritated at the president. . . . It almost gave you confidence to be with a man with so much sheer sense of power even though you know some of it—-maybe most of it?—was self-inflated. I felt he was the most powerful person in the United States at this moment." Anne Morrow Lindbergh, *The War Within and Without: Diaries and Letters of Anne Morrow Lindbergh, 1939–1944*, November 12, 1940, 152–53. A few weeks after Kennedy's interview, three pacifist members of the British House of Commons introduced a motion calling for immediate peace and compromise with Germany. Their motion was voted down, 342 to 4. Because these appeasers were permitted to speak in Parliament, the *New York Times* editorialized, "What now becomes of the fatuous idea that British democracy is dead or dying? Can any free country do better than this to prove that its freedom still lives?" *New York Times*, December 6, 1940, "Democracy at Its Best." Michael Beschloss, *Kennedy and Roosevelt: The Uneasy Alliance* (New York: Norton, 1980), 228–30; *New York Review of Books*, November 18, 1971, "Eleanor," by Gore Vidal; *New York Times*, December 2, 1940, "Kennedy Resigns as London Envoy to Combat War"; *Atlanta Constitution*, December 6, 1940, "The Capital Parade," by Joseph Alsop and Robert Kintner.

27. *Chicago Daily Tribune*, January 19, 1941, "Don't Enter War—Kennedy."

28. *New York Times*, January 26, 1941, "Administration Strong in Lease-Lend Battle"; *New York Times*, January 22, 1941, "Kennedy Opposes Full Power Given in Lease-Lend Bill"; Beschloss, *Kennedy and Roosevelt*, 235–38. Warren Kimball noted that Kennedy's testimony was confused and contradictory. He "refused either to condemn or support the Lend-Lease Bill but instead repeatedly stated that Britain had to be aided as quickly

and efficiently as possible. Yet during the same testimony he expressed the fear that America might be drawn into a war for which she was not prepared." Kimball, *The Most Unsordid Act*, 191. David Kaiser, *No End Save Victory* (New York: Basic Books, 2014), 325.

29. Kenneth S. Davis, *FDR: Into the Storm* (New York: Random House, 1993), 504; Marc Wortman, *1941: Fighting the Shadow War* (New York: Atlantic Monthly, 2016), 135.

30. *New York Times*, January 24, 1941, "Urges Neutrality."

31. Ibid.; *New York Times*, February 1, 1941, The Lease-Lend Bill"; *New York Times*, January 24, 1941, "Lindbergh's Formal Statement Before the House Committee"; *Los Angeles Times*, February 7, 1941, "Lindbergh Talks Again." On aid to Britain, Lindbergh said: "Our aid is not going to be sufficient and I believe we have encouraged a war in Europe that is not going to be successful." *Time*, February 3, 1941, "The Congress: Voices on 1776"; *New York Times*, October 27, 1940, "Text of Secretary Hull's Address"; Lindbergh, *Wartime Journals*, December 7 and 8, 1941, 560–61; Paul Seabury, "Charles A. Lindbergh and the Politics of Nostalgia," *History*, 1960, 143; *Los Angeles Times*, June 21, 1941, "Text of Lindbergh Plea for Isolation." As late as November 1941, Lindbergh published an article in the isolationist magazine *Scribner's Commentator* making the argument that "England and France were never in a position to win this war" and that "the only way our American life and ideals can be preserved is by staying out of this war."

32. *New York Times*, January 24, 1941, "Urges Neutrality."

33. *New York Times*, January 24, 1941, "Peace When There Is No Peace"; *New York Times*, January 24, 1941, "Lindbergh Called Pro-Nazi in Britain"; *Atlanta Constitution*, February 16, 1941, "Hitler's Lost War—III," by Dorothy Thompson; *New York Times*, January 25, 1941, "Lindbergh Praised by Reich Official"; *Washington Post*, January 25, 1941, "German Officials Take Their Hats Off to Lindbergh."

34. Lindbergh, *Wartime Journals*, January 6, 1941, 437. The *New York Times* referred to Lindbergh as "a blind young man." *New York Times*, May 20, 1940, "Col. Lindbergh's Broadcast"; *New York Times*, January 31, 1941, "Few Voters Back Lindbergh Views."

35. *New York Times*, January 23, 1941, "Thomas Pictures Democracy Upset"; *Time*, February 3, 1941, "The Congress: Voices on 1776"; *Christian Science Monitor*, January 22, 1941, "MacNider, McNary, Thomas Assail Bill." MacNider was one of the founders of the American Legion, which took a very anti-isolationist stance. MacNider was one of the few isolationists in the organization.

36. Raymond Daniell, *Civilians Must Fight* (Garden City, NY: Doubleday, 1941), 321. Daniell anticipated the story line of Philip Roth's 2004 novel *The Plot against America* in which Lindbergh wins the presidency in 1940 with Burton Wheeler as his vice-president.

37. *New York Times*, January 31, 1941, "America Acclaims Roosevelt at 59."
38. *Boston Globe*, January 31, 1941, "25,000 Jam Garden for Birthday Ball"; *New York Times*, January 31, 1941, "Celebration at Warm Springs"; *Washington Post*, January 31, 1941, "Diplomats and Statesmen."
39. *Washington Post*, January 31, 1941, "41,000 Throng Record District Celebrations of President's Birthday."
40. Langer and Gleason, *The Undeclared War*, 273; *Hartford Courant*, January 29, 1941, "Marshall Says Britain Can Whip Germany If Aided." Warren Kimball discusses the Roosevelt administration's avoidance of the issue of convoys: "The Administration still managed to avoid any discussion of the real question—would it order the convoying of the ships bringing Lend-Lease goods to Britain?" Kimball, *The Most Unsordid Act*, 180–81.
41. *New York Times*, January 31, 1941, "Textual Excerpts from the Speech by Reichsfuehrer Adolf Hitler"; *New York Times*, January 31, 1941, "A Reply to Roosevelt"; *London Times*, January 31, 1941, "Hitler Asks for Loyalty" and "The Decisive Phase."
42. *New York Times*, January 31, 1941, "Capital Is Cool to Hitler Threat"; *Atlanta Constitution*, January 31, 1941, "George Terms Hitler Speech a Morale-Builder"; *New York Times*, January 31, 1941, "When Hitler Threatens."
43. Floor Debate in House of Representatives, February 3, 1941, in McJimsey, *Documentary History of the Presidency of Franklin D. Roosevelt*, 2:215, 219. See also Document 105, 2:440–43.
44. *New York Times*, February 9, 1941, "House Votes Lease-Lend Bill"; *Washington Post*, February 10, 1941, "Taft Urges 7 Specific Restrictions."
45. *Washington Post*, February 10, 1941, "Text of Churchill Speech"; *Chicago Daily Tribune*, February 11, 1941, "Churchill Talk Was Aimed at Senate."
46. Wayne Cole, *America First: The Battle against Intervention* (Madison: University of Wisconsin Press, 1953), 47–49. During the election of 1940, Republicans also accused FDR of wanting to be a dictator. Sinclair Lewis, the author of *It Can't Happen Here*, a novel about a dictatorship in America, said that there was "no man in the world less likely to want, or to be able, to become dictator" than President Roosevelt. *Daily Boston Globe*, November 2, 1940, " 'Dictator' Cry Draws Sinclair Lewis' Fire."

The America First Committee's members distributed hundreds of thousands of pamphlets, automobile stickers, and buttons around the country. Money poured in, especially in the Midwest, from wealthy businessmen like Colonel Robert McCormick, the publisher of the *Chicago Daily Tribune*, William Regnery, a Chicago textile manufacturer, Sterling Morton, the president of Morton Salt Company, Lessing Rosenwald, the former chairman of Sears Roebuck, and Jay Hormel, the Minnesota meatpacker. There were small contributors, too—the twenty-four-year-old John F. Kennedy sent a check for $100 with a note saying, "What you are all doing is vital." Justus Doenecke, ed., *In Danger Undaunted: The*

Anti-Interventionist Movement of 1940–1941 (Stanford: Hoover Institution Press, 1990), 8, 37, 41, 409, 10, 16, 11; David Reynolds, *From Munich to Pearl Harbor* (Chicago: Ivan R. Dee, 2001), 111.

47. *Chicago Daily Tribune*, February 21, 1941, "Nye: 30 Senators for War!"

48. Lynne Olson, *Those Angry Days: Roosevelt, Lindbergh and America's Fight over World War II* (New York: Random House, 2013), 66.

49. *New York Times*, February 21, 1941, "Wheeler and Nye Carry Fight Here"; *Chicago Daily Tribune*, February 21, 1941, "Nye: 30 Senators for War!" It was later revealed that the AFC had received support from the German consulate in Washington. Hans Thomsen, the German chargé d'affaires, believed that it was important, as he informed the Foreign Office in Berlin, to continue supporting isolationist groups, "which consider Lindbergh to be their greatest protagonist." And he was especially pleased that "the German-American ethnic group in the Middle West . . . was persuaded by [our] agents to give backing to the America First Committee." Thomsen to German Foreign Ministry, February 9, 1941, in *Documents on German Foreign Policy, 1918–1945, Series D, 1937–1945*, 10 vols. (Washington, DC: U.S. Government Printing Office, 1947–), 8:61. An announcer on German shortwave radio asked Americans to cable him "collect"—the Germans would foot the bill—and indicate which radio programs they would like to receive from Germany. "We are always glad to get your suggestions as to our programs as a whole," he said. "Don't spare us any criticism you may have, and, of course, if you have any praise, we are only too glad to receive it." One responder expressed a wish for a broadcast of Hitler's funeral. *New York Times*, February 19, 1941, "Ill-Wishers Insult Hitler by Cable Collect."

50. *Chicago Daily Tribune*, February 1, 1941, "Mothers Assail Roosevelt"; Glen Jeansonne, *Women of the Far Right: The Mothers Movement and World War II* (Chicago: University of Chicago Press, 1996), 10, 74–79. For years, as Jeansonne writes, Dilling had been plying anti-Semitism, anti-Communism, and racism, asserting that Roosevelt was a puppet of Jewish Communists and should be put in jail for dragging the country toward war. On the other hand, she had only good things to say about the Nazis, especially about what she called their forbearance in the face of the "hysterical cries for war of New Deal officials." Dilling's backers included Henry Ford and other midwestern industrialists and also Hans Thomsen, the German chargé d'affaires in Washington. Thomsen informed the Foreign Ministry in Berlin on February 8 that he had taken "large propaganda steps" to influence the Lend-Lease debate. "There is being prepared, with our financial support," he wrote, "a women's march on Washington, accompanied by sensational publicity." His measures had incurred "considerable expense," but he assured his handlers in Berlin that they were a necessary "counteraction" to what he described as a massive British propaganda campaign of lies and bribes in an effort to

speed passage of FDR's proposal. *Documents on German Foreign Policy, 1918–1945, Series D, 1937–1945,* 12:60–61; *New York Times,* February 9, 1941, "Leaders of Youth Protest Aid Bill"; *Atlanta Constitution,* July 23, 1941, "Fiery Author, 2 Others Indicted in Plot." Other protesters included six thousand members of the American Youth Congress who gathered at the Washington Monument to protest against Lend-Lease. Document 74, Extracts from Testimony Before Senate Committee on Foreign Relations, Late February, in McJimsey, *Documentary History of the Franklin D. Roosevelt Presidency,* 2:309.

51. *New York Times,* February 20, 1941, "First Lady to Face War 'If Necessary.'"

52. *New York Times,* February 1, 1941, "Secretary Knox's Statement to Senate Group"; Langer and Gleason, *The Undeclared War,* 277.

53. *New York Times,* February 12, 1941, "Warns US of Axis."

54. Kimball, *The Most Unsordid Act,* 190; *New York Times,* February 7, 1941, "Lindbergh's Statement Before the Foreign Relations Committee"; *New York Times,* February 7, 1941, "Air Power the Crux."

55. *New York Times,* February 8, 1941, "Kansan Emphatic"; *New York Times,* February 9, 1941, "Text of Landon's Statement"; *Los Angeles Times,* February 9, 1941, "Landon Raps War Aid Bill."

56. *Chicago Daily Tribune,* February 8, 1941, "It's President's Own War! Editor Tells Senators"; *New York Times,* February 8, 1941, "New Yorkers Say Civil Uprising Will Come Here If We Enter War." Famed historian Charles Beard also testified; his book *A Foreign Policy for America* had come out in May 1940 and offered a defense of isolationism. There was not a single sentence in his book, remarked his fellow historian Allan Nevins, that gave "any indication whatever that the Western world is being shaken today by the mightiest conflict of moral forces in centuries; that democracy is struggling for its life against fascism." In his testimony Beard told the committee that the Lend-Lease bill was a measure "for waging an undeclared war" and said there was no guarantee that it would "buy peace or keep us out of war." *New York Times,* May 20, 1940, "Two Views of America's Part," by Allan Nevins; *Hartford Courant,* February 5, 1941, "Wheeler-Roosevelt Feud Flares Anew."

57. Willkie to Mark Sullivan, November 24 and 25, 1940, quoted in Steve Neal, *Dark Horse: A Biography of Wendell Willkie* (Garden City, NY: Doubleday, 1984), 179; Herbert Parmet, *Never Again: A President Runs for a Third Term* (New York: Macmillan, 1968), 278; *New York Times,* January 13, 1941, "Willkie Statement on the War Aid Bill." The isolationist *Chicago Daily Tribune* editorialized that Roosevelt's proposal "is a bill for the destruction of the American Republic" and for "unlimited dictatorship." *Chicago Daily Tribune,* January 12, 1941, "A Bill to Destroy the Republic." See also Kimball, *The Most Unsordid Act,* 156.

58. *Time,* February 24, 1941, "Republicans: The Undefeated."

59. *New York Times*, February 12, 1941, "Verbatim Testimony of Wendell Willkie."

60. Neal, *Dark Horse*, 204; *New York Times*, February 12, 1941, "Warns US of Axis."

61. Pa Watson, Memo to FDR, January 17, 1941, in McJimsey, *Documentary History of the Franklin D. Roosevelt Presidency*, 2:Document 24.

62. *Documents on German Foreign Policy, 1918–1945, Series D, 1937–1945*, February 11–June 22, 1941, 12:61–62.

63. Grace Tully, *F.D.R.: My Boss* (New York: Scribner's, 1949), 58.

64. *New York Times*, February 12, 1941, "Financial Markets"; *New York Times*, January 1, 1941, "Few Voters Back Lindbergh Views"; *Nation*, December 13, 1941, "The Future of the Republican Party," by Wendell Willkie et al., 609–12; *New York Times*, February 13, 1941, "Asks Positive Plan"; *Los Angeles Times*, February 13, 1941, "Willkie Challenges Republicans"; *Christian Science Monitor*, February 13, 1941, "Text of Willkie Talk to Republicans"; Neal, *Dark Horse*, 206.

65. *New York Times*, January 13, 1941, "Congress Reaction on Willkie Varies"; *Chicago Daily Tribune*, January 14, 1941, "Wheeler Warns Film Makers on War Propaganda"; *Christian Science Monitor*, January 14, 1941, "Wheeler Charges Newsreels." In September 1941, when the Senate held hearings on Hollywood movies, Wendell Willkie was the defense attorney for the Hollywood studio heads. In a statement to the committee members, Willkie wrote: "On behalf of the motion-picture industry and its personnel, I wish to put on the record this simple truth: We make no pretense of friendliness to Nazi Germany nor to the objectives and goals of this ruthless dictatorship. We abhor everything which Hitler represents. . . . In simple terms, the United States stands for the right of an individual to lead a decent life. Hitler and his Nazis stand for the opposite. The motion-picture industry wants no compromise between these two concepts. . . . The industry desires to *plead guilty* to sharing, with their fellow citizens, a horror of Hitler's Nazis; and to plead guilty to doing everything within its power to help the national-defense program." *New York Times*, September 9, 1941, "Willkie Attacks Inquiry on Films." See also *Propaganda in Motion Pictures, Hearings Before a Subcommittee of the Committee on Interstate Commerce*, United States Senate, Seventy-Seventh Congress, Sessions on S. Res. 152, September 1941 (Washington, DC: U.S. Government Printing Office, 1942), 18–19.

66. *New York Times*, June 21, 1940, "The Screen: 'The Mortal Storm,'" by Bosley Crowther; *New York Times*, January 19, 1941, "Shall the Screen Remain Free?"; *New York Times*, March 9, 1941, "Films for Defense"; *New York Times*, January 26, 1941, "Defense of the Arts," by Brooks Atkinson. As an example of Hollywood's superficiality, Atkinson quoted a remark made by a gentleman in *Andy Hardy's Private Secretary*, the latest

Mickey Rooney comedy. "When I see our three children going up the steps of that fine, big school building," says the man to Judge Hardy, "I know what is wrong with America." Naturally the judge inquires, "What?" The reply: "Absolutely nothing!" *New York Times*, November 3, 1940, "Problem in Defense," by Brooks Atkinson.

67. *The Secret Diary of Harold L. Ickes*, vol. 3, *The Lowering Clouds* (New York: Simon and Schuster, 1954), 447; *New York Times*, February 28, 1941, "President Calls Aid Bill Big Factor."

68. *New York Times*, February 16, 1941, "Mr. Goldwyn Bows Out"; *New York Times*, January 7, 1941, "Praised by Sergeant York."

Chapter Eight. Joint Talks

1. *New York Times*, January 10, 1941, "U.S. Aid Is Decisive, Churchill Asserts."

2. David Reynolds, *The Creation of the Anglo-American Alliance, 1937–1941* (Chapel Hill: University of North Carolina Press, 1982), 175–76.

3. Ibid.

4. Winston Churchill and Martin Gilbert, *The Churchill War Papers: The Ever-Widening War*, 3 vols. (New York: Norton, 2000), 3:52; Robert Sherwood, *Roosevelt and Hopkins* (New York: Harper and Brothers, 1948), 237. FDR's frequent correspondent the English political scientist Harold Laski also had confidence in Halifax. Writing in the *Washington Post*, Laski remarked that he sensed "something of the genuine saint" in the new British ambassador. Although Halifax "knows little or nothing of the working class, save as a great landlord; and he knows little or nothing of the middle class," Laski commended him for sharing with FDR "an ethical approach to politics." *Washington Post*, January 11, 1941, "Halifax's Character," by Harold Laski. Reynolds, *The Creation of the Anglo-American Alliance*, 175–76; Jonathan Schneer, *Ministers at War: Winston Churchill and His War Cabinet* (New York: Basic Books, 2015), 27–28, 54.

5. James R. Leutze, *Bargaining for Supremacy: Anglo-American Naval Collaboration, 1937–1941* (Chapel Hill: University of North Carolina Press, 1977), 220; *Christian Science Monitor*, January 25, 1941, "Halifax Outlines British Needs"; *Washington Post*, January 31, 1941, "Roosevelt's Pledge to Hitler Seen in Pledge to Halifax." Viscount Halifax was not Churchill's first choice to be the new British ambassador. See Reynolds, *The Creation of the Anglo-American Alliance*, 175–76.

6. *Hartford Courant*, January 25, 1941, "FDR Welcomes Halifax."

7. Sherwood, *Roosevelt and Hopkins*, 247; Thomas Parrish, *Roosevelt and Marshall* (New York: W. Morrow, 1989), 162.

8. Sherwood, *Roosevelt and Hopkins*, 230–31; Parrish, *Roosevelt and Marshall*, 127.

9. Lynne Olson, *Those Angry Days: Roosevelt, Lindbergh and America's Fight over World War II* (New York: Random House, 2013), 63; Sherwood, *Roosevelt and Hopkins,* notes at 948–49.

10. Parrish, *Roosevelt and Marshall,* 125, 155; Jon Meacham, *Franklin and Winston: An Intimate Portrait of an Epic Friendship* (New York: Random House, 2003), 94; Sherwood, *Roosevelt and Hopkins,* 25, 257; Lynne Olson, *Citizens of London: The Americans Who Stood with Britain in Its Darkest, Finest Hour* (New York: Random House, 2010), 64.

11. Sherwood, *Roosevelt and Hopkins,* notes at 949. The two leaders communicated directly with each other by telegram and by sending trusted emissaries, including Hopkins, back and forth across the Atlantic to serve as reporters, message bearers, negotiators, and administrators. Sometimes, when the prime minister wanted to learn the president's reaction to a new idea of his, he would write to Hopkins, saying, as Sherwood put it, "If you think well of it, perhaps you would ask our great friend for his opinion on the following proposal." And Hopkins, having sounded out Roosevelt, would reply that their friend didn't "think well of it," or "It is felt here that you should go ahead with your proposal." Those ad hoc methods permitted Churchill and Roosevelt to pursue their own instincts and ideas, to develop strategies and authorize experiments—in short, to do things each in his own way—and together. Sherwood, *Roosevelt and Hopkins,* 269.

12. *Washington Post,* January 26, 1941, "U. S. Observers Here to Report on British War"; *Atlanta Constitution,* January 25, 1941, "Lord Halifax Urges U.S. to Speed Aid."

    See also British and American Plans, http://www.history.army.mil/books/wwii/SP1941-42/chapter3.htm. Those British staff officers would remain in Washington as the permanent British Joint Staff Mission, which would evolve into the Combined Chiefs of Staff.

13. Reynolds, *The Creation of the Anglo-American Alliance,* 60–62.

14. George C. Marshall: Interviews and Reminiscences for Forrest C. Pogue, tape 9, 283, http://marshallfoundation.org/library/collection/george-c-marshall-interviews-reminiscences/#!/collection=341.

15. Stark to Marshall, November 29, 1940, in Leutze, *Bargaining for Supremacy,* 203. Admiral Stark received permission to show his memorandum to the British naval attaché, Captain Arthur W. Clarke.

16. Stark to Ghormley, November 16, 1940, in Leutze, *Bargaining for Supremacy,* 194–96, emphasis added. See also Mark A. Stoler, *Allies and Adversaries: The Joint Chiefs of Staff, the Grand Alliance, and U.S. Strategy in World War II* (Chapel Hill: University of North Carolina Press, 2000), 30–32, 37, 280, note 37. See Plan Dog Memo, https://en.wikisource.org/wiki/Plan_dog_memo. See also Steven T. Ross, *American War Plans, 1941–1945* (London: F. Cass, 1997), 281–300; Forrest C. Pogue, *George C. Marshall: Ordeal and Hope, 1939–1942,* 4 vols. (New York: Viking, 1965), 2:126ff.

17. Cabinet Meeting on Friday, November 29, 1940, in *The Secret Diary of Harold L. Ickes*, vol. 3, *The Lowering Clouds* (New York: Simon and Schuster 1954), 388–89. See also Leutze, *Bargaining for Supremacy*, 205; Sherwood, *Roosevelt and Hopkins*, 274.

18. Pogue, *George C. Marshall*, 2:128; Marshall, Interviews and Reminiscences, tape 9, 284; Leutze, *Bargaining for Supremacy*, 205; Mark M. Lowenthal, "Roosevelt and the Coming of War," *Journal of Contemporary History*, 16, 1981, 427.

19. The Henry Lewis Stimson Diaries, January 16, 1941, 109, Yale University Library; Mark Skinner Watson, *Chief of Staff: Prewar Plans and Preparations* (Washington, DC: Historical Division, U.S. Department of the Army, 1950), 124; FDR to Frank Knox, December 23, 1940, in *F.D.R.: His Personal Letters*, ed. Elliott Roosevelt (New York: Duell, Sloan and Pearce, 1950), 2:1089. See also James MacGregor Burns, *Roosevelt: The Soldier of Freedom* (New York: Harcourt Brace Jovanovich, 1970), 84; James MacGregor Burns, *Roosevelt: The Lion and the Fox* (New York: Harcourt Brace, 1956), 409.

20. Watson, *Chief of Staff*, 124–25; Memorandum for General Gerow, January 17, 1941, in *The Papers of George Catlett Marshall*, 6 vols., ed. Larry I. Bland et al. (Baltimore: Johns Hopkins University Press, 1986), 2:392; Stoler, *Allies and Adversaries*, 35; Leutze, *Bargaining for Supremacy*, 214.

21. Stoler, *Allies and Adversaries*, 13, 37; William T. Johnsen, *The Origins of the Grand Alliance: Anglo-American Military Collaboration from the Panay Incident to Pearl Harbor* (Lexington: University Press of Kentucky, 2016), 131–55; Leutze, *Bargaining for Supremacy*, 224, 207.

22. Leutze, *Bargaining for Supremacy*, 218, 223; Stoler, *Allies and Adversaries*, 10–14.

23. Burns, *Roosevelt: The Soldier of Freedom*, 86; Mark M. Lowenthal, *Leadership and Indecision: American War Planning and Policy Process, 1937–1942*, 2 vols. (New York: Garland, 1988), 1:449; Stetson Conn and Byron Fairchild, *The Framework of Hemisphere Defense* (Washington, DC: Office of the Chief of Military History, Department of the Army, 1960), 998.

24. FDR to Francis Sayre, December 31, 1940, in Roosevelt, *F.D.R.: His Personal Letters*, 2:1094.

25. Leutze, *Bargaining for Supremacy*, 234–35. In fact, the British had been asking the United States for a U.S. fleet in Singapore since 1938. See Johnsen, *The Origins of the Grand Alliance*, ch. 7, "Full Dress Talks."

26. Stoler, *Allies and Adversaries*, 38; Memo from Army Delegates to CofS, February 12, 1941, in Louis Morton, *Strategy and Command: The First Two Years* (Washington, DC: Center of Military History, U.S. Army, 2000), 88; Bland et al., *Papers of George Catlett Marshall*, February 12, 1941, 2:410, 426; Lowenthal, "Roosevelt and the Coming of War," 426.

27. Leutze, *Bargaining for Supremacy*, 244.

28. Samuel Eliot Morison, *Strategy and Compromise* (Boston: Little, Brown, 1958), 13.
29. Leutze, *Bargaining for Supremacy*, 211.
30. Churchill to A. V. Alexander and Admiral Pound, February 17, 1941, Secret, in Churchill and Gilbert, *The Churchill War Papers*, 3:235–36; Leutze, *Bargaining for Supremacy*, 241–42, 297, note 28; Johnsen, *The Origins of the Grand Alliance*, 140–42.
31. Johnsen, *The Origins of the Grand Alliance*, 143–46.
32. Leutze, *Bargaining for Supremacy*, 246, 248, 252; Bland et al., *Papers of George Catlett Marshall*, February 12, 1941, 2:426, 410.
33. Robert Sherwood, *Roosevelt and Hopkins*, 273; Leutze, *Bargaining for Supremacy*, 253. The British themselves hardly regarded the ABC agreements as "sacrosanct," noting that the Americans, "with their usual suspicious outlook," accused them of bad faith if they departed from it.
34. Morton, *Strategy and Command*, 79–84.
35. Churchill to Roosevelt, March 8, 1941, Correspondence C-64x, not sent, C-61x, 137, and C-62x, in Warren F. Kimball, ed., *Churchill and Roosevelt: The Complete Correspondence*, 3 vols. (Princeton: Princeton University Press, 1984), 1:141; Leutze, *Bargaining for Supremacy*, 252, 138–39.
36. Winston Churchill, *The Second World War*, vol. 2, *Their Finest Hour* (Boston: Houghton, Mifflin, 1949), 557.

Chapter Nine. The Flames of World Conflagration Lick Everywhere

1. *Life*, February 17, 1941, "The American Century," by Henry Luce.
2. Democrats Bennett Clark of Missouri and Guy Gillette of Iowa voted against Lend-Lease while Republican Wallace White of Maine voted for it.
3. *Washington Post*, February 18, 1941, "U.S. Will Fight Hitler If Necessary"; *Los Angeles Times*, February 18, 1941, "Senate Hears Cry of 'Fight If We Must!' "; *Atlanta Constitution*, February 18, 1941, "U.S. Will Not Let England Fall"; *Los Angeles Times*, February 26, 1941, "Senate Battles Eighth Day."
4. *Los Angeles Times*, February 26, 1941, "Senate Battles Eighth Day."
5. *Atlanta Constitution*, February 18, 1941, "U.S. Will Not Let England Fall"; *New York Times*, February 18, 1941, "Hitler Defeat Aim."
6. *Christian Science Monitor*, March 5, 1941, "Debate on Lease Amendments"; *New York Times*, February 22, 1941, "Aid Bill Means War, 3 Senators Assert"; *London Times*, February 25, 1941, "Hitler Threatens Again."
7. *Washington Post*, February 23, 1941, "Senate Poll Gives Aid Bill 52 Votes."
8. *New York Times*, February 25, 1941, "Aid Bill Is Delayed in the Senate"; *Atlanta Constitution*, March 5, 1941, "Nye Assails Great Britain as

Aggressor"; *Christian Science Monitor,* March 5, 1941, "Debate on Lease Amendments Promises Early Senate Vote"; *Christian Science Monitor,* February 20, 1941, "Senate Vote on Aid Bill Expected within Week"; Parrish, *Roosevelt and Marshall,* 195.

9. *Daily Boston Globe,* March 7, 1941, "Compton Asks Walsh, Lodge End Lease-Lend Discussion"; *Atlanta Constitution,* March 4, 1941, "The Capital Parade," by Joseph Alsop and Robert Kintner.

10. *Chicago Daily Tribune,* January 12, 1941, "A Bill to Destroy the Republic"; *Washington Post,* February 14, 1941, "The Gallup Poll"; *Washington Post,* February 12, 1941, "Four out of Five Sections Favor Lease-Lend Bill."

11. *New York Times,* February 20, 1941, "Liaison with Britain."

12. *Washington Post,* February 18, 1941, "President Sets Up Machinery to Expedite Aid to Britain"; William L. Langer and S. Everett Gleason, *The Undeclared War, 1940–1941* (New York: Harper and Brothers, 1953), 420–21; Winston Churchill, *The Second World War,* vol. 2, *Their Finest Hour* (Boston: Houghton, Mifflin, 1949), 573; Robert C. Stern, *The US Navy and the War in Europe* (Annapolis, MD: Naval Institute Press, 2012), 34; Lynne Olson, *Those Angry Days: Roosevelt, Lindbergh and America's Fight over World War II* (New York: Random House, 2013), 284, 73–74.

13. *New York Times,* March 1, 1941, "President Shapes Defense Ministry"; *New York Times,* March 5, 1941, "President to Run Defense Program"; Robert Sherwood, *Roosevelt and Hopkins* (New York: Harper and Brothers, 1948), 267–68.

14. Langer and Gleason, *The Undeclared War,* 282. The Senate committee had voted Ellender's proposal down, but he resurrected it during the debate on the Senate floor.

15. *New York Times,* February 26, 1941, "President Is Firm."

16. The Henry Lewis Stimson Diaries, March 2, 1941, 49–51, Yale University Library.

17. Ibid., 52; *New York Times,* January 30, 1941, "Four Amendments." The president of the Massachusetts Institute of Technology, Karl Compton, scolded the two Massachusetts senators, Democrat David Walsh and Republican Henry Cabot Lodge, pointing out the "serious dangers in further prolonged discussions of the bill."

18. *New York Times,* March 4, 1941, "Aid Bill Foes Balk."

19. *New York Times,* March 5, 1941, "Aid Bill Foes End 'General' Debate"; *Time,* March 10, 1941, "The Congress: Peacemongers"; Parrish, *Roosevelt and Marshall,* 257.

20. *New York Times,* March 7, 1941, "32 Major Changes Asked for Aid Bill."

21. Langer and Gleason, *The Undeclared War,* 281–83; *New York Times,* March 7, 1941, "Aid Bill's Backers Offer Substitute"; Stimson Diaries, March 4, 1941, 55; Warren F. Kimball, *The Most Unsordid Act: Lend-Lease, 1939–1941* (Baltimore: Johns Hopkins University Press, 1969), 211–16.

22. *New York Times*, March 8, 1941, "Convoy Ban Beaten"; Kimball, *The Most Unsordid Act*, 216.

23. *Daily Boston Globe*, March 9, 1941, "Bombs Trap Londoners in Night Club"; *New York Times*, March 10, 1941, "Nazis Strike Hard at London Again"; *Daily Boston Globe*, January 30, 1941, "Ernie Pyle in London."

24. James MacGregor Burns, *Roosevelt: The Soldier of Freedom* (New York: Harcourt Brace Jovanovich, 1970), 49.

25. It was fortunate for its success that Lend-Lease needed only a majority vote, for it was two votes short of a two-thirds majority. The Versailles Treaty that contained the provision for the League of Nations had also been approved by a simple majority in the Senate in 1920 but, with the opposition led by Senator Lodge's father, it failed to muster the two-thirds vote in the Senate that it needed. *Washington Post*, March 12, 1941, "End of an Era," by Ernest Lindley.

26. *Washington Post*, March 9, 1941, "Good Feeling Pervades Senate After Lend-Lease Bill Passes"; *New York Times*, March 9, 1941, "All Curbs Down"; *Time*, March 17, 1941, "Step into the Dark"; Marshall to Henry Cabot Lodge Jr., March 4, 1941, in *The Papers of George Catlett Marshall*, 6 vols., ed. Larry I. Bland et al. (Baltimore: Johns Hopkins University Press, 1986), 2:436. Democratic senator Allen Ellender of Louisiana voted for the bill, apparently not minding that his amendment had been voted down.

27. Kimball, *The Most Unsordid Act*, 220; *Chicago Daily Tribune*, March 12, 1941, "Dictator Bill Signed"; *Daily Boston Globe*, March 12, 1941, "McCormack and Martin Join in Dramatic Pleas for Unity." Explaining his unexpected switch to a yes vote, Fish claimed that the House had voted only on the Senate's amendments, not on the entire bill, which he continued to believe was a "dangerous delegation of power to the President." It was a strangely mistaken interpretation of a vote to reconcile House and Senate bills from a man who had served in the House since 1920.

28. *New York Times*, March 12, 1941, "Roosevelt Signs Aid Measure"; Kimball, *The Most Unsordid Act*, 220.

29. Stimson Diaries, March 11, 1941, 78; Text of Speech by Stimson to Conference of Public Relations Officers in the auditorium of Public Health Service, March 11, 1941, in Stimson Diaries, March 11, 1941, 80–82.

30. Stimson Diaries, March 11 and 12, 1941, 78, 85–86. In late March 1941, Congress approved FDR's request for $7 billion for military aid for nations fighting the Axis. In April 1941, the writers, artists, and musicians who belonged to the Dutch Treat Club held their annual dinner in the Waldorf-Astoria Hotel in New York. In one of the skits they performed after the dinner, the "president" made a speech in which he declared that he was so much greater than George Washington. The Republic's first president, he explained, was said to have thrown a silver dollar across the

Potomac, while "I have just thrown seven billion dollars across the Atlantic—and it didn't even interfere with my fishing!" *New York Times*, April 5, 1941, "Dutch Treat Puts Gridiron on Pan."

31. *Washington Post*, March 21, 1941, "The Gallup Poll"; Stimson Diaries, March 17, 1941, 94.

32. *New York Times*, March 20, 1941, "News Hitler Couldn't Kill"; *New York Times*, March 16, 1941, "America Acts"; *New York Times*, March 16, 1941, "Nazis See Imperialism Here."

33. *Atlanta Constitution*, March 17, 1941, "No Power Can Save England"; *New York Times*, March 17, 1941, "Derides U.S. Help"; *New York Times*, March 17, 1941, "The Text of Hitler's Memorial Day Address."

34. *New York Times*, March 13, 1941, "British Grateful"; *Daily Boston Globe*, March 13, 1941, "Churchill Hails Aid Bill"; *Time*, March 24, 1941, "Foreign News: The World and H.R. 1776"; *New York Times*, March 19, 1941, "Mr. Churchill's Address." An original copy of Magna Carta had been displayed at the 1939 New York World's Fair in Queens, New York. Later it would be housed for safekeeping at Fort Knox until after the war, along with original copies of the Declaration of Independence and the American Constitution. *New York Times*, February 4, 1941, "Our Peril Pictured"; *New York Times*, January 11, 1946, "Copy of Magna Carta on Way Home Today."

35. *Time*, March 24, 1941, "Foreign News: The World and H.R. 1776"; *New York Times*, March 19, 1941, "Mr. Churchill's Address"; *Time*, March 24, 1941, "The Presidency: Decision." British songwriter George Formby wrote the song; it was first performed on January 23, 1941, accompanied by ukulele and orchestra. https://www.youtube.com/watch?v=Og3EKwG5WKU. Representative Martin Sweeney of Ohio, opposed to Lend-Lease, wrote another song, sung to the tune of "God Bless America": "God save America from British rule . . . / God save America / From a king named George." Kimball, *The Most Unsordid Act*, 187.

36. *New York Times*, March 2, 1941, "King George Goes to Greet Winant"; *New York Times*, March 2, 1941, "Press Emphasizes Gesture"; *Los Angeles Times*, March 2, 1941, "Formality Ignored by King"; *Time*, March 10, 1941, "Foreign News: King's Greeting." In the fall of 1940, the CBS radio correspondent in Berlin, William Shirer, lunched with Winant and reported that "more than any other American in public life whom I know he understands the social forces and changes that have been at work in the last decade both at home and in Europe." William Shirer, "The Hour Will Come When One of Us Will Break," September 1940, in *Reporting World War II*, 2 vols., ed. Samuel Hynes et al. (New York: Library of America, 1995), 1:113.

37. *New York Times*, February 16, 1941, "Conant Off to Head War Science Study"; Stimson Diaries, February 10, 1941, 20. On June 18, 1940, Churchill warned the House of Commons that the Nazis were using "the

lights of perverted science" to create the "new Dark Age" they wanted to impose on mankind. He may have been referring to new weapons—for example, chemical weapons and proximity fuses—or to eugenics. Churchill, *Their Finest Hour*, 226.

38. Sherwood, *Roosevelt and Hopkins*, 265.

39. Ibid., 266–67.

40. Ibid.

41. *New York Times*, March 16, 1941, "Heavy Barrage Guards London"; *Time*, March 24, 1941, "The Presidency: Decision"; *Washington Post*, March 16, 1941, "Fun Lightens Correspondent Corps Dinner"; *New York Times*, March 16, 1941, "All Must Sacrifice."

42. *New York Times*, March 16, 1941, "President's Address on Aid to Democracies."

43. *New York Times*, February 14, 1941, "Sentiment for Bill Rising"; *New York Times*, March 15, 1941, "Roosevelt Trend at Record High." In March 1941, 80 percent of Americans believed that American entry in the war in Europe was inevitable. In April, when voters were asked, "If it appeared certain that there was no other way to defeat Germany and Italy except to go to war against them, would you be in favor of the United States going into the war?" 68 percent answered yes.

44. *Time*, March 24, 1941, "The Presidency: Decision"; Sherwood, *Roosevelt and Hopkins*, 267.

45. *New York Times*, August 13, 1919, "Lodge Outlines Five Reservations to League Plan"; *New York Times*, August 16, 1919, "Report Wilson Bound to Carry Treaty Unaltered."

46. James MacGregor Burns, *The Workshop of Democracy* (New York: Knopf, 1985), 411.

47. George Wickersham, "The Senate and Our Foreign Relations," *Foreign Affairs*, 2, 2, December 1923, 177; Allan Nevins, *America in World Affairs* (New York: Oxford University Press, 1942), 9.

48. *New York Times*, August 13, 1919, "Lodge Outlines Five Reservations to League Plan." An example of FDR's realism: he chose not to veto the Neutrality Acts of 1935 and 1937, but he did convince Congress to repeal the arms embargo in 1939.

49. *New York Times*, March 12, 1941, "We Shall Not Turn Back." A Gallup poll revealed that 56 percent of Americans supported passage of Lend-Lease, with 20 percent opposed and the rest undecided. Among young men of draft age, 55 percent supported the bill, with 24 percent opposed. *New York Times*, March 7, 1941, "Men of Draft Age Favor Lease-Lend Bill." See also *Daily Boston Globe*, February 21, 1941, "The American Century," by Dorothy Thompson; Henry L. Stimson, "The Challenge to Americans," *Foreign Affairs*, 26, 1, October 1947, 6, 14.

50. Samuel I. Rosenman, *Working with Roosevelt* (New York: Da Capo, 1967), 273.

Chapter Ten. The Third Hundred Days

1. In his speeches and press conferences, the president did not hesitate to lash out at the isolationist rearguard, exposing the barrenness of the anti-interventionist movement. The isolationists, however, continued their assaults on Roosevelt until the attack on Pearl Harbor. But after Lend-Lease became law, isolationists lost much credibility and acquired the taint of the un-American. Even Charles Lindbergh lost the aura and glamour of heroic patriotism.

2. The Henry Lewis Stimson Diaries, March 17, 1941, 94, Yale University Library; *New York Times*, May 24, 1941, "Lindbergh Joins in Wheeler Plea"; *Washington Post*, April 24, 1941, "Crowd Beats Lindbergh's Detractors."

3. Samuel I. Rosenman, *Working with Roosevelt* (New York: Da Capo, 1967), 272; Stimson Diaries, March 17, 1941, 94.

4. Justus D. Doenecke, "An Ambiguous Legacy," in *Debating Franklin D. Roosevelt's Foreign Policies, 1933–1945*, ed. Justus D. Doenecke and Mark A. Stoler (Lanham, MD: Rowman and Littlefield, 2005), 38. FDR's critics—Taft, Wheeler, and others—insisted that FDR was actively steering the country into war. *New York Times*, October 29, 1941, "Roosevelt 'Trick' Charged by Taft." James MacGregor Burns wrote that FDR "had become hostage to Hitler's strategy.... The president was imprisoned in his policy of aid short of war." Burns, *The Crosswinds of Freedom* (New York: Knopf, 1989), 170.

5. William Manchester, *The Last Lion: Winston Churchill* (Boston: Little, Brown 1983), 392.

6. Kenneth S. Davis, *FDR: The War President, 1940–1943* (New York: Random House, 2000), 274.

7. Jon Meacham, *Franklin and Winston: An Intimate Portrait of an Epic Friendship* (New York: Random House, 2003), 120; Davis, *FDR: The War President*, 274.

8. William L. Langer and S. Everett Gleason, *The Undeclared War, 1940–1941* (New York: Harper and Brothers, 1953), 680–81.

9. The Atlantic Charter: Official Statement on Meeting between the President and Prime Minister Churchill, August 14, 1941, in *Public Papers and Addresses of Franklin D. Roosevelt* (hereafter *PPA*), 13 vols., ed. Samuel I. Rosenman (New York: Macmillan, 1941), 10:314–15; Daniel Todman, *Britain's War: Into Battle, 1937–1941* (Oxford: Oxford University Press, 2016), 681–83.

10. James MacGregor Burns, *Roosevelt: The Soldier of Freedom* (New York: Harcourt Brace Jovanovich, 1970), 129–31; Todman, *Britain's War*, 548, 673.

11. One newspaper called the charter "in effect an Anglo-American trusteeship for world security." *Christian Science Monitor*, August 15, 1941, "U.S.

and Britain: Trustees for Future Peace." Frankfurter to FDR, August 18, 1941, quoted in Burns, *Roosevelt: The Soldier of Freedom*, 131.

12. Meacham, *Franklin and Winston*, 121; *New York Times*, September 14, 1941, "Two Men with One Idea."

13. *New York Times*, August 22, 1941, "The President's Message"; Universal Declaration of Human Rights, http://www.un.org/en/universal-declaration-human-rights/. See also Elizabeth Borgwardt, *A New Deal for the World* (Cambridge, MA: Harvard University Press, 2007), 29. In his autobiography, Nelson Mandela wrote: "Change was in the air in the 1940's. . . . Inspired by the Atlantic Charter and the fight of the Allies against tyranny and oppression, the A.N.C. created its own charter, called African Claims, which called for full citizenship for all Africans, the right to buy land, and the repeal of all discriminatory legislation." *New York Times*, November 30, 1994, "How a Leader Emerged."

14. Roosevelt, Fireside Chat, December 9, 1941, in *PPA*, 10:528.

15. Henry L. Stimson, "The Challenge to Americans," *Foreign Affairs*, 26, 1, October 1947, 6.

16. Alan Brinkley, *The Publisher: Henry Luce and His American Century* (New York: Knopf, 2010), 273; Henry Lewis Stimson and McGeorge Bundy, *On Active Service* (New York: Harper, 1948), 360–63; The Henry Lewis Stimson Diaries, March 17, 1941, 82, Yale University Library. See also Reinhold Niebuhr, "The Death of the President," *Christianity and Crisis*, 5, April 30, 1945, 4–6.

   In June 2015, former president George W. Bush said: "One of my big concerns is about the tendencies in United States to be isolationist. That has happened throughout our history. I mean World War II is a classic example where the 'America First' policy basically said 'who cares what happens in Europe.' As a result, there were terrible times. Isolation, and a certain fatigue, could come along with protectionist sentiments. The president is trying to pass a trade bill, and you see protectionist tendencies trying to fight off the trade bill, and there is a nativist element too. In the 1920s there was a period when we were isolationists. It was said we had too many Jews and too many Italians. Therefore we decided against immigration. And you begin to see the reverberations of history in 2015. Do they all relate to each other? I happen to think they do. I think it requires leadership to explain to the American people why our involvement overseas is important. Which is one of the real lessons of 9/11—that human conditions elsewhere matter to our security." *Wall Street Journal*, June 18, 2015, "Notable & Quotable," excerpt from Bush's interview in an Israeli daily newspaper, June 12, 2015.

17. *New York Times*, December 7, 1947, "Strong Brief for the Marshall Plan." Eichelberger was also a member, along with Dean Acheson and Allen Dulles, of the executive committee of the Citizens' Committee for the Marshall Plan.

18. FDR, Press Conference, April 15, 1941, in *PPA*, 10:113.

Acknowledgments

I AM DEEPLY GRATEFUL for the generous assistance and sage counsel I received on this project from a stellar crew of friends and colleagues. Milton Djuric contributed his astounding knowledge of the period, his linguistic gifts, and his indispensable editorial assistance at every stage of this project. Mark Stoler, George Marshall scholar and editor of *The Papers of George Catlett Marshall*, offered invaluable suggestions on many questions of military and foreign policy. Bruce Miroff, author of *Icons of Democracy* and *Presidents on Political Ground*, shared penetrating insights on subjects ranging from presidential leadership and labor relations to British imperial ambitions. Michael Beschloss, author of *The Conquerors* and *Kennedy and Roosevelt*, provided key information about FDR, Henry Stimson, and Henry Morgenthau. I was once again the beneficiary of the massive archive of historical documents compiled by the late J. Garry Clifford, author of *The First Peacetime Draft*. Three deans of faculty at Williams College—Denise Buell, William Wagner, and Thomas Kohut—have my warmest appreciation for their collegial support of my research and my teaching. And I will always be immensely thankful for the wisdom, humanity, and wit of Joseph Ellis, Robert Dalzell, Victor Brombert, and the late Conor Cruise O'Brien, who years ago took me under their wings.

This is very much a book for Yale University Press. I am indebted to Professor Ian Shapiro of the Political Science Department at Yale for his kind invitation to deliver the Henry L. Stimson Lectures on World Affairs at Yale's MacMillan Center in November 2016 on FDR's third Hundred Days as well as for his warm welcome to Yale and our energizing conversations. And once again I greatly benefited from the unsurpassed editing and probing questions of William Frucht, my wonderful editor at Yale University Press, from the expert help of his assistant Karen Olson and his former assistant and now associate editor Jaya Chatterjee, and from the sensitive suggestions of my copyeditor Robin DuBlanc and senior editor Margaret Otzel. My enthusiastic agents Ike

Williams and Katherine Flynn and their masterful colleague Hope Denekamp always cheered me on.

One of the great pleasures of working on this book was returning again and again to the FDR Library and Museum in Hyde Park, where director Paul Sparrow and archivist Robert Clark steered me through miles of documents. Robin Keller, my skillful and inventively resourceful departmental assistant at Williams College, aided me countless times. Alison O'Grady at the college library quickly tracked down many obscure works in far-flung places, and librarians Susan Lefaver, Mary Dzbenski, Rebecca Ohm, and Walter Komorowski ably fielded hundreds of queries. Terri-Lynn Hurley, Lynn Melchiori, Michael Richardson, and Seth Rogers at the Williams Office of Information Technology rescued me and my Mac during fraught moments of electronic crisis. And the Williams College basketball team capped many a winter week with their spirited Friday evening games.

And finally, I will forever be infinitely grateful to the late James MacGregor Burns. His brilliant work on Franklin D. Roosevelt—*Roosevelt: The Lion and the Fox* and *Roosevelt: The Soldier of Freedom*—and his Rooseveltian generosity of spirit inspired me as well as this book.

Credits

Prime Minister Winston Churchill views the bombed-out ruins of Coventry Cathedral in November 1940. (Library of Congress)

U.S. Army Chief of Staff General George C. Marshall (*left*) confers with Secretary of War Henry L. Stimson. (Bettmann/Getty Images)

A page from FDR's draft of his January 1941 Four Freedoms speech. (Franklin D. Roosevelt Presidential Library & Museum)

Four Freedoms poster, Federal Art Project. (Library of Congress, United States Works Progress Administration)

General George C. Marshall leads the inauguration day parade on January 20, 1941, on his bay gelding, King Story. (Alfred Eisenstaedt/Getty Images)

The military extravaganza at President Roosevelt's inauguration day parade. (Keystone/Hulton Archive/Getty Images)

1940 GOP presidential candidate Wendell Willkie views the damage to the Guildhall in London in January 1941. (George W. Hales/Getty Images)

Cartoonist Fred Seibel makes the point that aid to Britain serves American self-interest. (*Richmond Times-Dispatch*)

Isolationists Burton Wheeler, Charles Lindbergh, Kathleen Norris, and Norman Thomas at an America First rally in 1941 in Madison Square Garden in New York City. (Associated Press)

"Relatives? Naw . . . Just three fellers going along for the ride!" 1941. Cartoon by Dr. Seuss. (Special Collections & Archives, UC San Diego Library)

This cartoon by Clifford Kennedy Berryman lampoons former ambassador to Great Britain Joseph Kennedy's tendency to take contradictory positions, sometimes supporting Roosevelt for reelection and endorsing his policies and sometimes favoring isolationism. (Library of Congress)

President Roosevelt signs the Lend-Lease Act on March 11, 1941. (© Corbis via Getty Images)

At the York Safe and Lock Company in York, Pennsylvania, workers assemble guns and gun mounts. (Howard Hollem/Library of Congress, Prints & Photographs Division, FSA/OWI Collection, LC-USE6-D-002597)

Ford Motor Company workers and their children picket at the company's River Rouge plant in April 1941, carrying signs comparing Henry Ford to Hitler. (Walter P. Reuther Library, Archives of Labor and Urban Affairs, Wayne State University)

Ford Motor Company's hired thugs beat up striking employees at the company's River Rouge plant in April 1941. (Walter P. Reuther Library, Archives of Labor and Urban Affairs, Wayne State University)

President Roosevelt and Prime Minister Churchill aboard the HMS *Prince of Wales* during the Atlantic Conference in Placentia Bay, Newfoundland, in August 1941. (Franklin D. Roosevelt Presidential Library & Museum)

Index